1001
QUESTIONS &
ANSWERS

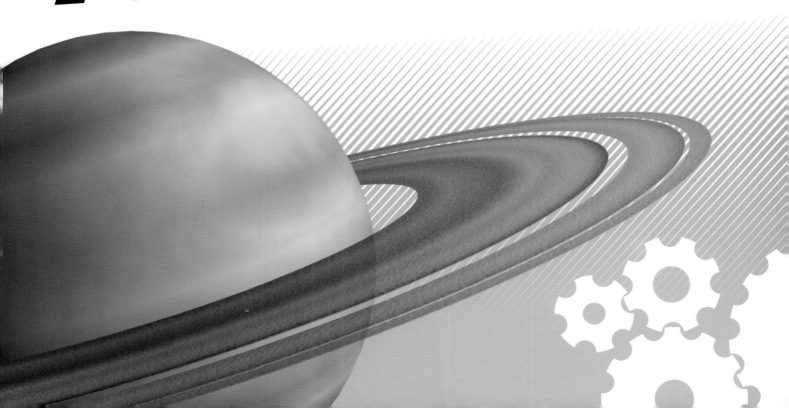

Written by: John Farndon, Ian James, Jinny Johnson, Fiona Macdonald,
Claudia Martin, Angela Royston, Philip Steele, and Martin Walters
Consultants: Sarah Durant, Philip Parker, Benjamin Robinson,
Ade Scott Colson, Tony Sizer, John Williams, and Astrid Wingler

This edition published by Parragon Books Ltd in 2016 and distributed by

Parragon Inc.
440 Park Avenue South, 13th Floor
New York, NY 10016
www.parragon.com

ISBN 978-1-4748-6720-7

Printed in China

Discovery KIDS™

1001

QUESTIONS & ANSWERS

about absolutely everything

PaRragon

Bath · New York · Cologne · Melbourne · Delhi
Hong Kong · Shenzhen · Singapore

Contents

WHAT IS GLOBAL WARMING?

WHY IS THE SKY BLUE?

WHICH

WHEN DID PEO

WHAT IS A TSUNA

WHIC

WHAT IS THE BIGG

HOW MUC

HOW BIG ARE ATOMS?
HOW DID LIFE BEGIN?
HOW OLD ARE THE PYRAMIDS?
COUNTRY HAS THREE CAPITALS?
PLE FIRST LIVE ON EARTH?
MI?
WHERE DO RIVERS START?
IS THE WORLD'S LONGEST ROAD?
EST THING IN THE UNIVERSE?
WHAT IS ENERGY?
WHY IS BLOOD RED?
RAIN FALLS IN THE RAIN FOREST?
HOW MANY STARS ARE THERE?

Introduction

Have you ever wanted to know how the Universe began? Or if it might come to an end? Did you ever wonder when human beings first walked on the Earth? Or how many people live on our crowded planet today? Do you know which is the biggest animal? Or which is the longest bone in the human body? In this book you will discover the incredible answers to 1001 of the questions you've always wanted to ask—covering everything from sharks to digestion, from Einstein to Shakespeare, from the pyramids to the Moon landings, from erupting volcanoes to splitting atoms.

The Solar System

Formation of the Earth ›

Our planet has not always existed. In fact, the Earth is a relatively young planet. Scientists believe that the Universe may be 13.8 billion years old. But Earth—along with the rest of our Solar System—was born only about 4.6 billion years ago.

PLANET BIRTH
Our Solar System formed from a gas and dust cloud.

HOW DID THE EARTH BEGIN?

Around 4.6 billion years ago, a cloud of gas and dust swirled around our newly formed Sun. Gradually, the grains of dust and gas were pulled together into clumps by their own gravity. These clumps became the Earth and the other planets in our Solar System.

SOLAR SYSTEM
Scientists have built up a picture of our Solar System's birth, as the planets were slowly formed around the Sun.

❯ HOW BIG IS THE EARTH?
Satellite measurements show it is 24,873 miles around the equator and 7,927 miles across. The diameter between the poles is slightly less, by 27 miles.

❯ WHAT WAS THE EARLY EARTH LIKE?
The early Earth was a fiery ball. It took half a billion years for its surface to cool and form a hard crust. As it cooled, the Earth gave off gases and water vapor, which formed the atmosphere.

❯ WHAT IS THE EARTH MADE OF?

The Earth has a core consisting mostly of iron, and a rocky crust made mostly of oxygen and silicon. In between is the soft, hot mantle of metal silicates, sulfides, and oxides.

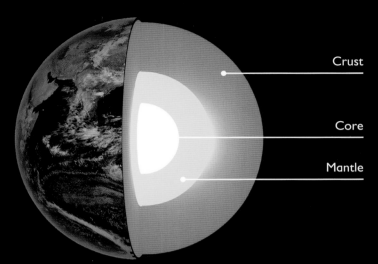

Crust

Core

Mantle

❯ WHAT SHAPE IS THE EARTH?

The Earth is not quite a perfect sphere. The spinning of the planet causes it to bulge at the equator. Scientists describe Earth's shape as "geoid," which simply means Earth-shaped! The poles, the Earth's northernmost and southernmost spots, are the points the Earth spins around.

❯ HOW OLD ARE OCEANS?

The oceans were formed between 4.2 and 3.8 billion years ago. As the Earth cooled, clouds of steam became water, creating vast oceans.

OLD ROCK

The Earth's oldest rock is about 4.4 billion years old.

Our special planet >

The Earth is the largest of the four inner planets, which lie closest to the Sun and are mostly made of rock. These four planets are Mercury, Venus, Earth, and Mars, with our planet being third from the Sun. The Earth is the only planet in the Universe on which life is known to exist.

> HOW LONG IS A DAY?

A day is the time the Earth takes to turn once. The stars move to the same place in the sky every 23 hours, 56 minutes, and 4.09 seconds (the sidereal day). Our day (the solar day) is 24 hours, because the Earth is moving around the Sun, and must turn an extra 1 degree for the Sun to be in the same place in the sky.

> DOES THE EARTH SPIN?

The Earth spins on its axis once a day, while also orbiting, or traveling around, the Sun.

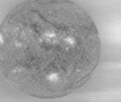

SUMMER AND WINTER

As the Earth orbits the Sun, the hemisphere of the planet tilted toward the Sun has its summer.

❯ HOW LONG IS A YEAR?

The Earth travels around the Sun every 365.24 days, which gives us our calendar year of 365 days. To make up the extra 0.24 days, we add an extra day to our calendar at the end of February in every fourth year, which is called a leap year—and then we have to knock off a leap year every four centuries.

❯ WHAT'S SPECIAL ABOUT THE EARTH?

The Earth is the only planet where temperatures are right for liquid water to exist on the surface. It is also the only planet with oxygen in its atmosphere. Both water and oxygen are needed for life to exist.

❯ WHAT IS THE ATMOSPHERE?

The Earth's atmosphere, or "air," is a layer of gases—including nitrogen, oxygen, argon, and carbon dioxide—that surrounds the planet.

SUNSET

The Earth turns on its axis once every 24 hours, so the Sun appears to rise in the east and move across the sky to set in the west.

WHO WAS COPERNICUS?

In the 1500s, most people thought the Earth was fixed in the center of the Universe, with the Sun and the stars revolving around it. Nicolaus Copernicus (1473–1543) was the Polish astronomer who first suggested the Earth was moving around the Sun.

The Moon >

The Moon is the Earth's natural satellite. Natural satellites, or moons, are objects that orbit a planet or other body in space. Our Moon is a rocky ball about a quarter of the Earth's diameter. It is held in its orbit around the Earth by gravity.

> WHAT IS THE MOON?

The Moon has circled the Earth for 4.5 billion years. Most scientists believe that the Moon formed when, early in Earth's history, a planet smashed into it. The impact was so great that nothing was left of the planet but a few splashes thrown back up into space. These splashes and material from the battered Earth were drawn together by gravity to form the Moon.

MOON DUST

The Moon's surface is covered with a fine layer of dust. Beneath lies a crust of rock.

ARE THERE OTHER MOONS?

As many as 182 bodies, all in our Solar System, are classified as moons. Other stars and their planets are likely to have moons, but none have yet been observed.

WHAT IS MOONLIGHT?

The Moon is by far the brightest thing in the night sky. But it has no light of its own. Moonlight is simply the Sun's light reflected off the dust on the Moon's surface.

TIDES

As the Earth spins, the Moon's gravity makes the oceans rise.

TOP QUESTION?

WHAT ARE TIDES?

Tides are caused by the oceans, on the side of the Earth facing the Moon, being pulled by the Moon's gravity more than the solid Earth itself. On the opposite side of the Earth, the water is actually pulled less than the Earth. This creates a bulge of water on each side of the world. This bulge stays under the Moon as the Earth turns.

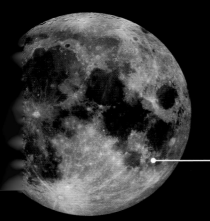

LUNAR SEAS

People once thought these dark patches were filled with water. In fact, they are formed from lava.

WHY DOES THE MOON HAVE CRATERS?

The Moon's surface is covered with impact craters. These form when asteroids and comets crash into the Moon. Most of the craters were made about 3.4 billion years ago.

WHAT ARE THE MOON'S SEAS?

The dark patches on the Moon's surface are called seas, but in fact they are not seas at all. They were formed about 3 billion years ago when lava from inside the Moon flowed into huge craters and then solidified.

Our nearest neighbor

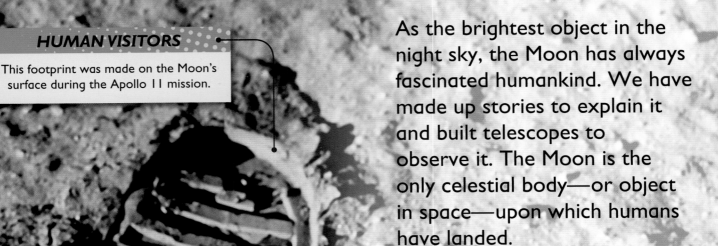

HUMAN VISITORS

This footprint was made on the Moon's surface during the Apollo 11 mission.

As the brightest object in the night sky, the Moon has always fascinated humankind. We have made up stories to explain it and built telescopes to observe it. The Moon is the only celestial body—or object in space—upon which humans have landed.

› WHO WERE THE FIRST PEOPLE ON THE MOON?

The first men on the Moon were Neil Armstrong and Buzz Aldrin of the U.S. Apollo 11 mission. They landed on the Moon on July 20, 1969. As Armstrong set foot on the Moon, he said: "That's one small step for (a) man, one giant leap for mankind."

LUNAR ECLIPSE

As the Moon passes through the Earth's shadow, the Sun's blue light is scattered by Earth's atmosphere. The remaining red light is refracted, or bent, into Earth's shadow. This makes the Moon appear red.

PHASES OF THE MOON

The Moon appears to wax (grow) and wane (shrink) every 29.53 days, as we see its sunny side from different angles.

> HOW LONG IS A MONTH?

It takes the Moon 27.3 days to circle the Earth, but 29.53 days from one full moon to the next, because the Earth is moving as well. A lunar month is the 29.53 days cycle. Our calendar months are entirely artificial.

> WHAT IS A LUNAR ECLIPSE?

As the Moon goes around the Earth, sometimes it passes right into Earth's shadow, where sunlight is blocked off. This is a lunar eclipse. If you look at the Moon during this time, you can see the dark disk of the Earth's shadow creeping across the Moon.

> WHAT IS WAXING?

Over the first two weeks of each month, we see more and more of the Moon's bright side until full moon. As the Moon appears to grow, we say that it is waxing.

WHAT IS A NEW MOON?

The Moon appears to change shape during the month because, as it circles the Earth, we see its bright, sunny side from a different angle. At the new moon, the Moon lies between the Earth and the Sun, and we catch only a crescent-shaped glimpse of its bright side.

> WHAT IS A HARVEST MOON?

The harvest moon is the full moon nearest the autumnal equinox (when night and day are of equal length). This moon hangs bright above the eastern horizon for several evenings, providing a good light for people harvesting crops.

The Sun >

The Sun is the star at the center of our Solar System. The Earth and the other planets orbit the Sun, which makes up 99% of the Solar System's mass. Sunlight and heat from the Sun support all life on Earth. Without the Sun, there would be no life at all.

> WHAT IS THE SUN?

The Sun is an average star, just like countless others in the Universe. It was formed from a cloud of gas and dust, plus material thrown out by one or more exploding stars. Now, in middle age, the Sun burns yellow and quite steadily—giving the Earth daylight and fairly constant temperatures. Besides heat and light, the Sun sends out deadly gamma rays, X-rays, and ultraviolet rays, as well as infrared and radio waves.

THE BOILING SURFACE

The Sun's visible surface is called the photosphere. It is a sea of boiling gas that gives the heat and light we experience on Earth.

> WHAT MAKES THE SUN BURN?

The Sun gets its heat from nuclear fusion. Huge pressures deep inside the Sun force the nuclei (cores) of hydrogen atoms to fuse together to make helium atoms, releasing vast amounts of nuclear energy.

WHAT IS A SOLAR ECLIPSE?

A solar eclipse is when the Moon moves in between the Sun and the Earth (shown on the left), creating a shadow a few hundred miles wide on the Earth's surface.

HOW BIG IS THE SUN?

The Sun is a small- to medium-sized star 864,949 miles in diameter. It weighs about 2 trillion trillion trillion tons.

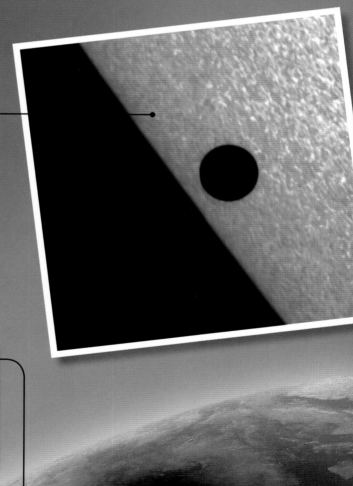

MERCURY IN TRANSIT
The last transit of Mercury took place on May 9, 2016.

WHAT IS A TRANSIT?

Mercury and Venus are the two planets closer to the Sun than Earth. Occasionally, they can be seen crossing, or in transit over, the face of the Sun. Mercury crosses 13 or 14 times a century; Venus crosses twice every 120 years.

WHAT IS THE SUN'S CROWN?

The Sun's crown is its corona, its glowing white-hot atmosphere. It is seen only as a halo when the rest of the Sun's disc is blotted out by the Moon in a solar eclipse.

ECLIPSE
During an eclipse, the Moon's shadow can be seen on the Earth. Up to five eclipses occur each year.

Ball of fire →

While the Solar System orbits the Sun, the Sun itself is orbiting the center of our Galaxy, the Milky Way. The Sun is moving at an orbital speed of 156 miles every second. It takes the Solar System about 225 to 250 million years to complete one orbit of the Galaxy.

LIGHT DISPLAY

The northern lights often appear as a greenish glow or a faint red. They can occur as arcs or bands.

❯ WHAT IS THE SOLAR WIND?

The solar wind is the stream of particles constantly blowing out from the Sun at hundreds of miles per second. The Earth is protected from the solar wind by its magnetic field, but at the poles the solar wind interacts with Earth's atmosphere to create the *aurora borealis* or northern lights, and the *aurora australis* or southern lights.

❯ HOW HOT IS THE SUN?

The surface of the Sun is a phenomenal 9,900°F, and would melt absolutely anything. But its core is thousands of times hotter at over 27 million°F!

❯ HOW OLD IS THE SUN?

The Sun is a middle-aged star. It probably formed about 4.6 billion years ago. It will probably burn for another 5 billion years and then die in a blaze so bright that the Earth will be scorched right out of existence.

❯ WHAT ARE SUNSPOTS?

Sunspots are dark blotches seen on the Sun's surface (right). They are thousands of miles across, and usually occur in pairs. They are dark because they are slightly cooler than the rest of the surface. As the Sun rotates, they slowly cross its face—in about 31 days at the equator and 27 days at the poles.

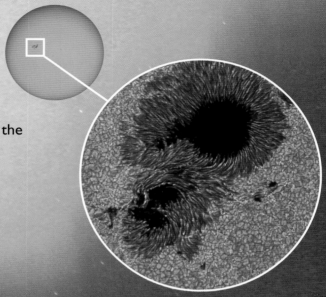

❯ WHAT IS THE SOLAR CYCLE?

The average number of sunspots and flares seems to reach a maximum every 11 years. Some scientists think that these peaks in the Sun's cycle are linked to stormier weather on Earth.

TOP QUESTION ?

WHAT ARE SOLAR FLARES?

Flares are eruptions on the Sun's surface that release energy into space with the power of one million atom bombs for about five minutes. Solar prominences are giant flamelike tongues of hot hydrogen that loop up to 20,000 miles into space.

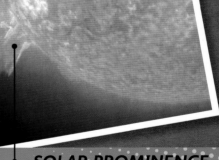

SOLAR PROMINENCE

Prominences form in about a day and may last as long as several months.

Venus and Mercury ›

Along with Earth and Mars, Venus and Mercury make up the inner planets. These planets all have an atmosphere, but each is very different. Mercury orbits the Sun at a distance of 29–43 million miles, while Venus has an average distance from the Sun of 67 million miles.

› WHAT ARE THE INNER PLANETS MADE OF?

Each of the inner planets is formed a little bit like an egg—with a hard "shell" or crust of rock, a "white" or mantle of soft, semimolten rock, and a "yolk" or core of hot, often molten, iron and nickel.

› WHAT IS THE ATMOSPHERE LIKE ON VENUS?

Venus' atmosphere would be deadly for humans. It is very deep, so the pressure on the ground is huge. It is made mainly of poisonous carbon dioxide and is also filled with clouds of sulfuric acid.

VENUS

Venus is the second brightest object in the night sky, after the Moon.

VENUS' SURFACE

This computer-generated image was created using data supplied by the Magellan space probe.

> COULD YOU BREATHE ON MERCURY?

Not without your own oxygen supply. Mercury has almost no atmosphere—just a few wisps of sodium—because gases are burned off by the nearby Sun.

> HOW HOT IS MERCURY?

Temperatures on Mercury veer from one extreme to the other because it has too thin an atmosphere to insulate it. In the day, temperatures soar to 770°F; at night they plunge to -300°F.

> HAVE ANY SPACECRAFT VISITED MERCURY?

Approaching Mercury is difficult because it lies so close to the Sun. A mission there is planned for 2017.

TOP QUESTION

WHY IS VENUS CALLED THE EVENING STAR?

Venus reflects sunlight so well that it shines like a star. Because it is quite close to the Sun, we can see it in the evening, just after the Sun sets. We can also see it just before sunrise.

MERCURY

Mercury's surface is pitted with craters like the Moon. It also has mountains and valleys.

Mars >

The fourth of the inner planets is Mars, which orbits the Sun every 687 days. It is often called the "Red Planet" because of its reddish appearance. Martian temperatures range from -220°F during winter at its poles to up to 70°F during its summers.

❯ WHY IS MARS RED?

Mars is red because it is rusty. The surface contains a high proportion of iron dust, and this has been oxidized by small amounts of oxygen in the atmosphere.

❯ IS THERE LIFE ON MARS?

In the 1970s, unmanned landers of the Viking missions found no trace of life. Then, in 1996, microscopic fossils of what might be mini-viruses were found in a rock from Mars. But these turned out not to be signs of life after all.

MARTIAN SOIL

The soil on Mars is similar to Earth's. But the dust is often whipped up into huge dust storms that can cover the whole planet.

VALLES MARINERIS

As Mars cooled after its formation, this giant canyon opened up.

WHO DISCOVERED MARS' MOONS?

In 1877, American astronomer Asaph Hall decided to have an early night. But his wife encouraged him to stay up and work—and that night he discovered Mars' two moons. He named them Phobos and Deimos after the attendants of the Roman war god, Mars.

WHICH CANYON IS BIGGER THAN THE GRAND CANYON?

A canyon on Mars! The planet has a great chasm, discovered by the Mariner 9 space probe and called the Valles Marineris. It is more than 2,000 miles long and four times as deep as the Grand Canyon. It is the largest known chasm in the Solar System.

WILL HUMANS EVER LAND ON MARS?

NASA intends to launch a manned mission to Mars in the 2030s.

WHERE IS THE BIGGEST VOLCANO?

Mars has a volcano called Olympus Mons which is 16 miles high—three times higher than Mount Everest. It was created by lava welling up beneath Mars' surface.

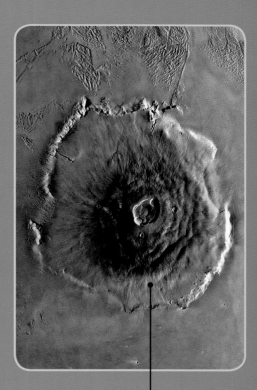

OLYMPUS MONS

This volcano is the highest mountain in the Solar System and is just one of many volcanoes on the planet.

Jupiter >

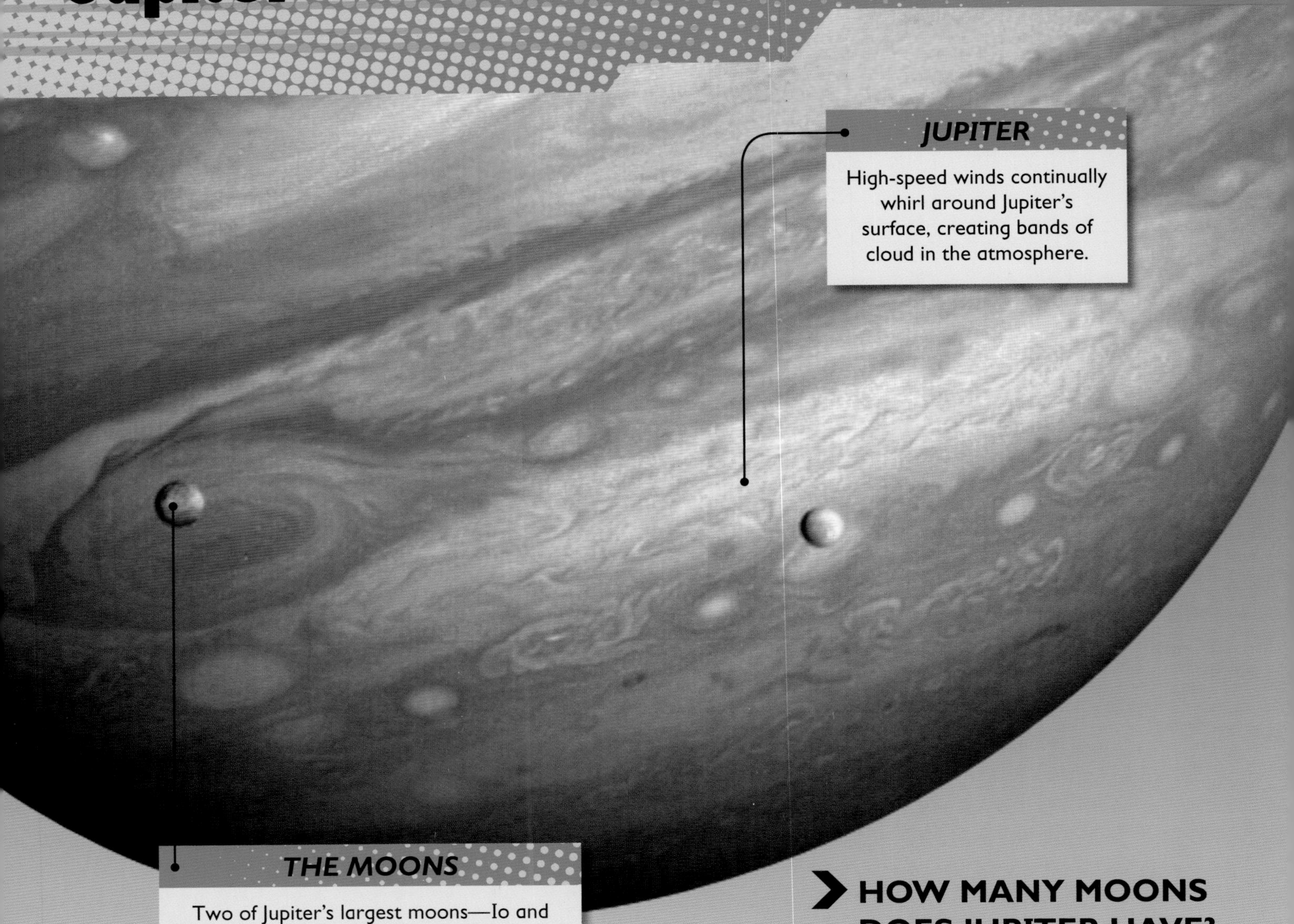

→

JUPITER

High-speed winds continually whirl around Jupiter's surface, creating bands of cloud in the atmosphere.

THE MOONS

Two of Jupiter's largest moons—Io and Europa—can be seen in orbit. They are both close to the size of Earth's Moon.

The largest planet in the Solar System is Jupiter, the fifth planet from the Sun. Along with Saturn, Uranus, and Neptune, Jupiter is called a gas giant. These planets do not have a solid surface because they are not made of rock or other hard materials.

> HOW MANY MOONS DOES JUPITER HAVE?

Jupiter has 67 moons. Many of them are very small—47 are less than 6 miles in diameter. The four largest are called Io, Europa, Ganymede, and Callisto.

> HOW BIG IS JUPITER?

Very big. Even though Jupiter is largely gas, it weighs 320 times as much as the Earth and is 86,881 miles in diameter.

➤ WHAT IS JUPITER MADE OF?

Unlike the rocky inner planets, the gas giants are made largely of gas. Jupiter is made mostly of hydrogen and helium. Internal pressures are so great that most of the hydrogen is turned to metal.

➤ COULD YOU LAND ON JUPITER?

No. Even if your spaceship could withstand the enormous pressures, there is no surface to land on—the atmosphere merges unnoticeably into deep oceans of liquid hydrogen.

➤ HOW FAST DOES JUPITER SPIN?

Jupiter spins faster than any other planet. Despite its huge size, it turns right around in just 9 hours 55 minutes, which means the surface is moving at 28,000 miles an hour!

IO

Io has more than 300 volcanoes, making it the most geologically active object in the Solar System. Here an eruption can be seen on its surface.

TOP QUESTION

WHAT IS JUPITER'S RED SPOT?

The Great Red Spot or GRS is a huge swirling storm in Jupiter's atmosphere. It is 16,000 miles across and has been going on for at least 330 years.

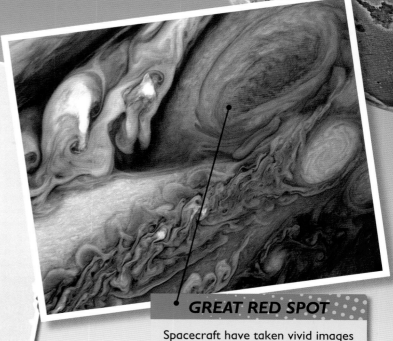

GREAT RED SPOT

Spacecraft have taken vivid images of the storm, with its red center and wavy cloud formations.

Saturn

RING SYSTEM

Some scientists think that the rings are the remains of a moon that was hit by a comet.

SATURN

Saturn is nine times bigger than the Earth, with a diameter of 72,492 miles.

The gas giant Saturn is the sixth planet from the Sun. It takes Saturn 10,759 days to orbit the Sun. The planet is composed mainly of hydrogen and a little helium. It is best known for its ring system, which can be seen from Earth with a good pair of binoculars.

HOW HEAVY IS SATURN?

Saturn may be big, but because it is made largely of hydrogen, it is also remarkably light, with a mass of 627 billion trillion tons. If you could find a big enough bathtub to put it in,

HOW WINDY IS SATURN?

Saturn's winds are even faster than Jupiter's and roar around the planet at up to 1,100 miles an hour. But Neptune's are even faster, at 1,300 miles an hour!

➤ HOW MANY MOONS DOES SATURN HAVE?

Saturn has 53 moons, including Lapetus, which is dark on one side and light on the other.

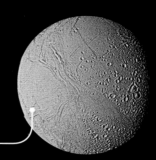

ENCELADUS

Saturn's moon Enceladus is composed of ice and rock.

➤ WHAT IS THE CASSINI DIVISION?

Saturn's rings occur in broad bands, referred to by the letters A to G. In 1675, the astronomer Cassini spotted a dark gap between rings A and B. This is now called the Cassini division, after him.

➤ WHAT ARE SATURN'S RINGS?

Saturn's rings are the planet's shining halo, first seen by Galileo Galilei (1564–1642), who invented a simple telescope in 1609. The rings are incredibly thin—no more than 170 feet deep—yet they stretch 175,000 miles into space.

ICE CHIPS

The rings are made of billions of chips of ice and dust.

➤ WHY ARE ASTRONOMERS EXCITED ABOUT TITAN?

Saturn's moon Titan is very special because it is the only moon in the Solar System with a dense atmosphere, which is vital for supporting life.

Neptune and Uranus →

Neptune and Uranus are the two planets farthest from the Sun. Like Jupiter and Saturn, they are composed mostly of gas. These two planets are sometimes known as ice giants because they contain a large amount of icy water, methane, and ammonia.

NEPTUNE

Neptune has 17 times the mass of Earth and is slightly heavier than its sister planet, Uranus, which is only 15 times heavier.

> WHAT COLOR IS NEPTUNE?

Neptune appears greeny-blue because of the methane gas in its atmosphere. This gas absorbs red light in the spectrum, making it seem that Neptune is a vivid, azure blue-green. The same effect can be seen with Uranus, which also has a lot of methane in its atmosphere, although that planet appears to be a much paler shade of turquoise blue.

> HOW LONG IS A YEAR ON NEPTUNE?

Neptune is so far from the Sun—about 2.8 billion miles—that its orbit takes about 165 Earth years. So one year on Neptune lasts for 165 Earth years.

> WHO FOUND NEPTUNE?

Two mathematicians, John Couch Adams in England and Urbain le Verrier in France, predicted where Neptune should be from the way its gravity disturbed Uranus' orbit. Johann Galle in Berlin was the first to spot it on September 23, 1846.

NEPTUNE'S WINDS

Space probes have sent back images of Neptune's high winds.

> WHEN WAS URANUS DISCOVERED?

Uranus was first discovered in 1781 by the astronomer William Herschel. He thought at first that it was a comet, but Uranus was soon proved to be a planet.

TOP QUESTION

?

DOES URANUS HAVE RINGS?

Like the other gas giants, Uranus has a ring system (below). Currently 13 rings have been identified.

URANUS

Uranus is the seventh planet from the Sun and is named after the Greek god of the sky.

> WHAT'S STRANGE ABOUT URANUS?

Unlike any of the other planets, Uranus does not spin on a slight tilt. Instead it is tilted right over and rolls around the Sun on its side, like a giant bowling ball.

Other objects →

As well as the 8 planets and 146 known moons, the Solar System holds dwarf planets, asteroids, icy Kuiper Belt objects, meteoroids, comets, and dust. All these objects are held in orbit around the Sun by gravity.

❯ WHAT IS THE KUIPER BELT?

It is a region of the Solar System that lies beyond Neptune. Thousands of relatively small, frozen objects orbit there.

PLUTO

Pluto was called a planet until 2006, when it was reclassified.

❯ WHAT IS AN ASTEROID?

Asteroids are the thousands of rocky lumps that circle around the Sun in a big band between Mars and Jupiter. Some venture outside this zone. Unlike the frozen Kuiper Belt objects, asteroids are mostly made of rock and metal. More than 5,000 asteroids have been identified so far.

❯ WHAT ARE DWARF PLANETS?

There are five dwarf planets currently known in the Solar System. They are Pluto, Ceres, Makemake, Haumea, and Eris. These bodies are large enough to be made rounded by their own gravity but not large enough to have cleared the area around them of other bodies.

METEOR CRATER

Meteor Crater, in northern Arizona, was made by a meteorite 165 feet across.

NUCLEUS

At the heart of a comet is a nucleus of ice and rock, often shaped like a lumpy potato and just a few miles across.

WHAT IS A METEORITE?

Meteorites are lumps of rock from space big enough to penetrate the Earth's atmosphere and reach the ground without burning up.

❯ WHAT IS A COMET?

Comets are just dirty iceballs. Normally, they circle the outer Solar System. But occasionally, one of them is drawn in toward the Sun. As it hurtles along, material from its surface is blown away from the Sun by the solar wind. We may see this tail in the night sky, shining in the sunlight until it swings out of sight.

❯ HOW LONG IS A COMET'S TAIL?

It can be millions of miles long. If a comet's path crosses Earth's path, there may be meteor showers of debris.

METEORITE

More than 50,000 meteorites have been found on the Earth. Some are as small as marbles.

Stars and galaxies

Birth of the Universe ➤

Scientists define the Universe as absolutely everything that physically exists. But the Universe has not always existed. It is believed that the Universe was created by the Big Bang, when it started to grow from a tiny point that contained all matter and energy.

➤ WHAT WAS THE UNIVERSE LIKE AT THE BEGINNING?

The early Universe was very small, but it contained all the matter and energy in the Universe today. It was a dense and chaotic soup of tiny particles and forces. But this original Universe lasted only a split second—just three trillionths of a trillionth of a trillionth of a second.

➤ WHAT WAS THERE BEFORE THE UNIVERSE?

No one knows. Some people think there was an unimaginable ocean, beyond space and time, of potential universes continually bursting into life or failing. Ours succeeded.

➤ CAN WE SEE THE BIG BANG?

Astronomers can see the galaxies still hurtling away from the Big Bang in all directions. They can also see the afterglow—low-level microwave radiation coming at us from all over the sky, called background radiation.

COSMIC RADIATION

This image taken by the Cosmic Background Explorer satellite shows the radiation created by the Big Bang.

YOUNG UNIVERSE

This artist's impression shows how the young Universe may have looked as stars burst into being like fireworks.

NEW GALAXY

As it started to form, 13.5 billion years ago, our own galaxy may have looked like this.

TOP QUESTION

WHAT WAS THE BIG BANG?

In the beginning, all the Universe was squeezed into an unimaginably small, hot, dense ball. The Big Bang was when this suddenly began to swell explosively, allowing first energy and matter, then atoms, gas clouds, and galaxies to form. The Universe has been swelling ever since.

❯ HOW DO WE KNOW WHAT THE EARLY UNIVERSE WAS LIKE?

Machines called colliders and particle accelerators can recreate conditions in the early Universe by using magnets to accelerate particles to astonishing speeds and then crashing them together.

❯ HOW HOT WAS THE BIG BANG?

As the Universe grew from smaller than an atom to the size of a soccer ball, it cooled to nearly 20 billion billion billion°F.

Growing Universe >

The Universe has continued to expand ever since the Big Bang. Scientists are not sure if it will carry on growing forever, beyond what we can possibly observe, or whether it will eventually come to a stop and end in a Big Crunch.

> WHAT IS INFLATION?

Inflation was when dramatic expansion and cooling took place just a tiny fraction of a second after the Big Bang.

> HOW LONG WILL THE UNIVERSE LAST?

It depends how much matter it contains. If there is more than the "critical density," gravity will put a brake on its expansion, and it may begin to contract again to end in a Big Crunch. If there is much less, it may go on expanding forever.

TOP
?
QUESTION

HOW DID THE FIRST GALAXIES FORM?

They formed from lumps of clouds of hydrogen and helium, as concentrations within the clumps drew together. The youngest known galaxy (right) is just 500 million years old and typical of the galaxies of the early Universe.

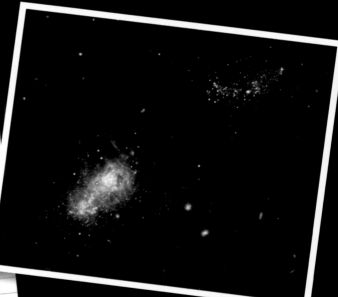

> WHAT SHAPE IS THE UNIVERSE?

Scientists do not yet know—just as early humankind had no way of knowing the shape of our own Earth. Perhaps the Universe is flat, perhaps it is a curve, or perhaps even a sphere.

SPEEDING APART

All the galaxies are speeding apart from each other, rather like raisins in a continuously rising loaf of bread.

❯ HOW DO WE KNOW THAT THE UNIVERSE IS GETTING BIGGER?

We can tell the Universe is getting bigger because distant galaxies are speeding away from us. Yet the galaxies themselves are not moving—the space in between them is stretching.

❯ HOW OLD IS THE UNIVERSE?

We know that the Universe is getting bigger at a certain rate by observing how fast distant galaxies are moving apart. By working out how long it took everything to expand to where it is now, we can work out that the Universe may be about 13.8 billion years old.

DISTANT GALAXIES

As their light takes time to reach us, distant galaxies seen through a telescope are seen as they were millions of years ago.

Matter and particles >

Matter is simply anything that has mass and takes up space. All matter is made up of tiny particles, such as protons, neutrons, and electrons. Particles are the building blocks of the Universe.

> WHAT IS THE UNIVERSE MADE FROM?

The stars and clouds in space are made almost 100% of hydrogen and helium, the lightest and simplest atoms, or elements. All the other elements are quite rare. But some, such as carbon, oxygen, silicon, nitrogen, and iron, can form important concentrations, as in the rocky planets like Earth, where iron, oxygen, and magnesium are among the most common elements.

ATOM

A cloud of particles called electrons surrounds the atom's nucleus.

> WHAT ARE QUARKS?

Quarks are tiny particles much smaller than atoms. They were among the first particles to form at the birth of the Universe.

> HOW WERE ATOMS MADE?

Atoms of hydrogen and helium were made in the early days of the Universe when quarks in the matter soup joined together. All other atoms were made as atoms were fused together by the intense heat and pressure inside stars.

NUCLEUS

The nucleus, or center, of an atom is made of protons and neutrons, which are themselves made of quarks.

ATOM SMASHER

A particle accelerator propels particles at immense speeds to investigate their nature.

WHAT IS THE SMALLEST KNOWN PARTICLE?

The smallest particle inside the nucleus is the quark. It is less than 10^{-20} meters across, which means a line of ten billion billion of them would be less than a meter (3.3 feet) long.

▶ WHAT ARE PARTICLES?

Particles are the basic units of matter that make up everyday objects. There are hundreds of kinds of particles, but all apart from the atom and molecule are too small to see, even with the most powerful microscope.

▶ WHAT IS ANTIMATTER?

Antimatter is the mirror image of ordinary matter. If matter and antimatter meet, they destroy each other. Fortunately, there is no antimatter on Earth.

SCATTERED ATOMS

The paths of subatomic particles, such as quarks, can be seen after colliding atoms at great speed.

The birth of stars >

Stars are gigantic glowing balls of gas, scattered throughout space. They burn for anything from a few million to tens of billions of years. The closest star to the Earth is our Sun.

> HOW ARE STARS BORN?

Stars are born when clumps of gas in space are drawn together by their own gravity, and the middle of the clump is squeezed so hard that temperatures reach 18 million°F, so a nuclear fusion reaction starts. The heat makes the star shine.

> WHERE ARE STARS BORN?

Stretched throughout space are vast clouds of dust and gas called nebulae. These clouds are 99% hydrogen and helium with tiny amounts of other gases and minute quantities of icy, cosmic dust. Stars are born in the biggest of these nebulae, which are called giant molecular clouds.

EAGLE NEBULA

Stars are being formed in the Eagle Nebula, which was photographed by the Hubble Space Telescope.

STAR BIRTH
New stars are seen glowing as bright spots.

➤ HOW CLOSE ARE THE STARS?

The nearest star, apart from the Sun, is more than 25 trillion miles away. The stars are all so distant that we can see them only as pinpoints of light in the night sky.

➤ CAN WE SEE NEBULAE FROM EARTH?

Some nebulae can be seen through telescopes because they shine as they reflect starlight. Others, called dark nebulae, are seen as inky black patches. A few, called glowing nebulae, glow as the gas within them is heated by nearby stars.

➤ HOW DOES A STAR BURN STEADILY?

In medium-sized stars, like our Sun, the heat generated in the core pushes gas out as hard as gravity pulls it in, so the star burns steadily for billions of years.

➤ WHICH IS THE CLOSEST NEBULA TO EARTH?

It is the Orion Nebula (below right), which is 1,500 light-years, or 8.8 thousand million million miles, away.

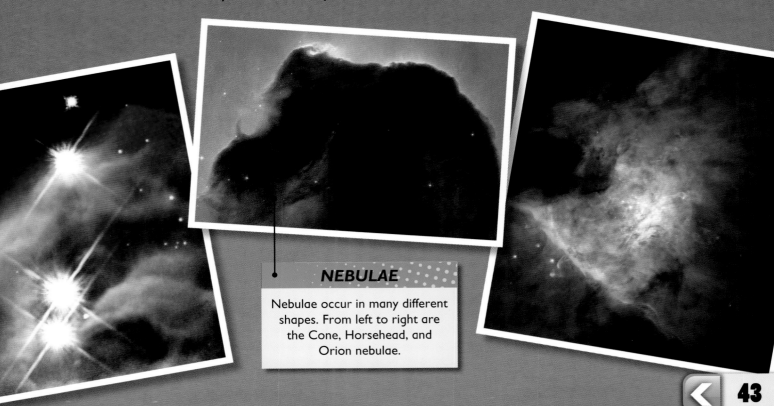

NEBULAE
Nebulae occur in many different shapes. From left to right are the Cone, Horsehead, and Orion nebulae.

Shining stars →

Many stars are visible in the night sky, when they are not outshone by the Sun. Humankind has studied the stars for millennia, with the oldest known star chart dating back 3,500 years. Today, the position of the stars is still used for navigation.

› WHAT ARE CONSTELLATIONS?

Constellations are small patterns of stars in the sky, each with its own name. They are often named after the object or figure that they resemble, such as a lion or cross. Different cultures identify different constellations. The stars in a constellation may not be very close to each other in reality—they only appear to be close when viewed from Earth.

ORION

The constellation of Orion is one of the brightest in the night sky.

› WHERE IS THE POLE STAR?

The Pole Star is a bright star that lies directly over the North Pole. With a long camera exposure, the stars seem to rotate about the Pole Star as the Earth turns (above).

TOP ? QUESTION

WHERE IS THE HUNTER?

The constellation of Orion looks like a hunter holding a sword. The hunter's head, shoulders, three-starred belt, legs, and sword can be seen.

❯ HOW HOT IS A STAR?

The surface temperature of the coolest stars is below 6,300°F; that of the hottest, brightest stars is over 70,000°F.

❯ WHAT COLORS ARE STARS?

It depends how hot they are. The color of medium-sized stars varies along a band on a graph called the main sequence—from hot and bright blue-white stars to cool and dim red stars.

❯ WHAT MAKES STARS GLOW?

Stars glow because the enormous pressure deep inside generates nuclear fusion reactions in which hydrogen atoms are fused together, releasing huge quantities of energy.

RED STAR

Older stars are often cooler and dimmer and take on a reddish glow.

WHITE STARS

Young stars often burn hot and bright and can be seen as blue-white lights in the night sky.

Star giants and dwarfs >

VARIABLE STAR

The star Eta Carinae brightens
and dims over a period of years.

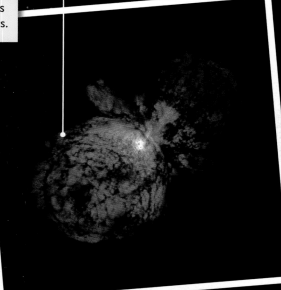

Stars can be classified depending on their
size and how brightly they are burning.
Large stars burn their fuel very fast and are
short-lived. Small stars burn their fuel slowly
and can last for billions of years.

> HOW MANY STARS ARE THERE?

It is hard to know how many stars there are in the
Universe—most are much too far away to see. But
astronomers guess there are about 1,000 billion billion.

> WHAT IS A RED DWARF?

A red dwarf is a small and fairly cool star with a mass
of less than 40% that of the Sun. The majority of stars are
believed to be red dwarfs.

> WHICH STARS THROB?

The light from variable stars flares
up and down. "Cepheid" stars are
big old stars that pulsate over a few
days or a few weeks. "RR Lyrae"
variables are old yellow stars that
vary over a few hours.

PERSEUS

The constellation of Perseus contains a variable star called Algol. Its brightest star is a supergiant called Mirfak.

STAR SIZES

The size of stars is measured in solar masses—or how many times the size of our Sun they are.

TOP QUESTION

WHAT IS A RED GIANT?

It is a huge, cool star, formed as surface gas on a medium-sized star near the end of its life swells up.

WHAT MAKES STARS TWINKLE?

Stars twinkle because the Earth's atmosphere is never still, and starlight is distorted as the air wavers. Light from the nearby planets is not distorted as much, so they don't twinkle.

WHICH IS THE BIGGEST STAR?

The biggest stars are the supergiants. Antares is 700 times as big as the Sun. There may be a star in the Epsilon system in the constellation of Auriga that is 2 billion miles across—4,000 times bigger than the Sun.

Red dwarf
0.4 solar masses

Sun
1 solar mass

Blue-white giant
150 solar masses

Red giant
5 solar masses

The death of stars >

CAT'S EYE NEBULA

This nebula is created by a dying star at its center, throwing out gas and plasma.

Stars make energy by turning hydrogen into helium. When the hydrogen is used up, they then use any other nuclear energy. When a star's supplies of energy are all gone, it dies.

> HOW OLD ARE STARS?

Stars are dying and being born all the time. Big, bright stars live for only 10 million years. Medium-sized stars like our Sun live for 10 billion years.

> WHAT HAPPENS WHEN STARS DIE?

When a star has used up all its energy, it either blows up, shrinks, goes cold, or becomes a black hole. Just how long it takes to reach this point depends on the size of the star. The biggest stars have lots of nuclear fuel, but live fast and die young. The smallest stars have little nuclear fuel, but live slow and long. A star twice as big

HOW WILL OUR SUN DIE?

The Sun will exhaust its supply of hydrogen fuel in about 4 billion years. Its core will crash inward and become hot enough to ignite its helium atoms. The Sun will then swell up to become a red giant. The outer layers will drift off, making a planetary nebula, leaving behind the core of the Sun. This will gradually cool off.

WHAT IS A PULSAR?

Pulsars are stars that flash out intense radio pulses every ten seconds or less as they spin rapidly. They are thought to be very dense dying stars called neutron stars.

WHAT IS A WHITE DWARF?

White dwarfs are the small dense stars formed when the outer layers of a star like the Sun are blown off during the last parts of the red giant stage.

EXPLODED STAR

This image taken by a telescope shows the remains of a star after it has blown up in a supernova.

TOP QUESTION ?

WHAT IS A SUPERNOVA?

A supernova is a gigantic explosion. It finishes off a supergiant star. For a few minutes, the supernova flashes out with the brilliance of billions of suns. Supernovae are usually visible only through a telescope. But in 1987, for the first time in 400 years, a supernova (Supernova 1987A) was visible to the naked eye.

SUPERNOVA

The supernova explosion known as Cassiopeia A took place in the Milky Way Galaxy about 11,000 light-years away.

Star groups ➤

In addition to single stars, stars exist in multi-star groups that orbit around each other. Larger groups called star clusters also occur. Stars are not spread uniformly across the Universe: they are normally grouped in galaxies.

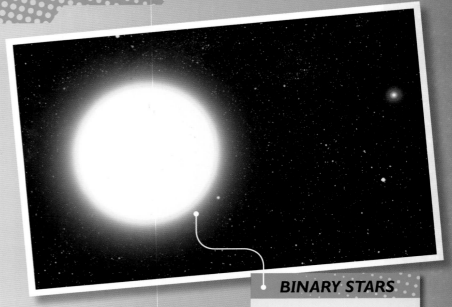

BINARY STARS

The star Sirius A has a small companion called Sirius B.

➤ WHAT ARE CLUSTERS?

Stars are rarely entirely alone within a galaxy. Many are concentrated in groups called clusters. Globular clusters are big and round. Galactic clusters are small and formless.

➤ WHAT ARE DOUBLE STARS?

Our Sun is alone in space, but many stars have one or more nearby companions. Double stars are called binaries.

WHAT ARE THE PLEIADES?

The Pleiades are a group of 400 stars, seven of which are visible to the naked eye, that formed in the same cloud of dust and gas. The stars are held loosely together by gravity.

THE MILKY WAY

Our Galaxy looks like a milky band in the night sky, but if we could view it from above, we would see that the Milky Way is a giant spiral.

> WHAT IS A GALAXY?

Our Sun is just one of 200 billion stars arranged in a shape like a fried egg, 100,000 light-years across. This star group is our Galaxy, which is just one of billions of galaxies scattered throughout space.

> WHAT IS THE MILKY WAY?

Our Galaxy is called the Milky Way. This is because it can be seen stretching across the night sky in a blotchy white band. This is our edge-on view of the Galaxy. Since our own Galaxy was the first one that astronomers knew about, they came up with the word "galaxy," which comes from the Greek word for milky.

> WHAT IS THE BIGGEST THING IN THE UNIVERSE?

The biggest structure in the Universe is a huge ring of galaxies five billion light-years across.

Types of galaxies >

A galaxy is a massive system of stars, gas, and dust, held together by gravity. Galaxies are classified by their shape, which may be spiral, elliptical, or irregular. Sometimes, galaxies can merge or collide with each other.

> WHAT ARE SPIRAL GALAXIES?

Spiral galaxies are spinning Catherine wheel spirals like our Milky Way. Barred spiral galaxies have a bar crossing the center with arms trailing from it.

> WHAT ARE IRREGULAR GALAXIES?

Irregular galaxies are galaxies that have no particular shape at all.

> WHERE IS THE EARTH?

The Earth is just over halfway out along one of the spiral arms of the Milky Way Galaxy, about 30,000 light-years from the center. The Galaxy is whirling rapidly, sweeping us round at 60,000 miles an hour.

SPIRAL GALAXY

The neat spiral galaxy named M81 has perfect arms spiraling into its center.

IRREGULAR GALAXY

Most irregular galaxies were once spiral or elliptical but have been pulled apart by gravity.

ELLIPTICAL GALAXY

The elliptical galaxy known as Fornax A is at the edge of a cluster of galaxies known as the Fornax Cluster.

WHAT ARE ELLIPTICAL GALAXIES?

Elliptical galaxies are shaped like footballs. There is no gas and dust remaining in an elliptical galaxy, so no new stars can form.

ARE GALAXIES IN GROUPS?

Yes! Most galaxies are in clusters, which can form larger groups called superclusters. And superclusters are grouped into sheets and threadlike filaments, which surround huge voids in the Universe.

HOW MANY GALAXIES ARE THERE?

There are currently estimated to be about 125 billion galaxies in the Universe, but there may be many, many more than this.

Black holes →

A black hole is a region that has such an immense gravitational pull that it sucks space into a "hole" like a funnel. Not even light can escape the pull of a black hole, which is why it is called "black." The hole's interior cannot be seen.

❯ HOW IS A BLACK HOLE FORMED?

When a large star goes supernova, the center of the star is violently compressed by the shock of the explosion. As it compresses, it becomes denser and denser and its gravity becomes more and more powerful—until it shrinks to a single tiny point of infinite density called a singularity. The singularity sucks space into a black hole.

❯ HOW CAN WE SEE A BLACK HOLE?

The black hole contains so much matter in such a small space that its gravitational pull even drags in light. We may be able to spot a black hole from the powerful radiation emitted by stars being ripped to shreds as they are sucked in. A giant black hole may exist at the center of our Galaxy.

HOLE AT THE CENTER •

It is believed that the galaxy Centaurus A, like many galaxies, has a black hole at its center.

→ WHAT HAPPENS INSIDE A BLACK HOLE?

Nothing that goes into a black hole comes out. Everything is torn apart by the immense gravity.

→ HOW MANY BLACK HOLES ARE THERE?

No one really knows. Because they trap light, they are hard to see. But there may be as many as 100 million black holes in the Milky Way.

→ HOW BIG IS A BLACK HOLE?

The singularity at the heart of a black hole is infinitely small. The size of the black hole is usually taken to be the size of the volume of space from which light cannot escape. The black hole at the heart of our Galaxy may be the size of the Solar System.

WHAT IS GRAVITY?

Gravity is the mutual attraction between every bit of matter in the Universe. The more matter there is, and the closer it is, the stronger the attraction. A big planet pulls much more than a small one, or one that is far away. The Sun is so big, it makes its pull felt over millions of miles.

BLACK HOLE

This artist's impression shows what a black hole at the center of a galaxy might look like.

Distances in the Universe →

It is difficult to measure distances directly in the wider Universe, as very few spacecraft have traveled beyond our Solar System. Astronomers can perform complicated calculations to work out the distances of faraway stars.

❯ WHAT IS A LIGHT-YEAR?

A light-year is 5,879,000,000,000 miles. This is the distance light can travel in a year, at its constant rate of 186,000 miles per second.

❯ HOW FAR IS IT TO THE NEAREST STAR?

The nearest star is Proxima Centauri, which is 4.3 light-years away, or 25 trillion miles.

CLOSEST STAR

Since Proxima Centauri is so close to us, its diameter can be calculated as about an eighth of the Sun's.

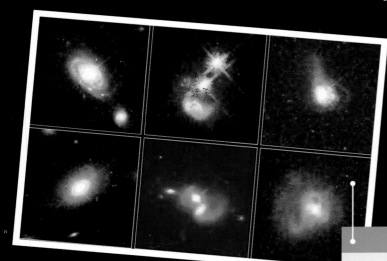

❯ WHAT ARE STANDARD CANDLES?

When measuring the distance to a middle-distance stars, astronomers compare the star's brightness to stars that they know, or "standard candles." The dimmer the star looks in comparison, the farther away it is.

QUASARS

Some of the farthest objects we can see with telescopes are quasars, which may be 13 billion light-years away. Quasars probably surround black holes.

❯ WHAT IS THE FARTHEST OBJECT WE CAN SEE?

The farthest object visible with the naked eye is the Andromeda Galaxy, which is about 2.5 million light-years away. It is visible as a smudge in the night sky. A better view is gained with binoculars or a telescope.

❯ WHAT IS A PARSEC?

A parsec is 3.26 light-years. Parsecs are parallax distances—distances worked out geometrically from slight shifts of a star's apparent position as the Earth moves around the Sun.

❯ WHAT IS RED SHIFT?

When a galaxy is moving away from us, the waves of light become stretched out— that is, they become redder. The greater this red shift, the faster the galaxy is moving.

ANDROMEDA

The Andromeda Galaxy is the closest large galaxy to the Milky Way. Both galaxies are part of the Local Group of galaxies.

STELLAR DISK

It is estimated that the Andromeda Galaxy's disk of stars may be 220,000 light-years across.

Life in the Universe >

As far as we know, Earth is the only planet in the Universe on which life exists. But perhaps in other galaxies there are planets in orbit around a star, just as the Earth orbits the Sun. Could there be life on such planets?

> HOW DID LIFE BEGIN?

Scientific experiments in the 1950s showed how lightning flashes might create amino acids, the basic chemicals of life, from the waters and gases of the early Earth. But no one knows how these chemicals were able to make copies of themselves. This is the key to life, which remains a mystery.

> WHAT IS LIFE MADE OF?

Life is based on compounds of the element carbon, known as organic chemicals. Carbon compounds called amino acids link up to form proteins, and proteins form the chemicals that build and maintain living cells.

> WHAT IS SETI?

SETI is the Search for Extra-Terrestrial Intelligence project, designed to continually scan radio signals from space and pick up any signs of intelligence. It looks for signals that have a pattern, but are not completely regular, like those from pulsating stars.

SEARCHING FOR LIFE

These vast radio telescopes in New Mexico in the United States constantly scan the Universe for radio waves.

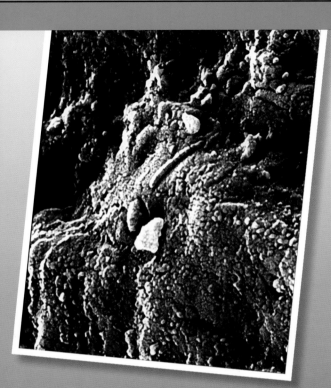

➤ WHERE DID THE MATERIALS OF LIFE COME FROM?

It used to be thought that organic chemicals all originated on Earth, but many complicated organic compounds, including amino acids, have been detected in molecular clouds.

➤ HOW DO WE LOOK FOR EXTRATERRESTRIAL LIFE?

Since possible fossils of microscopic life were seen in a Martian meteorite found on Earth in 1996 (above), scientists have hunted for other signs of organisms in rocks from space.

MARS ROVER

Robotic probes are currently looking for signs that there was once life on Mars. Today, the planet is uninhabitable.

TOP ? QUESTION

IS THERE LIFE ON OTHER PLANETS?

In such a large Universe there are probably many planets, like Earth, suitable for life. But no one knows if life arose on Earth by a unique chance or whether it is fairly likely to happen given the right conditions.

A crowded world >

All human beings are basically the same, wherever they live. We may speak different languages and have different ideas. Our parents may give us dark or pale skin, blue eyes or brown. But in the end we are all members of the same family, living on our increasingly crowded Earth.

MANY PEOPLES

Many nationalities compete in the Olympic Games.

> WHO ARE THE WORLD'S PEOPLES?

Human beings who share the same history or language make up a "people" or "ethnic group." Sometimes many different peoples share a country. More than 120 peoples live in Tanzania, Africa.

> WHICH COUNTRY HAS THE MOST PEOPLE?

More people live in China than anywhere else in the world. They number over 1.3 billion and most live in the big cities of the east and the south. In the far west of China there are empty deserts and lonely mountains.

> HOW MANY PEOPLE LIVE IN THE WORLD?

Billions! The population of the world is now approximately 7.5 billion. That's more than twice as many as 50 years ago.

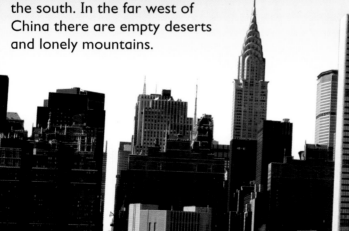

TOP QUESTION ?

WHERE ARE THE MOST CROWDED PLACES IN THE WORLD?

Tiny countries and large cities may house millions of people. Bangladesh is one of the most crowded places in the world. There are more than 1,000 people per square mile.

> ## IS THERE ENOUGH ROOM FOR EVERYBODY?

Just about! But sometime in the future, people may have to live in towns under the ocean or even on other planets, where they would need a special supply of air to stay alive.

> ## ARE THERE MORE AND MORE PEOPLE?

Every minute, about 260 babies are born around the world. Imagine how they would cry if they were all put together! By the year 2050 there will probably be 9.7 billion people in the world.

NEW YORK

In busy cities where land is scarce, people have built tall skyscrapers.

The world's population

Some parts of the world are rich in natural resources such as good soil for growing crops, or oil that can be used for powering machinery. Such resources make countries wealthy. Elsewhere, people may live in poverty and be forced to migrate in search of work and food.

TOP QUESTION ?

HAVE PEOPLE ALWAYS LIVED WHERE THEY LIVE NOW?

During history many peoples have moved huge distances, or migrated. The Polynesians may have taken 2,500 years to cross the Pacific Ocean and settle its islands. In modern times, many people have traveled to the USA in search of better lives.

AFRICAN LAND

Many parts of Africa suffer from poor soil and lack of rain.

❯ HAVE HUMANS CHANGED OUR PLANET?

Over the ages, humans have changed the face of the world we live in. They have chopped down forests and dammed rivers. They have built big cities and roads.

❯ WHY ARE SOME LANDS RICHER THAN OTHERS?

Some lands have good soil, where crops can grow. Some have oil, which is worth a lot of money. But other countries have poor soil, little rain, and no minerals. However hard people work there, they struggle to survive.

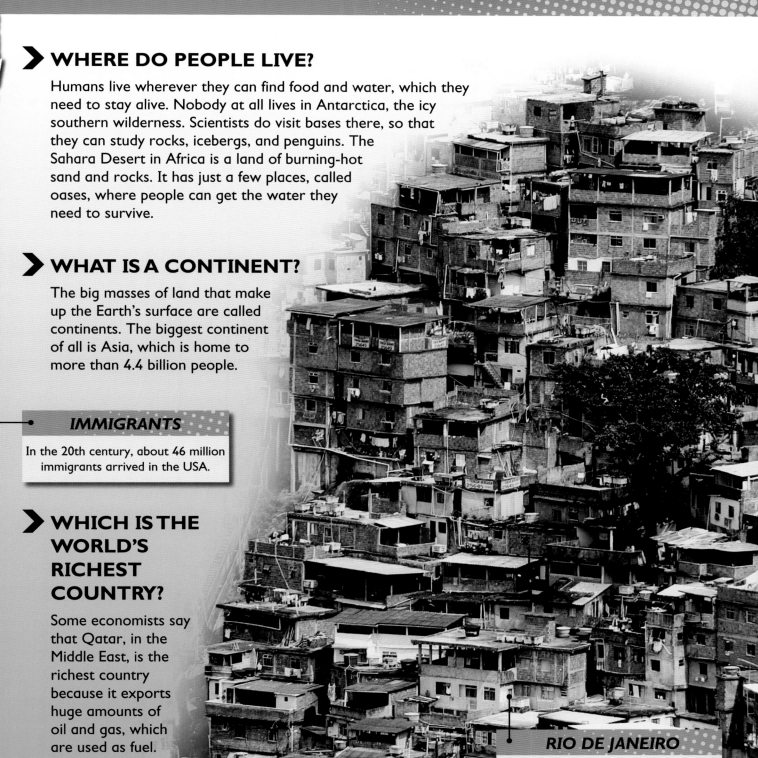

❯ WHERE DO PEOPLE LIVE?

Humans live wherever they can find food and water, which they need to stay alive. Nobody at all lives in Antarctica, the icy southern wilderness. Scientists do visit bases there, so that they can study rocks, icebergs, and penguins. The Sahara Desert in Africa is a land of burning-hot sand and rocks. It has just a few places, called oases, where people can get the water they need to survive.

❯ WHAT IS A CONTINENT?

The big masses of land that make up the Earth's surface are called continents. The biggest continent of all is Asia, which is home to more than 4.4 billion people.

IMMIGRANTS

In the 20th century, about 46 million immigrants arrived in the USA.

❯ WHICH IS THE WORLD'S RICHEST COUNTRY?

Some economists say that Qatar, in the Middle East, is the richest country because it exports huge amounts of oil and gas, which are used as fuel.

RIO DE JANEIRO

Many people in Rio, in Brazil, live in packed shanty towns called *favelas*.

Countries and flags >

There are around 200 countries in the world. Some of these nations rule themselves, while some are ruled by other countries. The number of countries constantly changes as some join together to make a single nation, while others break up into smaller states.

> WHAT IS A COUNTRY?

A country is an area of land under the rule of a single government. Its borders have to be agreed with neighboring countries, although this sometimes leads to arguments. Countries that rule themselves are called independent. Countries that are ruled by other countries are called dependencies.

> DO ALL PEOPLES HAVE A COUNTRY THEY CAN CALL THEIR OWN?

No, the ancient homelands of some peoples are divided up between other countries. The lands of the Kurdish people are split between several nations.

> WHERE CAN YOU SEE ALL THE FLAGS OF THE UNITED NATIONS?

Rows of flags fly outside the headquarters of the United Nations in New York City. Most of the world's countries belong to this organization, which tries to solve all kinds of problems around the globe.

➤ WHICH COUNTRY FITS INSIDE A CITY?

The world's smallest nation is an area within the city of Rome, in Italy. It is called Vatican City and is the headquarters of the Roman Catholic Church. Fewer than 1,000 people live there.

VATICAN CITY

The Pope is the head of government of Vatican City, which is only 0.17 square miles.

➤ WHY DO COUNTRIES HAVE FLAGS?

Flags show bold patterns and bright colors. Many flags are symbols of a nation, or of its regions. The designs on flags often tell us about a country or its history. The flag of Kenya includes a traditional shield and spears, while the flag of Lebanon includes a cedar tree—cedar trees were plentiful there in ancient times.

➤ WHICH IS THE OLDEST NATIONAL FLAG?

The oldest flag still in use is Denmark's. It is a white cross on a red background and was first used in the 14th century. It is called the Dannebrog, meaning "Danish cloth."

UNITED NATIONS

Today 193 countries belong to the United Nations. The organization's own flag is blue.

Nations of the world →

The world's countries range from tiny independent island nations to vast countries made up of numerous states or provinces. Some nations are ruled by countries that lie on the other side of the world, like the British Virgin Islands in the Caribbean Sea.

CANADIAN QUEEN

Canada was once part of the British Empire. Today it is independent, but Britain's Queen Elizabeth II is still on banknotes as the state's figurehead.

❯ WHAT IS AN EMPIRE?

An empire is a country that rules over many other countries and nations. The British Empire was the world's largest empire. In 1922 it covered over a quarter of the world's land.

RUSSIAN LANDS

Russia shares land borders with 14 other countries, from Norway in the west to China in the east. It covers all of northern Asia and takes up 40% of Europe.

❯ HOW MANY INDEPENDENT COUNTRIES ARE THERE?

Currently there are more than 190 independent countries in the world—the number changes from one year to the next.

❯ WHICH IS THE BIGGEST COUNTRY IN THE WORLD?

The gigantic Russian Federation takes up more than 6.5 million square miles of the Earth's surface. It spreads into two continents, Europe and Asia, and its clocks are set at 11 different times.

WHAT ARE COUNTIES AND STATES?

If you look at the map of a country, you will see that it is divided up into smaller regions. These often have their own local laws and are known as states, provinces, counties, or departments.

➤ WHO RULES ANTARCTICA?

Antarctica has no government and belongs to no country. Several different countries have claimed territory in Antarctica, including Britain and France.

➤ HOW MANY DEPENDENCIES ARE THERE IN THE WORLD?

Around 58 of the world's nations are still ruled by other countries. They include many tiny islands in the Caribbean Sea and in the Atlantic and Pacific Oceans.

UNITED STATES

The United States of America is composed of 50 states.

Types of government >

The countries of the world are governed in many different ways. In a democracy, people vote for a political party to make the decisions. In some countries, people do not have the right to vote freely and are ruled over by a dictator.

> HOW DO YOU RECOGNIZE KINGS AND QUEENS?

For ceremonies kings and queens wear traditional robes, and some wear crowns and carry symbols of royal power, such as golden scepters. The traditional rulers of the Yoruba people of Nigeria wear a beaded crown.

> HOW DOES ANYONE GET TO BE A KING OR QUEEN?

Normally you have to be a prince or princess, born into a royal family. In the past, kings and queens were powerful. Today their role is more as the nation's figurehead. They visit hospitals and meet other heads of state, as representatives of their country.

TOP QUESTION

WHAT IS A REPUBLIC?

It's a country that has no king or queen. France is a republic. Over 200 years ago the French king had his head chopped off, during a revolution. The United States of America was ruled by the British king until it fought the Revolutionary War (1775–83).

REVOLUTIONARY WAR
British troops in the Revolutionary War wore red coats.

CROWN JEWELS

The British Crown Jewels include all the crowns owned by the royal family.

WHAT IS A GOVERNMENT?

The members of the government run the country. They pass new laws on everything from schools to hospitals and businesses. Countries where the people can choose their government by voting for a political party are called democracies. Some countries are ruled by dictators. These countries do not hold free elections or have a choice of political parties.

WHAT IS A HEAD OF STATE?

The most important person in a country is the head of state. This may be a king or a queen or an elected president. The head of state takes part in ceremonies and often rides in a big car with a flag on it.

WHICH IS THE WORLD'S OLDEST ROYAL FAMILY?

The Japanese royal family has produced a long line of 125 reigning emperors over a period of thousands of years.

JAPANESE ROYALTY

Emperor Akihito reads from a scroll during a ceremony to make him Emperor of Japan in 1990.

Elections and laws >

Every country has laws. These are a system of rules that govern everything from how we elect our leaders to how we should behave towards each other. Laws are created by governments, while judges and courts decide what should happen when laws are broken.

> ## WHO RULES THE BIRDS?

Traditionally, the king or queen of England owns all the swans on the River Thames, except for those marked in a special ceremony that takes place each summer.

ANTHEM

French soccer players sing along to their national anthem at the 2006 World Cup.

> ## WHAT ARE "JANA-GANA-MANA" AND "THE STAR-SPANGLED BANNER"?

Both of them are national anthems or songs. The first tune is played to show respect to India, the second to the United States. National anthems are played at important occasions, such as the Olympic Games.

➤ WHERE DO JUDGES WEAR BIG WIGS?

In Great Britain judges wear old-fashioned wigs. This is meant to show that the judge is not in court as a private person but as someone who stands for the law of the land.

➤ WHERE IS THE BIGGEST GENERAL ELECTION?

More than 815 million people are eligible to vote in general elections in India. They can cast their votes at one of more than a million Electronic Voting Machines around the country.

ENGLISH JUDGES

The wigs worn by judges are in the style fashionable in 18th-century London.

➤ WHICH IS THE WORLD'S OLDEST PARLIAMENT?

A parliament is a meeting place where new laws are discussed and approved. The oldest parliament is in Iceland. Called the Althing, it was started by Viking settlers in AD 930.

PERICLES OF ATHENS

Pericles, who lived in the 5th century BC, passed laws allowing poorer people to take part in democracy.

TOP ? QUESTION

WHO INVENTED DEMOCRACY?

The people of ancient Athens, in Greece, started the first democratic assembly nearly 2,500 years ago. It wasn't really fair, as women and slaves weren't given the right to vote.

Language >

Around 6,900 languages are spoken in the world. The language spoken by the most people is Mandarin Chinese, which is used daily by around a billion people. English is the most widespread language: the 470 million English-speakers are dotted through every single country.

> WHAT'S IN A NAME?

In Norway there's a village called Å. In New Zealand there's a place called Taumatawhakatangihangak-oauauotamateaturipukaka-pikimaungahoronukupokaiwhe-nua-kitanatahu.

> DO WE USE DIFFERENT WAYS OF WRITING?

Many different kinds of writing have grown up around the world, using all sorts of lines and pictures. This book is printed in the Roman alphabet, which has 26 letters and is used for many languages. Chinese writers normally use about 4,000 different symbols, or characters.

CHINESE HANZI

Chinese characters, called *hanzi*, make single syllables, such as "han" and "zi."

← 800

SACRAMENTO

唐 人 街

▶ DOES EVERYBODY IN ONE COUNTRY SPEAK THE SAME LANGUAGE?

Not often. For example, families from all over the world have made their homes in the United States. In San Francisco, for example, many thousands of Chinese people live in an area called Chinatown. The street signs give the names in both English and Chinese (right).

▶ COULD WE INVENT ONE LANGUAGE FOR THE WHOLE WORLD?

It's already been done! A language called Esperanto was invented more than 100 years ago. Only about 100,000 people have learned to speak it fluently.

▶ WHICH IS THE LEAST SPOKEN LANGUAGE?

Akuntsu is spoken only by the five remaining members of the Akuntsu tribe in Brazil. It is one of around 3,000 endangered languages that may soon die out.

▶ DO WE ALL READ LEFT TO RIGHT?

The Arabic language is read right-to-left, and traditional Japanese top-to-bottom.

ARABIC CALLIGRAPHY

Arabic craftspeople often decorate buildings with beautiful writing, or calligraphy, on tiles or carved in stone.

Communication ➤

Telephones, computers, and radios allow us to keep in touch with family and friends—or to do business with people who live on the other side of the world. A television in London can show live images of celebrations or wars taking place in Sydney or Timbuktu.

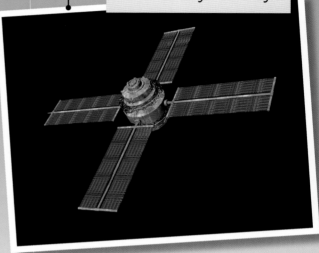

TOP QUESTION ?

CAN WE TALK WITHOUT WORDS?

People who are unable to hear or speak can sign with their hands. Various sign languages have been developed around the world, from China to the United States.

➤ HOW DO WE TALK THROUGH SPACE?

Satellites are machines sent into space to circle the Earth. They can pick up telephone, radio, or television signals from one part of the world and beam them down to another.

➤ WHAT IS THE MOST UNUSUAL WAY TO COMMUNICATE?

In some parts of Central America, Turkey, and the Canary Islands, people worked out a way of communicating using whistles instead of words.

SIGN LANGUAGE

Deaf people of different nationalities can talk to each other using International Sign.

❯ WHAT IS BODY LANGUAGE?

Movements of the head and hands can be a kind of language. Be careful! In some countries wagging the hand palm down means "come here", but in others it means "go away." Shaking the head can mean "yes" in some countries and "no" in others.

❯ WHAT IS EMAIL?

Email, or "electronic mail," is a way of sending and receiving messages by electronic communications systems, such as computers. The first email was sent in 1972.

❯ WHAT HAS MADE THE WORLD SHRINK?

The planet hasn't really got smaller—it just seems that way. Today, telephones, emails, and the internet make it possible to send messages around the world instantly. Once, letters were sent by ship and took many months to arrive.

PHONES

There are almost as many cell phone subscriptions as there are people on Earth—6.8 billion!

Cities of the world

PARTHENON

The great temple of the Parthenon was built in the Doric style, with simple and elegant columns.

Towns first grew up when people stopped being hunter-gatherers and learned how to farm, which meant staying in one place. The first cities were built in southwest Asia. Çatal Hüyük in Turkey was begun about 9,000 years ago. Today, more than half the world's population lives in a city.

WHICH CITY IS NAMED AFTER A GODDESS?

Athens, the capital of Greece, shares its name with an ancient goddess named Athena. Her beautiful temple, the Parthenon, still towers over the modern city. It was built in the mid-5th century BC.

WHICH IS THE HIGHEST CITY?

Potosí in Bolivia stands at 13,350 feet above sea level. The city lies beneath the Cerro Rico ("Rich Mountain"), which is a source of silver ore.

POTOSÍ

The city was founded as a silver-mining town in the 16th century.

ATHENS

In the 1990s, Athens was one of the most polluted cities in the world. The city has now taken steps to reduce traffic fumes.

WHERE ARE THE BIGGEST CITIES IN THE WORLD?

In Japan, where big cities have spread and joined up! Japan is made up of islands that have high mountains, so most people live on the flat strips of land around the coast. In order to grow, cities have had to stretch out until they merge into each other. More than 20 million people live in the capital, Tokyo (below).

> WHAT PROBLEMS DO CITIES CAUSE?

Too much traffic in cities often blocks up the roads and fills the air with fumes. In some cities, there isn't enough work for everyone and some people live in poor conditions.

TOKYO

The megacity of Tokyo encompasses 26 other cities and 5 towns.

> WHO LIVES AT THE ENDS OF THE EARTH?

One of the world's most northerly settlements is Ny-Ålesund, in the Norwegian Arctic territory of Svalbard. The southernmost city is Puerto Williams in Tierra del Fuego, Chile.

> WHICH COUNTRY HAS THREE CAPITALS?

The most important city in a country is called the capital. South Africa has three of them! Cape Town is the legislative capital. Pretoria is the executive capital. Bloemfontein is the judicial capital.

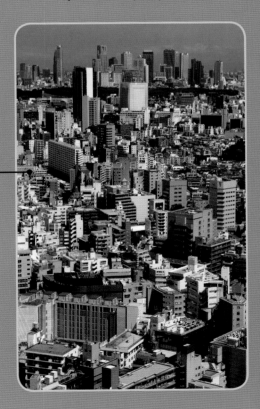

Trade and money

Through the ages, all kinds of things have been used as money around the world—shells, stones, beads, and sharks' teeth. These had no value in themselves, but neither do the metal, paper, or plastic we use today. They are just tokens of exchange.

> WHAT ARE CURRENCIES?

A currency is a money system, such as the Japanese yen, the U.S. dollar, the Mongolian tugrik, or the Bhutanese ngultrum. The exchange rate is what it costs to buy or sell one currency for another.

> WHERE WERE BANKNOTES INVENTED?

Paper money was first used in China 1,000 years ago.

> WHO MAKES MONEY?

The mint—that's the place where coins and banknotes are made. The U.S. mints in Philadelphia and Denver produce billions of new coins each year.

TOP QUESTION

WHERE IS THE SILK ROAD?

This is an ancient trading route stretching from China through Central Asia to the Mediterranean Sea. Hundreds of years ago, silk, tea, and spices were transported along this road to the West by camel trains.

❯ WHERE DO PEOPLE DO BUSINESS?

In Nigeria, money changes hands every day in the busy street markets. Customers haggle about the price of goods. In England, trading might take place in a big store. In Switzerland, bankers watch their computer screens to check their profits. In the New York Stock Exchange, traders grab their telephones as they buy and sell shares in companies.

❯ WHO CATCHES SMUGGLERS?

If you wish to take some goods from one country to another, you may have to pay a tax to the government. Customs officers may check your luggage to see that you are not sneaking in— or smuggling— illegal goods.

COSTLY SILK

In the Middle Ages, Chinese silk was sold for great prices in Europe.

STOCK EXCHANGE

The New York Stock Exchange is over 200 years old and is the largest in the world.

Crops of the world →

The world's land is cultivated to grow crops for people to eat, while fishermen cast nets into the oceans to catch cod and haddock to sell. Some climates are ideal for growing citrus fruit or sugar cane, while other regions are famous for their herds of sheep or cattle.

› WHAT DO BILLIONS OF PEOPLE EAT EVERY DAY?

Billions of people eat rice every day, especially in Asia. Grains of rice are the seeds of a kind of grass that grows in flooded fields called paddies.

PADDY FIELD

Rice grows best in warm and wet river valleys.

› WHERE ARE THE WORLD'S BIGGEST RANCHES?

The world's biggest sheep and cattle stations are in the Australian outback. The best way to cross these lands is in a light aircraft.

› WHAT IS A CASH CROP?

It is any crop that is sold for money. However, many small farmers around the world can only grow enough food to feed themselves and their families—there is no surplus left to sell.

WHEAT HARVEST

Combine harvesters cut the wheat and separate out the grain.

➤ WHICH WERE THE FIRST ALL-AMERICAN CROPS?

About 500 years ago, nobody in Europe had ever seen potatoes, corn, or tomatoes. These important food crops were first developed by the peoples who lived in the Americas before European settlers arrived.

➤ WHO ARE THE GAUCHOS?

The cowboys of the Pampas—the grasslands of Argentina. Today, the *gauchos* still round up the cattle on big ranches called *estancias*.

TOMATO PLANT
The tomato is native to western South America. Today it is grown worldwide.

TOP QUESTION

WHERE ARE THE WORLD'S BREADBASKETS?

Important wheat-producing areas are called "breadbaskets," because they provide our bread! Wheat is a kind of grass, so it grows best in areas that were once natural grasslands, such as the North American prairies.

Transportation around the world >

One of the world's most important inventions was the wheel, which developed in Mesopotamia more than 6,000 years ago. Since then, humankind has invented steam ships, cars, trains, and airplanes in order to travel the world to meet, trade, and learn.

> WHERE IS THE WORLD'S BIGGEST AIRPORT?

Riyadh airport in Saudi Arabia is bigger than some countries. It covers 87 square miles of the Arabian desert.

> WHERE ARE THE LONGEST TRUCKS?

In the outback, the dusty back country of Australia, the roads are long and straight and pretty empty. Trucks can hitch on three or four giant trailers to form a "road train."

> WHICH IS THE WORLD'S LONGEST ROAD?

The Pan-American Highway. It covers 30,000 miles, from Alaska right down to the tip of South America. There is still a bit missing in the middle, but the road starts up again and carries on through South America to Chile (below), Argentina and Brazil.

➤ WHERE CAN YOU CATCH A TRAIN INTO THE SKY?

In the Andes Mountains of South America. One track in Peru climbs to about 15,744 feet above sea level. In Salta, Argentina, you can catch a locomotive known as the "Train to the Clouds."

➤ WHERE ARE BOATS USED AS BUSES?

In the beautiful Italian city of Venice, there are canals instead of roads. People travel from one part of the city to another by boat.

➤ HOW CAN YOU TRAVEL BENEATH THE ALPS?

The Alps are snowy mountains that run across France, Italy, Switzerland, and Austria. They soar to 15,777 feet above sea level at Mont Blanc. Tunnels carry trains and cars through the mountains. The Gotthard Base Tunnel in Switzerland is 35 miles long.

VENETIAN GONDOLAS

A traditional Venetian rowing boat is called a gondola and it is propelled by an oarsman known as a gondolier.

ROAD TRAIN

Road trains more than 160 feet long cruise the highways of Australia's bush.

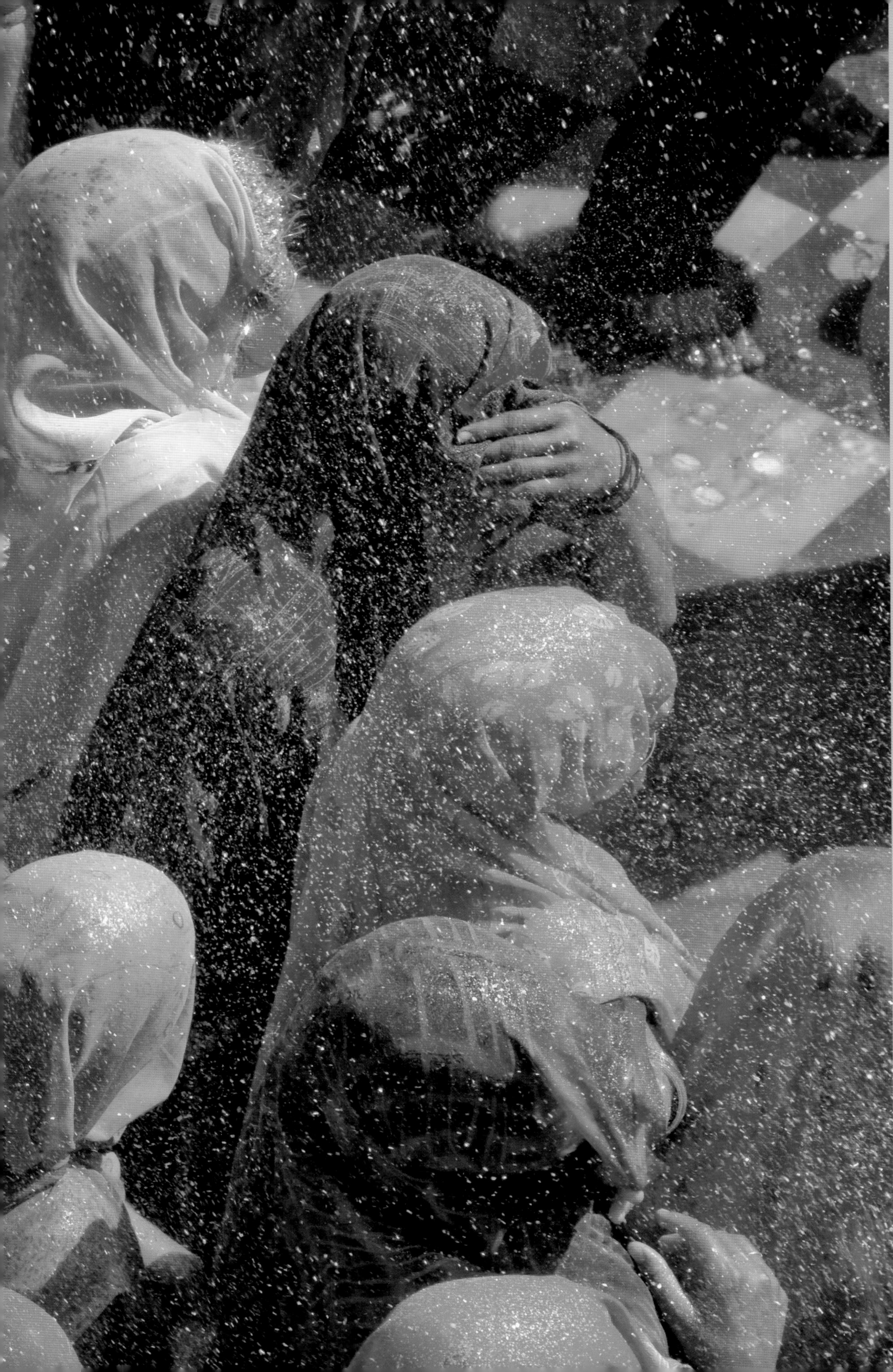

Religion and culture

The world's religions →

Major world religions include Islam, Hinduism, Buddhism, and Judaism. The religion with the most believers—a third of the world's population—is Christianity. All faiths have their own beliefs about the nature of the world and special ways of praying and worshipping.

> WHERE DO YOUNG BOYS BECOME MONKS?

In Burma a four-year-old boy learns about the life of Buddha at a special ceremony. He is dressed as a rich prince and is then given the simple robes of a Buddhist monk.

> WHICH CITY IS HOLY TO THREE FAITHS?

Jerusalem is a holy place for Jews, Muslims, and Christians. Sacred sites include the Western Wall, the Dome of the Rock, and the Church of the Holy Sepulcher.

BUDDHIST MONKS

Boy monks dressed in simple robes hold their traditional bowls ready for lunch.

> WHAT ARE PARSIS?

The Parsis belong to a sect of the Zoroastrian religion, which began long ago in ancient Persia, now Iran. Today, Parsis live in India and Pakistan.

> ## WHICH COUNTRY HAS THE MOST MUSLIMS?

Indonesia is the largest Islamic country in the world, although some parts of it, such as the island of Bali, are mostly Hindu.

JERUSALEM

Muslims worship at the Dome of the Rock in the center of Jerusalem.

WHAT IS SHINTO?

This is the ancient religion of Japan. At its holy shrines, people pray for happiness and to honor their ancestors. Many Japanese people also follow Buddhist beliefs.

> ## WHY IS MOUNT ATHOS IMPORTANT?

Mount Athos is a rocky headland in northern Greece, holy to Christians of the Eastern Orthodox faith. Monks have worshipped there since the Middle Ages.

EMA TABLETS

Ema tablets are covered with written wishes at a Shinto shrine in Tokyo.

A question of faith ➤

Most religions set down moral codes that say how believers should behave. These rules might govern how we should treat people and animals. Religious scriptures, or holy books, also tell believers how they should worship, through prayer, fasting, or pilgrimage.

➤ WHICH MONKS COVER THEIR MOUTHS?

Some monks of the Jain religion, in India, wear masks over their mouths. This is because they respect all living things and do not wish to harm or swallow even the tiniest insect that might fly into their mouths.

➤ WHO WAS CONFUCIUS?

This is the English name given to the Chinese thinker Kong Fuzi (551–479 BC). His beliefs in an ordered society and respect for ancestors became very popular in China.

CONFUCIUS

Confucius taught that we must treat others as we would like to be treated.

➤ WHY DO PEOPLE FAST?

In many religions people fast, or go without food, as part of their worship. If you visit a Muslim city such as Cairo during Ramadan, the ninth month of the Islamic year, you will find that no food is served during daylight hours.

➤ WHERE DO PILGRIMS GO?

Pilgrims are religious people who travel to holy places around the world. Muslims try to travel to the sacred city of Mecca, in Saudi Arabia, at least once in their lifetime. Hindus may travel to the city of Varanasi, in India, to wash in the holy waters of the River Ganges. Some Christians travel to Bethlehem, the birthplace of Jesus Christ.

MECCA PILGRIMS

Muslim pilgrims ritually walk round and round the Kaaba ("cube") shrine, which is the holiest place in Islam.

➤ WHAT IS THE TAO?

Pronounced "dow," it means "the way." It is the name given to the beliefs of the Chinese thinker Lao Zi, who lived about 2500 years ago. Taoists believe in the harmony of the Universe.

SIKH PARADE

Sikh men wearing traditional turbans hold their daggers, or Kirpans.

TOP ? QUESTION

WHAT ARE THE FIVE "K"s?

Sikh men honor five religious traditions. Kesh is uncut hair, worn in a turban. They carry a Kangha or comb, a Kara or metal bangle, and a Kirpan or dagger. They wear an undergarment called a Kaccha.

Festivals >

Religious festivals are times of special importance in the year. They often commemorate, or remember, important events in holy stories, such as the birth of Christ or the triumph of the Hindu god Krishna over demons. Festivals can be times of joy or solemn remembrance.

> WHEN DO PEOPLE THROW PAINT?

During the Hindu festival of Holi, people crowd into the streets to joyfully throw multicolored water over each other. The festival celebrates the triumph of good over evil.

LIGHTED LAMPS

Diwali means "rows of lighted lamps." To celebrate, Hindus light small oil lamps around the home.

> WHAT IS DIWALI?

This is the time in the fall when Hindus celebrate their New Year and honor Lakshmi, goddess of good fortune. Candles are lit in windows and people give each other cards and presents.

➤ WHAT IS HANUKKAH?

This Jewish festival of light lasts eight days. Families light a new candle each day on a special candlestick called a menorah (right). Hanukkah celebrates the recapture of the temple in Jerusalem in ancient times.

➤ WHERE IS NEW YEAR'S DAY ALWAYS WET?

In Burma, people celebrate the Buddhist New Year by splashing and spraying water over their friends!

➤ WHEN ARE MUSLIMS ALLOWED CANDIES?

The Muslim festival of Eid-ul-Fitr marks the end of a month's fasting during Ramadan. People send special cards and children enjoy eating traditional candies.

DIWALI

During Diwali people set off fireworks and prepare traditional meals and candies. Homes are cleaned and windows are opened.

➤ WHERE DO DRAGONS DANCE?

Wherever Chinese people get together to celebrate their New Year or Spring Festival. The lucky dragon weaves along the streets, held up by the people crouching underneath its long body. Firecrackers are set off to scare away evil spirits. The festival is a chance for families to get together.

DRAGON DANCE

Chinese dragons dance as drums beat and cymbals clash. The deafening noise and the fierce face of the dragon were traditionally believed to banish evil spirits on the first day of the new year.

Party time

In every country, people like to get together at certain times of year to dance and dress up. These public parties may be in honor of particular people or they may commemorate a historical event. Sometimes they are just good reasons to practice traditional arts and music.

WHO RIDES TO THE *FERIA*?

Each April the people of Seville, in Spain, ride on horseback to a fair by the River Guadalquivir. They wear traditional finery and dance all night.

WHO REMEMBERS THE FIFTH OF NOVEMBER?

People in Great Britain. The date recalls the capture of Guy Fawkes, who plotted to blow up the Houses of Parliament in London in 1605. The night is marked by fireworks and blazing bonfires.

WHO GETS TO SIT IN THE LEADER'S CHAIR?

In Turkey, April 23 is Children's Day. There are puppet shows and dances. One child gets the chance to sit at the desk of the country's prime minister!

GREEN RIVER

The Chicago River is dyed green on St. Patrick's Day.

VENETIAN MASKS

In Venice people celebrate Carnival by wearing costumes.

WHO WEARS GREEN ON ST PATRICK'S DAY?

St. Patrick's Day, on March 17, is the national day of Ireland. It is celebrated wherever Irish people have settled over the ages, from the United States to Australia. People wear green clothes and green shamrock leaves.

➤ WHAT IS A POWWOW?

It means "a get-together." The Native American peoples of the United States and the First Nations of Canada meet up at powwows each year to celebrate their traditions with dance and music.

POWWOW

A Native American man wearing a celebratory traditional-style outfit dances to the accompaniment of singing and drumming.

TOP QUESTION ?

WHAT IS CARNIVAL?

In ancient Rome there was a rowdy winter festival called Saturnalia. People copied this idea in the Middle Ages. They feasted before Lent began, when Christians had to give up eating meat. People still celebrate Carnival today. In New Orleans, Louisiana, jazz bands parade.

The arts >

The arts include painting, music, theater, and dance. Every country has its own traditional art forms, from the flamenco dancers of Spain and the opera singers of Italy to the Punch and Judy puppet shows of England.

> WHERE DO THEY DANCE LIKE THE GODS?

Kathakali is a kind of dance-drama performed in Kerala, southern India. Dancers in makeup that looks like a mask and gorgeous costumes act out ancient tales of gods and demons.

> WHO PLAYS THE PANS?

People in the Caribbean, at Carnival time. The "pans" are steel drums, which can produce beautiful dance rhythms and melodies.

KATHAKALI MAKEUP

Green makeup shows that the actor is playing a noble character.

ELABORATE COSTUME

The style of costume tells the audience immediately that this character is a hero.

TOP ? QUESTION

WHAT IS KABUKI?

Kabuki is an exciting type of drama that became popular in Japan in the 1600s and can still be seen today. The actors, who are always male, wear splendid makeup and costumes. Kabuki performances last for a whole day and feature several plays, from histories to romances.

WHERE IS STRATFORD?

There are two famous Stratfords. Four hundred years ago, Stratford-upon-Avon, in England, was the home of the great playwright William Shakespeare. The other Stratford, in Ontario, Canada, holds a drama festival in his honor.

WHO MAKES PICTURES FROM SAND?

The Navajo people of the southwestern United States make beautiful patterns using many different colored sands.

KABUKI ACTOR

As tradition demands, this male actor dressed in a kimono is playing a female role.

WHAT IS MORRIS DANCING?

Morris dancing is an English folk dance that probably dates back to the 15th century. The dancers bang sticks together and jingle bells tied to their legs, while stepping in time to traditional music (left).

More arts >

Art can be used to express feelings and communicate ideas. Some of the oldest art forms tell stories about the Earth's creation and the myths of gods and goddesses. Today, artists, musicians, dancers, and playwrights still use art to entertain, inspire, and educate us.

> WHERE IS THE WORLD'S OLDEST THEATER?

The oldest theater building still in use is probably the Teatro Olimpico, in Vicenza, Italy. It opened over 400 years ago. But people were going to see plays long before that. In ancient Greece people went to see masked actors appear in some of the funniest and saddest plays ever written, at stone open-air theaters that are sometimes used for performances today.

GAUGUIN IN RUSSIA

This 1899 painting called *Tahitian Woman with Blossom* was painted by the French artist Paul Gauguin. It hangs in the Hermitage Museum.

TAMA DRUM

The tama is beaten with a curved wooden stick.

> WHERE DO DRUMS TALK?

In Senegal and Gambia, in Africa, the tama is nicknamed the "talking drum." Its tightness can be varied while it is being played, making a strange throbbing sound.

TOP QUESTION
?

WHERE ARE THERE 3 MILLION WORKS OF ART?

At St. Petersburg in Russia, in an art gallery made up of two great buildings, the Hermitage and the Winter Palace.

> WHO SINGS IN BEIJING?

Beijing opera is a spectacular performance. Musicians clash cymbals and actors sing in high voices. They take the part of heroes and villains in ancient Chinese tales. Their faces are painted and they wear beautiful costumes, some decorated with pheasant feathers.

> WHO DANCES A HAKA?

In New Zealand, young Maori people have kept alive many of their traditional dances. A haka was often danced by warriors, to bring them strength to face battle.

> WHO PAINTS THE DREAMTIME?

Australia's Aborigines look back to the Dreamtime, a magical age when the world was being formed, along with its animals and peoples. Many paintings (below) show the landscape and how it was molded by animals such as the Rainbow Serpent.

Food around the world >

The food people eat depends not just on the crops they can grow, the animals they can raise, or the fish they can catch, but also on their traditional customs and religious beliefs. Many people in the world, for example in southern India, do not eat meat—they are vegetarian.

> ## WHO EATS THE MOST CHEESE?

The French eat the most cheese, with the average person consuming 57.2 pounds every year.

> ## WHO MAKES THE WORLD'S HOTTEST CURRIES?

The people of southern India. A mouthwatering recipe might include fiery spices such as red chili pepper and fresh hot green chilies, ginger, garlic, turmeric, and curry leaves.

SPICES

Spices are dried seeds, fruits, roots and barks used as flavorings and preservatives.

HAGGIS

A traditional dish in Scotland is haggis with "neeps and tatties," or mashed yellow turnips and potatoes.

➤ WHO WROTE A POEM TO HIS HAGGIS?

Robert Burns, Scotland's greatest poet, who lived in the 1700s. The haggis is a traditional dish from Scotland made of lamb's heart, liver and lungs, suet, onions, and oatmeal, cooked inside—guess what—a sheep's stomach!

➤ WHERE DO YOU BUY MILK BY WEIGHT?

In the Russian Arctic it is so cold in winter that milk is sold in frozen chunks rather than by the bottle.

➤ HOW DO YOU EAT WITH CHOPSTICKS?

Chopsticks are popular in China and Japan. They can be used by holding them between the thumb and fingers in one hand.

HOW DO WE KEEP FOOD FRESH?

Today, butter can be sent across the world, kept cool by refrigeration. The first ever refrigerator ship was invented in 1876 to carry beef from Argentina. But how did people keep food fresh before that? The old methods were simpler—pickling, smoking, or drying. Traditional methods are still used today to produce some of the world's tastiest foods, such as Japanese pickles (below).

World delicacies

Sushi is considered a great delicacy in Japan. In Great Britain, many people think there is nothing tastier than roast beef. The food we like is a question of personal taste. Sheep's eyeballs and pigs' ears are considered mouthwatering delicacies somewhere in the world!

WHAT IS JAMBALAYA?

Rice and peppers with meat or shrimp, all in an amazing hot, spicy sauce. Where is this served up? In New Orleans, which has a rich cooking tradition.

SUSHI

In Japan, sushi is rice wrapped in sheets of seaweed and topped with meat, fish, or vegetables.

CAVIAR

Black caviar is the salted eggs of the sturgeon fish, while red caviar is the eggs of the salmon. Both varieties are considered a great delicacy.

WHAT IS CAVIAR?

One of the most expensive foods in the world. It is made of eggs from a fish called the sturgeon, which lives in lakes and rivers in Russia and other northern lands.

WHAT IS YERBA MATÉ?

It is a bitter but refreshing hot drink, made from the leaves of the Paraguay holly. It is sipped from a gourd (a kind of pumpkin shell) through a silver straw, and is very popular in Argentina.

CAN YOU EAT SEAWEED?

Various seaweeds are eaten in Japan, and in South Wales seaweed makes up a dish called laverbread. A seaweed called carrageen moss is often used to thicken ice cream and milk puddings.

WHO EATS SPIDERS?

Spiders are a delicacy in Cambodia. The tastiest are plucked straight from their burrow and fried with loads of garlic and salt.

WHO INVENTED NOODLES?

Which noodles came first—Italian spaghetti or Chinese chow mein? Some people say that the traveler Marco Polo brought the secret of noodle-making back to Italy from China in the Middle Ages. Others say the Romans were making pasta in Italy long before that.

SINGAPORE NOODLES

Singapore noodles are a tasty mix of shrimp, red pepper, eggs, and seasoning.

Clothes of the world

We are so used to wearing clothes that we rarely think about why we wear them! People wear clothes to protect themselves from the weather, for modesty, and for comfort. We also choose our clothes to reflect who we are.

TUAREG DRESS

The Tuareg of the Sahara Desert cover their heads to keep out sun and sand.

WHERE DO PANAMA HATS COME FROM?

Actually, Panama hats were first made in Ecuador, where they were plaited from the leaves of the toquilla palm. But they were first exported, or shipped abroad, from Panama.

HOW DO PEOPLE DRESS IN HOT COUNTRIES?

In hot countries people protect their heads from the sun with broad-brimmed hats, from the Mexican sombrero to the cone-shaped hats worn by farm workers in southern China and Vietnam.

WHAT ARE CLOTHES MADE FROM?

Clothes today may be made from natural fibers, such as wool or cotton, or from artificial fibers such as nylon.

BATIK

Intricately patterned batik cloth is made in Java, in Indonesia.

TOP QUESTION ?

WHERE IS THE CAPITAL OF FASHION?

Milan, London, New York, and many other cities stage fantastic fashion shows each year. But Paris, in France, has been the center of world fashion for hundreds of years.

❯ WHAT IS BATIK?

This is a way of making pretty patterns on cloth. Wax is put on the fiber so that the dye sinks in only in certain places. This method was invented in Southeast Asia. In Indonesia, batik is considered a national art form and patterns are handed down over generations of craftspeople.

❯ HOW DO WE KEEP WARM AND DRY?

Since prehistoric times, people have used fur and animal skins to keep out the cold. Today, clothing for polar expeditions uses wool and feathers, plus man-made fibers that are very warm but not too heavy.

PARIS FASHION SHOW

People from all over the world go to see the gorgeous fashions.

National costumes ➤

Most people today wear T-shirts and jeans, skirts or suits. Only on special occasions do they still put on traditional, regional costumes. But in some countries, people still wear local dress regularly. This might be the elaborate kimono of Japan or the colorful sari of India.

➤ WHO WEARS FEATHERS TO A SINGSING?

A singsing is a big festival in Papua New Guinea. Men paint their faces and wear ornaments of bone and shell and long bird-of-paradise feathers. Traditional dress may include skirts made of leaves and grass.

➤ WHICH LADIES WEAR TALL LACE HATS?

The Breton people of northwest France are proud of their costume, which they wear for special occasions. The men wear vests and big black hats. The women wear lace caps, some of which are high and shaped like chimneys.

➤ WHO ARE THE TRUE CLOGGIES?

A hundred years ago wooden shoes, or clogs, were worn in many parts of Europe. The most famous clogs were the Dutch ones (above), which are still worn today by farmers and market traders in the Netherlands.

SILK WEAVING

Beautiful silk is still woven by hand in some parts of Asia.

TOP QUESTION ?

WHO INVENTED SILK?

The Chinese were the first people to make silk, from the cocoons of silkworms, thousands of years ago. Today silk may be used to make bright Indian wraps called saris and Japanese robes called kimonos.

➤ WHERE DO SOLDIERS WEAR SKIRTS?

Guards of honor in the Greek army are called Evzónes. Their uniform is based on the old-fashioned costume of the mountain peoples—a white skirt, woolen leggings, and a cap with a tassel.

➤ WHAT IS A KILT?

The Scottish kilt is a knee-length skirt that is based on traditional male dress in the Highlands of Scotland. Kilts are woven in tartan patterns that are linked with particular families or regions.

Homes around the world →

Houses must shelter people from cold and heat, rain and snow, storms and floods. Around the world, people have come up with different solutions for their homes, depending on the materials they have to build with and the weather conditions that they face.

› WHY DO PEOPLE LIVE UNDERGROUND?

To stay cool! At Coober Pedy in Australia it is so hot that miners digging for opals built houses and even a church underground. These rock homes remain at a constant temperature all year.

› WHAT ARE HOUSES LIKE IN THE ARCTIC?

Today the Inuit people of Arctic North America live in houses, huts, and tents. Traditionally, they lived in igloos made out of blocks of snow. Igloos are still used today by Inuits on the move.

› WHAT ARE HOUSES MADE FROM?

Mud, stone, slate, boulders, bricks, branches, reeds, steel girders, sheets of iron, concrete, glass, timber, straw, turf, ice, bamboo, animal hides, cardboard boxes—you name it! All over the world, people make use of whatever materials they can find or produce to build homes. A building made of stone can remain standing for thousands of years, while wooden or hide houses may be rebuilt frequently.

IGLOO

Snow blocks are stacked into a sturdy dome shape.

LAKE TITICACA

Reed homes are built on floating islands made of reeds!

WHY DO CHALETS HAVE BIG ROOFS?

In the mountains of Switzerland, the wooden houses have broad roofs, designed for heavy falls of snow each winter.

➤ WHY BUILD REED HOUSES?

It makes sense to use the nearest building material to hand. Tall reeds grow around Lake Titicaca in Peru—so the local people use them to build their beautiful houses.

➤ WHY ARE HOUSES BUILT ON STILTS?

In many parts of the world, homes are built on stilts to protect them from flooding or to stop animals from running into the house.

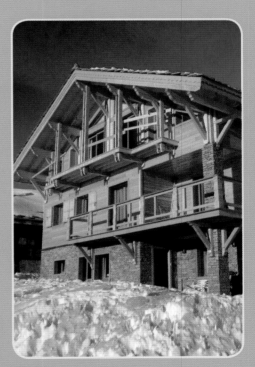

WARM AS SNOW

Snow is an excellent insulator so igloos are surprisingly warm inside, particularly when heated by a stove.

Somewhere to live →

Modern buildings look much the same wherever they have been built, from Los Angeles to Singapore. But all types of local houses can still be seen as well, from mud huts or homes carved from rock to the tents of the Bedouin nomads.

❯ WHERE DO PEOPLE LIVE IN FAIRY CHIMNEYS?

In Cappadocia in eastern Turkey, people have carved homes out of natural cone-shaped rock formations known as "fairy chimneys."

❯ WHERE IS THE BLUE CITY?

The Indian city of Jodhpur is known as the "Blue City" because many of its houses are painted blue (right). The inhabitants believe the color reflects heat and keeps away mosquitoes.

❯ WHERE DO THEY BUILD MUD HUTS?

Thatched huts with walls of dried mud can still be seen in parts of Africa, such as Mali. They are cheap to build, cool to live in, and often look beautiful too.

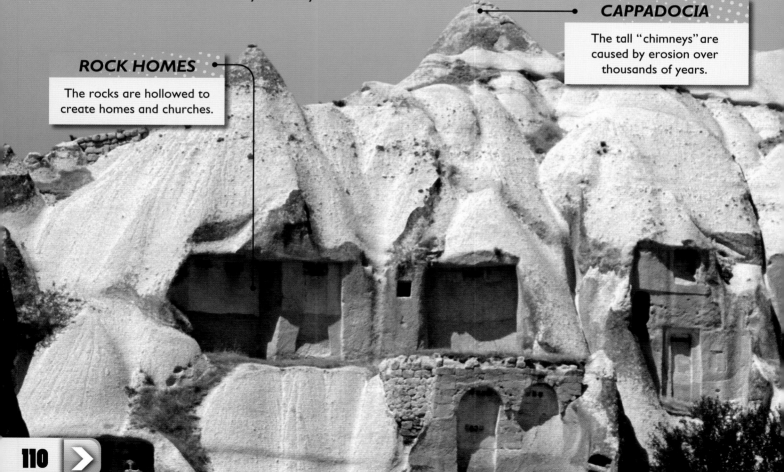

ROCK HOMES
The rocks are hollowed to create homes and churches.

CAPPADOCIA
The tall "chimneys" are caused by erosion over thousands of years.

➤ WHICH PEOPLE LIVE IN CARAVANS?

Many of Europe's Roma people live in caravans, moving from one campsite to another. The Roma, who are sometimes called Gypsies, arrived in Europe from India about 500 years ago.

➤ WHY WERE SKYSCRAPERS INVENTED?

So that more people could fit into a small area of city. High-rise buildings were first built in Chicago about 120 years ago. Newly invented elevators saved people a long climb!

TOP QUESTION ?

WHY DO PEOPLE LIVE IN TENTS?

In many parts of the world, there are people who do not live in the same place all year round. Instead, they follow their herds of sheep and goats from one pasture to another. Such people are called nomads. The Bedouin are nomads who live in North Africa. Their tents are woven from camel hair (below).

Ancient Egypt >

The ancient Egyptian civilization grew up along the River Nile, in northeastern Africa, from about 3150 BC. Under the rule of kings known as pharaohs, the Egyptians made great strides in building, art, and science.

> HOW OLD ARE THE PYRAMIDS?

The first pyramid was built between 2630 and 2611 BC. It had stepped sides and was built for King Djoser. Before then, pharaohs were buried in flat-topped mounds called mastabas. The last pyramid in Egypt itself was built about 1530 BC.

> WHY WERE THE PYRAMIDS BUILT?

The pyramids are huge tombs for pharaohs and nobility. The Egyptians believed that dead people's spirits could live on after death if their bodies were carefully preserved. It was specially important to preserve the bodies of dead pharaohs as their spirits would help the kingdom of Egypt to survive. So they made dead bodies into mummies, and buried them in these splendid tombs along with clothes and jewels.

PYRAMID OF KHAFRE

Pharaoh Khafre's pyramid was completed in about 2530 BC in Giza, near Cairo.

➤ HOW WAS A PYRAMID BUILT?

By man-power! Thousands of laborers worked in the hot sun to clear the site, lay the foundations, drag building stone from the quarry, and lift it into place. Most of the laborers were ordinary farmers, who worked as builders to pay their dues to the pharaoh. Expert craftsmen cut the stone into blocks and fitted them together.

➤ WHY DID EGYPTIANS TREASURE SCARABS?

Scarabs (beetles) collect animal dung and roll it into little balls. To the Egyptians, these dung balls looked like the life-giving Sun, so they hoped that scarabs would bring them long life.

➤ HOW WERE CORPSES MUMMIFIED?

Making a mummy was a complicated and expensive process. First, most of the soft internal organs were removed, then the body was packed in chemicals and left to dry out. Finally, it was wrapped in resin-soaked linen bandages, and placed in a beautifully decorated coffin.

WHY WAS THE RIVER NILE SO IMPORTANT?

Because Egypt got hardly any rain. But every year the Nile flooded the fields along its banks, bringing fresh water and rich black silt, which helped crops grow. Farmers dug irrigation channels to carry water to distant fields. All Egypt's great cities lay on the river, which was also a vital thoroughfare for boats carrying people and goods.

FELUCCA

Wooden boats called feluccas have sailed on the Nile for millennia.

MUMMY

After embalming, a body was wrapped in a sheet and placed in a coffin to keep it safe.

Ancient Greece and Rome >

From the 8th century BC, a great civilization began to grow in Greece, allowing architects, thinkers, and artists to thrive. But by the 3rd century BC, a new power was taking over in the region—the Romans.

WHY DID GREEK TEMPLES HAVE SO MANY COLUMNS?

The style may have been copied from ancient Greek palaces, which had lots of wooden pillars to hold up the roof.

> WHY DID THE ROMAN EMPEROR HADRIAN BUILD A WALL?

To help guard the frontiers of the Roman Empire, which then spread from Britain to North Africa. The wall ran from coast to coast across the north of Britain. Emperor Hadrian (ruled AD 117–138) made many visits to frontier provinces to encourage the Roman troops stationed there.

GREEK TEMPLE

Greek architecture was based on balance and order.

HADRIAN'S WALL

Roman soldiers were based along the wall, looking out for raiders from the lands beyond.

➤ WHY DID THE GREEKS BUILD SO MANY TEMPLES?

Because they worshipped so many different goddesses and gods! The Greeks believed each god needed a home where its spirit could live. And every god had special powers, which visitors to the temple prayed for. Zeus was the god of the sky and Aphrodite was the goddess of love.

➤ WHAT WERE THE ORIGINAL OLYMPIC GAMES?

The Greeks set up an athletics competition in the city of Olympia in 776 BC. It was held every four years, with athletes traveling from all over Greece to compete at events including running, boxing, and wrestling.

➤ WHO WERE ROMAN CENTURIONS?

Centurions were army officers. They dressed for parade in a decorated metal breastplate and a helmet topped with a crest of horsehair. They also wore shin guards, called greaves.

➤ DID THE ROMANS HAVE CENTRAL HEATING?

Yes. They invented a system called the "hypocaust." Hot air, heated by a wood-burning furnace, was circulated through pipes underneath the floor.

ROMAN SOLDIER

This reconstruction of a soldier's dress shows his armor, spear, and sword.

Vikings >

The Vikings came from Norway, Denmark, and Sweden. From around AD 800 until AD 1100, these terrifying warriors made raids right across Europe, killing, burning, and carrying away all they could manage.

> WERE THE VIKINGS GOOD SAILORS?

Yes. They sailed for thousands of miles across the icy northern oceans in open wooden boats, known as longboats. They learned how to navigate by observing the Sun and the stars.

LONGBOAT

A reconstruction of a Viking longboat shows the streamlined, lightweight design.

> WHAT GODS DID THE VIKINGS BELIEVE IN?

The Vikings prayed to many different gods. Thor sent thunder and protected craftsmen. Odin was the god of wisdom and war. Kindly goddess Freya gave peace and fruitful crops.

> WHAT WERE VIKING SHIPS MADE OF?

Narrow, flexible strips of wood, fixed to a solid wooden backbone called a keel. Viking warships were long and narrow, and could sail very fast. They were powered by men rowing, or by the wind trapped in big square sails.

➤ DID THE VIKINGS REACH AMERICA?

Yes, around AD 1000. A bold adventurer named Leif Ericsson sailed westward from Greenland until he reached "Vinland" (present-day Newfoundland, Canada). He built a farmstead there, but quarreled with the local people, and decided to return home.

LEIF ERICSSON

This adventurer was based in a Viking colony in Greenland.

➤ WHAT DOES "VIKING" MEAN?

The word "Viking" comes from the old Scandinavian word *vik*, which means a narrow bay beside the sea. That's where the Vikings lived. It was hard to make a living in the cold Viking homelands, so Viking men raided wealthier lands. But not all Vikings were raiders. Some traveled to new places to settle, and many were hunters and farmers who never left home.

WHAT DID VIKINGS SEIZE ON THEIR RAIDS?

All kinds of treasure. A hoard of silver (below), including coins and belt buckles, was buried by Vikings in the 10th century and discovered by workmen in Lancashire, England, in 1840. The Vikings also kidnapped people to sell as slaves.

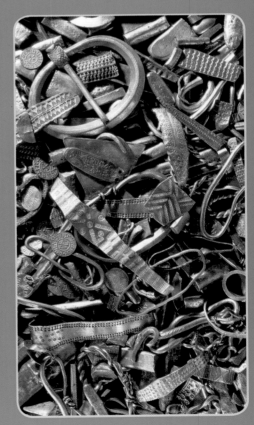

Aztecs, Maya, and Incas >

Before the Spanish conquest of the Americas in the 16th century, Central and South America were home to some of the world's greatest civilizations. Beautiful cities and pyramids were built, while scholars studied astronomy and mathematics.

> **WHO WERE THE INCAS?**

A people who lived in the Andes Mountains of South America (part of present-day Peru and Ecuador). They ruled a mighty empire from the early 15th century to the early 16th century AD.

MACHU PICCHU

This Inca city was built of polished stone around AD 1460.

➤ WHO BUILT PYRAMIDS TO STUDY THE STARS?

Priests of the Maya civilization, which was powerful in Central America between AD 200 and 900. They built huge, stepped pyramids, with temples and observatories at the top. The Maya were expert astronomers and mathematicians, and worked out very accurate calendars.

➤ WHO WERE THE AZTECS?

The Aztecs were wandering hunters who arrived in Mexico about AD 1200. They fought against the people already living there, built a city called Tenochtitlan on an island in a marshy lake, and soon grew rich and strong.

CHICHEN ITZA

This step pyramid is topped by a temple dedicated to the Maya serpent god Kukulkan.

➤ WHO WROTE IN PICTURES?

Maya and Aztec scribes. The Maya used a system of picture symbols called glyphs. Maya and Aztecs both wrote in stitched books, called codices, using paper made from fig-tree bark.

➤ HOW DID THE MAYA, AZTECS, AND INCAS LOSE THEIR POWER?

They were conquered by soldiers from Spain, who arrived in America in the early 16th century, looking for treasure, especially gold.

TOP QUESTION ?

WHY WERE LLAMAS SO IMPORTANT?

Because they could survive in the Incas' mountain homeland, more than 10,000 feet above sea level. It is cold and windy there, and few plants grow. The Incas wove cloth from llama wool, and used llamas to carry loads up steep mountain paths.

The Islamic World >

From about AD 700 to 1200, the Islamic World experienced a period of great power. It led the rest of the globe in learning, invention, and architecture. Islamic leaders controlled lands from southern Spain to northwest India.

> WHAT IS ISLAM?

The religious faith taught by the Prophet Muhammad. People who follow the faith of Islam are called Muslims. Muhammad was a religious leader who lived in Arabia from AD 570 to 632. He taught people to worship Allah, the one God. At its peak, the vast Islamic World—stretching from Spain and North Africa, through Central Asia to northwest India—was ruled by Muslim princes and governed by Islamic laws.

> WHO WERE THE MONGOLS?

They were nomads who roamed over Central Asia. In AD 1206, the Mongol tribes united under a leader known as Genghis Khan ("Supreme Ruler") and set out to conquer the world. At its peak, the Mongol Empire spread from China to eastern Europe.

LA MEZQUITA

The Muslim rulers of Spain built a great mosque in the city of Córdoba from AD 784.

➤ WHO INVENTED THE ASTROLABE?

The astrolabe was perfected by Muslim scientists who lived and worked in the Middle East in the 8th century. Astrolabes were scientific instruments that helped sailors find their position when they were at sea. They worked by measuring the height of the Sun above the horizon.

➤ WHO LIVED IN A CIRCULAR CITY?

The citizens of Baghdad, which was founded in AD 762 by the caliph (ruler) al-Mansur. He employed builders and architects to create a huge circular city, surrounded by strong walls. There were palaces, government offices, mosques, hospitals, schools, libraries, and gardens.

ASTROLABE

Astrolabes can be used for navigation and timekeeping.

➤ WHAT WERE SHIPS OF THE DESERT?

Camels owned by merchants who lived in Arabia. They were the only animals that could survive long enough without food and water to make journeys across the desert, laden with goods to sell. They stored enough nourishment in their humps to last several days.

TOP QUESTION

WHAT WERE THE CRUSADES?

A series of wars fought between Christian and Muslim soldiers for control of the area around Jerusalem (in present-day Israel), which was holy to Muslims, Christians, and Jews. The Crusades began in 1095, when a Christian army attacked (right). Their main period ended in 1291, when Muslim soldiers forced the Christians to leave.

China and Japan →

China was one of the earliest centers of human civilization, with its first cities founded more than 4,000 years ago. On the islands of Japan, people were making decorated pottery an amazing 12,000 years ago. Pottery found there is among the oldest in the world.

❯ WHAT MADE CHINA SO RICH?

The inventions of Chinese farmers and engineers made the land productive. In the Middle Ages, the Chinese made spectacular strides in agriculture. They dug networks of irrigation channels to bring water to the rice fields. They built machines such as a foot-powered pump to lift water to the fields. The emperor and government officials also ruled China very effectively, allowing it to grow wealthy.

❯ HOW DID CHINA GET ITS NAME?

From the Qin (pronounced "chin") dynasty, the first dynasty to rule over a united China. Founded by Qin Shi Huangdi, China's first emperor, it lasted from 221 to 206 BC. It was responsible for the standardization of Chinese script, weights and measures, and the construction of the Great Wall.

GOLDEN TEMPLE

The temple was built in the 14th century in Kyoto, Japan.

❯ WHERE WAS THE MIDDLE KINGDOM?

The Chinese believed their country was at the center of the world, so they called it the Middle Kingdom. Indeed, for centuries, China was one of the most advanced civilizations on Earth. Under the Tang and Song dynasties (AD 618–1279) Chinese cities like Chang'an (modern Xi'an) were the world's biggest.

FORBIDDEN CITY

Built from 1406, the palace, "forbidden" to outsiders, was home to China's emperors.

INNER COURT

A walkway leads to the Palace of Heavenly Purity, where the emperor received guests.

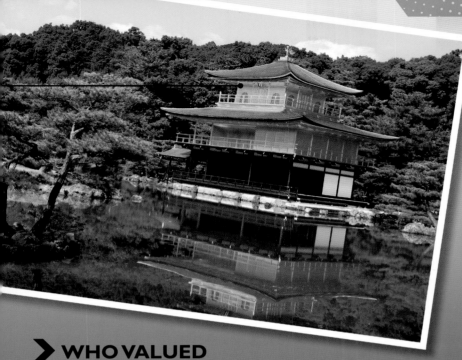

➤ WHO VALUED HONOR MORE THAN LIFE?

Japanese warriors, called samurai, who were powerful from around the 12th century. They were taught to fight according to a strict code of honor. They believed it was better to commit suicide rather than face defeat.

➤ WHICH RULERS CLAIMED DESCENT FROM THE SUN GODDESS?

The emperors of Japan. The first Japanese emperor lived about 660 BC. His descendants ruled until AD 1192. After that, shoguns (army generals) ran the government, leaving the emperors with only religious and ceremonial powers.

WHAT WAS CHINA'S BEST-KEPT SECRET?

How to make silk. For centuries, no one else knew how. Chinese women fed silk-moth grubs on mulberry leaves, and the grubs spun thread and wrapped themselves in it, to make cocoons. Workers steamed the cocoons to kill the grubs, unwound the thread, dyed it, and wove it into cloth.

SILKWORM

Silkworms have been kept in China for at least 5,000 years.

Europe >

After the Roman Empire lost its hold on the rest of Europe, the countries of Europe were ruled by kings, queens, and nobles. As they farmed the land, many ordinary people lived in great poverty.

> WHEN WERE THE MIDDLE AGES?

When historians refer to the Middle Ages, or the medieval period, they usually mean the time from the collapse of the Roman Empire, around AD 500, to about AD 1500.

> WHO FARMED LAND THEY DID NOT OWN?

Poor peasant families. Under medieval law, all land belonged to the king, or to rich nobles. The peasants lived in little cottages in return for rent or for work on the land. Sometimes the peasants protested or tried to run away.

> WHO DID BATTLE IN METAL SUITS?

Kings, lords, and knights who lived in Europe during the Middle Ages. In those days, men from noble families were brought up to fight and lead soldiers into battle. It was their duty, according to law. From about AD 1000, knights wore simple chain-mail tunics, but by about 1450, armor was made of shaped metal plates, carefully fitted together. The most expensive suits of armor were decorated with engraved patterns or polished gold.

ARMOR

Medieval armor covered the body from head to toe.

WHO BUILT CASTLES AND CATHEDRALS?

Kings, queens, and nobles. The first castles were wooden forts. Later, they were built of stone. Cathedrals were very big churches, in cities or towns. They were built to reflect God's glory and to bring honor to those who had paid for them.

❯ WHO WAS THE VIRGIN QUEEN?

Elizabeth I of England (above), who reigned from 1558 to 1603, at a time when many people believed that women were too weak to rule. Elizabeth proved them wrong. Under her leadership, England grew stronger. She never married, and ruled alone.

NOTRE DAME

The Bishop of Paris ordered the construction of the cathedral in 1163.

❯ WHICH RUSSIAN CZAR WAS TERRIBLE?

Ivan IV, who was known as Ivan the Terrible. He became czar, or emperor, in 1533, when he was three years old. He was clever but ruthless, and killed everyone who opposed him. He passed laws removing many of the rights of peasants, making them almost serfs, like slaves.

Africa and India >

By the Middle Ages, African cities were rich centers of learning and trade, with merchants traveling as far afield as India and Southeast Asia. And through its long history, India has been home to many great empires, from the Mauryans (322–185 BC) to the Mughals.

> WHERE DID DHOWS SAIL TO TRADE?

Dhows were ships built for rich merchants living in trading ports like Kilwa, in East Africa. They sailed to the Red Sea and the Persian Gulf to buy pearls and perfumes, across the Indian Ocean to India to buy silks and jewels, and to Malaysia and Indonesia to buy spices.

> WHICH AFRICAN CITY HAD A FAMOUS UNIVERSITY?

Timbuktu, in present-day Mali, West Africa. The city was founded in the 11th century and became a great center of learning for Muslim scholars from many lands. Timbuktu also had several mosques and markets, a royal palace, and a library.

DHOW
A traditional wooden dhow is powered by triangular-shaped sails.

> WHICH KINGS BUILT TALL TOWERS?

Shona kings of southeast Africa, who built a city called Great Zimbabwe. Zimbabwe means "stone houses." The city was also a massive fortress. From inside this fortress, the Shona kings ruled a rich empire from AD 1100 to 1600.

WHO FOUNDED A NEW RELIGION IN INDIA?

Guru Nanak, a religious teacher who lived in northwest India from 1469 to 1539. He taught that there is one God, and that people should respect one another equally, as brothers and sisters. His followers became known as Sikhs.

HOW LONG DID THE MUGHALS RULE INDIA?

For more than three centuries, from 1526 to 1858. The Mughal dynasty was descended from the great Mongol warrior Genghis Khan (Mughal is a north Indian way of writing Mongol). The last Mughal emperor was toppled when the British government took control of India.

GOLDEN TEMPLE OF AMRITSAR

The beautiful temple, begun in 1574, is one of the most important places of worship for Sikhs.

TAJ MAHAL

To construct the building, 20,000 workers were recruited from as far afield as Persia and Syria.

WHO BUILT THE TAJ MAHAL?

The Mughal emperor Shah Jahan (ruled 1628–58). He was so sad when his wife Mumtaz Mahal died that he built a lovely tomb for her, called the Taj Mahal. It is made of pure white marble decorated with gold and semi-precious stones.

Pacific Ocean lands >

Australia, New Zealand, and the Polynesian islands lie in the Pacific Ocean. They were probably first colonized by voyagers from Southeast Asia. From the 16th century, Europeans started to explore the Pacific lands.

> WHO WAS THE FIRST TO SAIL AROUND THE WORLD?

It was sailors in the ship *Victoria*, owned by Ferdinand Magellan, a Portuguese explorer. In 1519, he sailed westward from Europe, but was killed fighting in the Philippines. His captain, Sebastian Elcano, managed to complete the voyage, and returned home to Europe, weak but triumphant, in 1522.

HOW DID SAILORS HELP SCIENCE?

European sailors often observed the plants, fish, and animals as they traveled, and brought specimens home with them. When Captain James Cook explored the Pacific Ocean, he took artists and scientists with him to record what they saw.

CAPTAIN COOK

This drawing was made by Captain Cook's official artist, John Webber, when the expedition arrived in Hawaii in 1779.

> DID THE ABORIGINALS ALWAYS LIVE IN AUSTRALIA?

No, they probably arrived from Southeast Asia about 60,000 years ago, when the sea around Australia was shallower than today. They may have traveled by land or in small boats.

> WHAT WERE DINGOES USED FOR?

Dingoes are descended from dogs introduced to Australia by Aboriginal settlers. They were used as guard and hunting dogs, and to keep Aboriginal people warm as they slept around campfires in the desert, which is cold at night.

➤ WHO WERE THE FIRST PEOPLE TO DISCOVER NEW ZEALAND?

The Maoris. They began a mass migration from other Pacific Islands in about AD 1150, but remains dating back to AD 800 have been found in New Zealand.

MAORI CARVING

Wood carving—on buildings and decorative items—is an important part of traditional Maori culture.

➤ HOW DID THE POLYNESIAN PEOPLE CROSS THE PACIFIC OCEAN?

By sailing and paddling big outrigger canoes. They steered by studying the waves and the stars, and made maps out of twigs and shells to help themselves navigate.

POLYNESIAN CANOE

The canoe has an outrigger, or support, on one side for stability.

North America >

The earliest evidence for settlement of North America dates from 26,000 years ago. These ancestors of today's Native Americans were farmers, hunters, and traders. The first Europeans to settle in North America arrived in the mid-16th century.

> WHAT STORIES DO TOTEM POLES TELL?

Native American people who lived in the forests of northwest North America carved tall totem poles to record their family's history, and to retell ancient legends about the powerful spirits that lived in all rocks, mountains, wild animals, and trees.

> WHO LIVED IN TENTS ON THE GREAT PLAINS?

Native American hunters, like the Sioux and the Cheyenne. After Europeans arrived, bringing horses with them, Native Americans spent summer on the grasslands of the Great Plains, following herds of buffalo, which they killed for meat and skins. In winter, they camped in sheltered valleys. Before the Europeans brought horses, Native Americans were mainly farmers.

TOTEM POLE

The word "totem" comes from the Ojibwe people of Canada's word for family or tribe.

> WHY DID THE PILGRIMS LEAVE HOME?

The Pilgrims were a group of English families with strong religious beliefs, who quarreled with Church leaders and the government. In 1620 they sailed in the *Mayflower* to America, to build a new community where they could practice their religion in peace.

➤ WHEN DID THE USA BECOME INDEPENDENT?

On July 4, 1776, 13 English colonies (where most Europeans in America had settled) made a Declaration of Independence, refusing to be ruled by Britain any longer. They became a new nation, the United States of America. Britain sent more troops to win the colonies back, but was defeated in 1783.

LIBERTY BELL

According to tradition, the bell was rung to announce the Declaration of Independence in 1776.

➤ WHO WERE THE FIRST EUROPEANS TO SETTLE IN NORTH AMERICA?

Spanish colonists, who settled in present-day Florida and California from about 1540. English settlements began in Jamestown in 1607 and in Massachusetts in 1620.

WHY DID A CIVIL WAR BREAK OUT?

The Civil War (1861–65), between the northern and southern states, was caused mainly by a quarrel over slavery. The southern states relied on African slaves working on their cotton plantations. The northern states wanted slavery banned. After four years, the northern states won, and slavery was abolished.

The Industrial Revolution ❯

The Industrial Revolution was a huge change in the way people worked and goods were produced. Machines in large factories replaced craftspeople working by hand. It began around 1775 in Britain and spread slowly to Western Europe and the USA.

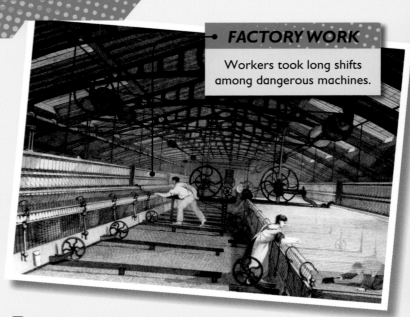

FACTORY WORK

Workers took long shifts among dangerous machines.

❯ WHEN DID THE FIRST TRAINS RUN?

Horse-drawn railway wagons had been used to haul coal and stone from mines and quarries since the 16th century, but the first passenger railroad was opened by George Stephenson in the north of England in 1825. Its locomotives were powered by steam.

❯ WHO WORKED IN THE FIRST FACTORIES?

Thousands of poor men and women moved from the countryside to live in fast-growing factory towns. They hoped to find regular work and more pay. Wages in factories were better than those on farms, but factories were often dirty and dangerous.

STEPHENSON'S ROCKET

In 1829, George Stephenson built a groundbreaking steam locomotive, called the *Rocket*.

> DID CHILDREN LEAD BETTER LIVES THEN?

No. Many worked 16 hours a day in factories and down mines. Large numbers were killed in accidents with machinery, or died from breathing coal dust or chemical fumes. After 1802, governments began to pass laws to protect child workers.

> WHY WERE DRAINS AND TOILETS SO IMPORTANT?

Because without them, diseases carried in sewage could spread quickly in crowded industrial towns. Pottery-making was one of the first mass-production industries—and the factories made thousands of toilets!

> HOW DID THE RAILROADS CHANGE PEOPLE'S LIVES?

They helped trade and industry grow, by carrying raw materials to factories, and finished goods from factories to shops. They carried fresh foods from farms to cities. They made it easier for people to travel and encouraged a whole new holiday industry.

WHY WAS STEAM POWER SO IMPORTANT?

The development of the steam engine was one of the key breakthroughs that allowed the Industrial Revolution to take place. A steam engine can do work—such as powering machines or trains —using hot steam. Steam power allowed quicker production of goods in factories (below) and then their swift transport to buyers.

The Modern Age >

Since 1900 the world has changed in many ways. Women now play an important part in government. Technology has revolutionized our lives. But wars and poverty still blight the world.

WAR GRAVES

Around 10 million soldiers died in World War I.

> WHAT WAS THE LONG MARCH?

A grueling march across China, covering 5,000 miles, made by around 100,000 Communists escaping their enemies. They were led by Mao Zedong, who became ruler of China in 1949.

> WHO FOUGHT AND DIED IN THE TRENCHES?

Millions of young men during World War I (1914–18). Trenches were ditches dug into the ground. They were meant to shelter soldiers from gunfire, but offered little protection from shells exploding overhead. Soon, the trenches filled up with mud, water, rats, and dead bodies.

TOP QUESTION ?

WHO DROPPED THE FIRST ATOMIC BOMB?

On August 6, 1945, the United States bombed Hiroshima in Japan, killing 66,000 people instantly. Two-thirds of the city's buildings were destroyed (right). Days later, Japan surrendered, ending World War II.

➤ WHO MADE FIVE-YEAR PLANS?

Joseph Stalin, the Russian Communist leader who ruled from 1924 to 1953. He reorganized the country in a series of Five-Year Plans. He built thousands of new factories, took land away from ordinary people, and divided it into vast collective farms. Critics of his policies were often killed.

➤ WHAT WAS THE COLD WAR?

A time of tension from the 1940s to the 1980s between the USA and the USSR. The USA believed in capitalism; the USSR was Communist—and the countries distrusted one another. The superpowers never fought face to face, but their enmity drew them into local conflicts around the globe.

MAN ON THE MOON

The American astronaut Buzz Aldrin (left) was the second man to set foot on the Moon. The first man on the Moon was his companion Neil Armstrong, who took this famous photo.

➤ WHO TOOK PART IN THE SPACE RACE?

The USSR and the USA. Each tried to rival the other's achievements in space. The USSR took the lead by launching the first satellite in 1957, but the United States won the race by landing the first man on the Moon in 1969.

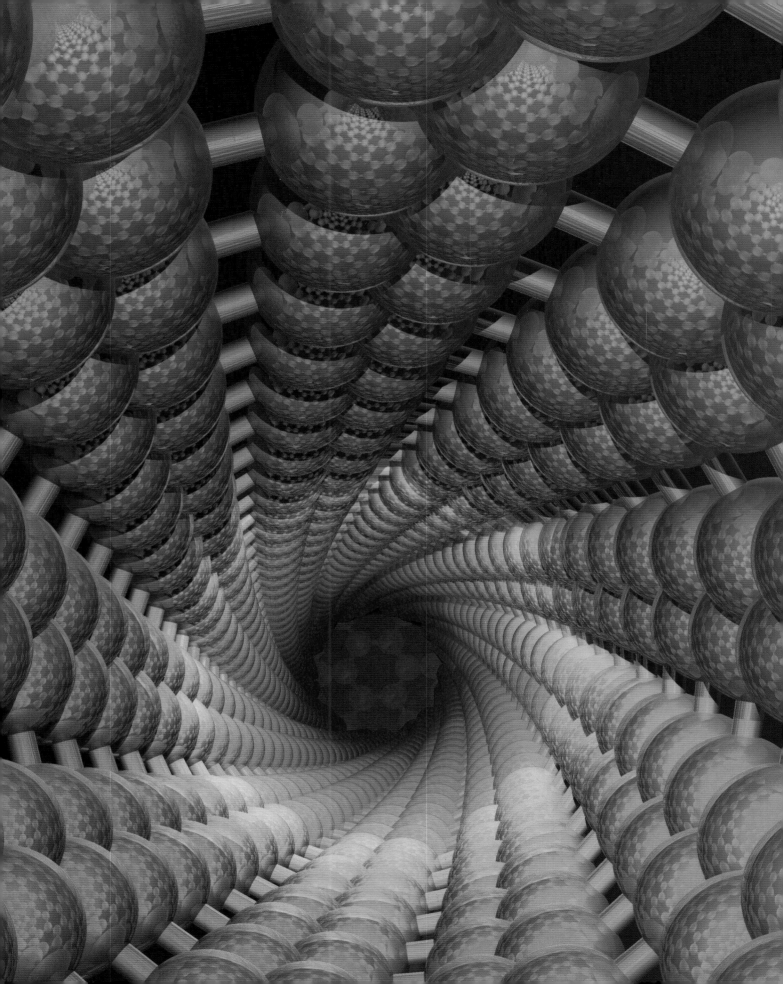

Elements and substances

Atoms and particles ›

Atoms are what every substance is made of. They are the smallest bit of any substance. Yet atoms are largely composed of empty space—and dotted with even tinier clouds of energy called subatomic particles.

› WHAT IS THE NUCLEUS?

Most of an atom is empty space, but at its center is a tiny area called the nucleus. This contains two kinds of nuclear particle—neutrons with no electrical charge, and protons with a positive electrical charge. A hydrogen atom contains no neutrons and one proton.

ELECTRON

A helium atom has two electrons. Their negative charge balances the positive charge of the protons.

› HOW BIG ARE ATOMS?

Atoms are about a ten millionth of a millimeter across and weigh 100 trillionths of a trillionth of a gram. The smallest atom is hydrogen; the most massive is ununoctium.

HELIUM ATOM

A helium atom contains two protons and two neutrons in its nucleus. It is the second smallest atom.

WHAT IS THE SMALLEST PARTICLE?

No one is sure. Atoms are made of protons, neutrons, and electrons. In turn, these are made of even tinier particles—quarks and leptons. Scientists know about more than 200 kinds of subatomic particle so far. But one day we might discover even smaller particles.

WHAT ARE ELECTRONS?

Electrons are the negatively electrically charged particles that whiz around inside an atom. They were discovered by the English physicist J.J. Thomson (1856–1940) in 1897 during some experiments with cathode ray tubes.

CATHODE RAY TUBE

A stream of electrons is fired into a vacuum, or totally empty, tube.

CAN ATOMS JOIN TOGETHER?

Yes! Electrons are held to the nucleus by electrical attraction, because they have an opposite electrical charge to the protons in the nucleus. But electrons can also be drawn to the nuclei of other atoms. This is when bonding takes place.

WHIZZING

Electrons whirl around inside the atom.

TOP QUESTION ?

WHO FIRST SPLIT THE ATOM?

In 1919, the physicist Ernest Rutherford (right) managed to break down nitrogen atoms into hydrogen and oxygen. In 1932, his students John Cockcroft and Ernest Walton managed to split the nucleus of an atom by firing protons at it.

Elements

An element is a substance that cannot be split up into other substances. Water is not an element because it can be split into the gases oxygen and hydrogen. Oxygen and hydrogen are elements because they cannot be split.

Hydrogen

WHAT IS AN ATOMIC NUMBER?

Every element has its own atomic number. This is the number of protons in its nucleus, which is balanced by the same number of electrons. Hydrogen, with one proton, is number 1.

WHAT ARE ELECTRON SHELLS?

Electrons behave as if they are stacked around the nucleus at different levels, like the layers of an onion. These levels are called shells, and there is room for a particular number of electrons in each shell. The number of electrons in the outer shell determines how the atom will react with other atoms. Carbon has four electrons in its outer shell and room for four more, so carbon atoms link very readily with other atoms.

WHAT IS ATOMIC MASS?

Atomic mass is the "weight" of one whole atom of a substance, which is of course very tiny! It includes both protons and neutrons.

Oxygen

WATER MOLECULE

A molecule of water is composed of two hydrogen atoms bonded to one oxygen atom by electrons.

SULFUR

The element sulfur has an atomic number of 16.

WHAT IS THE LIGHTEST ELEMENT?

The lightest element is hydrogen. It has one proton in its nucleus and has an atomic mass of just one. Hydrogen is the most common element in the Universe.

HYDROGEN AIRSHIP

Since hydrogen is lighter than air, it was once used in airships. However, it is also very flammable.

Hydrogen

❯ WHAT IS A MOLECULE?

Quite often, atoms join up with other atoms—either of the same kind, or with other kinds—to form chemical compounds. A molecule is the smallest part of a substance that can exist on its own.

❯ HOW MANY ELEMENTS ARE THERE?

New elements are sometimes discovered, but the total number identified so far is 118.

The periodic table

Elements can be ordered into a chart called the periodic table. Columns are called groups; rows are called periods. Elements in a group have the same number of electrons in the outer shell of their atoms and similar properties—such as being hard and shiny.

› WHAT ARE THE TRANSITION METALS?

Transition metals are the metals in the middle of the periodic table, such as gold, chromium, and silver (left). They are usually shiny and tough, but easily shaped.

› WHAT ARE NOBLE GASES?

The noble gases are in the farthest right-hand column of the periodic table. These gases do not readily react with other elements. But krypton, radon, and xenon do combine with fluorine and oxygen to form compounds.

› WHY ARE SOME ELEMENTS REACTIVE?

Elements are reactive if they readily gain or lose electrons. Elements on the left of the periodic table, called metals, lose electrons very easily. The farther left they are, the more reactive they are.

› WHAT IS A METAL?

A metal is hard, dense, and shiny, and goes "ping" when you strike it with another metal. It also conducts, or transfers, electricity and heat well. Chemists define a metal as an electropositive element, which means that metals easily lose negatively charged electrons. It is these lost, "free" electrons that make metals excellent conductors of electricity.

GROUP 2

The alkaline earth metals are silver-colored metals. They have two electrons in their outer shells.

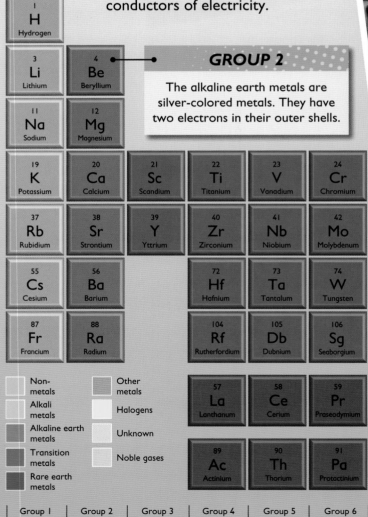

Non-metals	Other metals
Alkali metals	Halogens
Alkaline earth metals	Unknown
Transition metals	Noble gases
Rare earth metals	

| Group 1 | Group 2 | Group 3 | Group 4 | Group 5 | Group 6 |

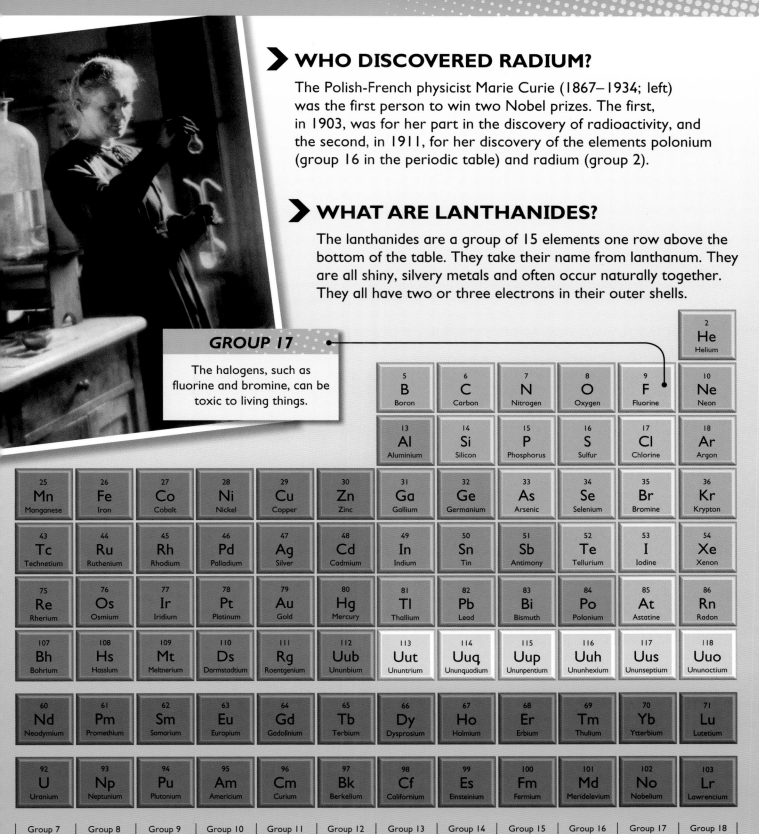

❯ WHO DISCOVERED RADIUM?

The Polish-French physicist Marie Curie (1867–1934; left) was the first person to win two Nobel prizes. The first, in 1903, was for her part in the discovery of radioactivity, and the second, in 1911, for her discovery of the elements polonium (group 16 in the periodic table) and radium (group 2).

❯ WHAT ARE LANTHANIDES?

The lanthanides are a group of 15 elements one row above the bottom of the table. They take their name from lanthanum. They are all shiny, silvery metals and often occur naturally together. They all have two or three electrons in their outer shells.

GROUP 17

The halogens, such as fluorine and bromine, can be toxic to living things.

											2 He Helium
5 B Boron	6 C Carbon	7 N Nitrogen	8 O Oxygen	9 F Fluorine	10 Ne Neon
13 Al Aluminium	14 Si Silicon	15 P Phosphorus	16 S Sulfur	17 Cl Chlorine	18 Ar Argon

25 Mn Manganese	26 Fe Iron	27 Co Cobalt	28 Ni Nickel	29 Cu Copper	30 Zn Zinc	31 Ga Gallium	32 Ge Germanium	33 As Arsenic	34 Se Selenium	35 Br Bromine	36 Kr Krypton
43 Tc Technetium	44 Ru Ruthenium	45 Rh Rhodium	46 Pd Palladium	47 Ag Silver	48 Cd Cadmium	49 In Indium	50 Sn Tin	51 Sb Antimony	52 Te Tellurium	53 I Iodine	54 Xe Xenon
75 Re Rherium	76 Os Osmium	77 Ir Iridium	78 Pt Platinum	79 Au Gold	80 Hg Mercury	81 Tl Thallium	82 Pb Lead	83 Bi Bismuth	84 Po Polonium	85 At Astatine	86 Rn Radon
107 Bh Bohrium	108 Hs Hasslum	109 Mt Meltnerium	110 Ds Darmstadtium	111 Rg Roentgenium	112 Uub Ununbium	113 Uut Ununtrium	114 Uuq Ununquadium	115 Uup Ununpentium	116 Uuh Ununhexium	117 Uus Ununseptium	118 Uuo Ununoctium
60 Nd Neodymium	61 Pm Promethium	62 Sm Samarium	63 Eu Europium	64 Gd Gadollnium	65 Tb Terbium	66 Dy Dysprosium	67 Ho Holmium	68 Er Erbium	69 Tm Thulium	70 Yb Ytterbium	71 Lu Lutetium
92 U Uranium	93 Np Neptunium	94 Pu Plutonium	95 Am Americium	96 Cm Curium	97 Bk Berkelium	98 Cf Californium	99 Es Einsteinium	100 Fm Fermium	101 Md Meridelevium	102 No Nobelium	103 Lr Lawrencium

| Group 7 | Group 8 | Group 9 | Group 10 | Group 11 | Group 12 | Group 13 | Group 14 | Group 15 | Group 16 | Group 17 | Group 18 |

Solids and liquids >

Substances can be solid, liquid, or gas. These are the different states of matter. Substances move from one state to another when they are heated or cooled, boosting or reducing the energy of their particles.

> WHAT ARE SOLIDS?

In solids, particles are locked together, so solids have a definite shape and volume. In liquids, particles move around a bit, so liquids can flow into any shape, while their volume stays the same. In gases, particles zoom about all over the place, so gases spread out to fill containers of any size or shape.

TOP QUESTION ?

WHAT SUBSTANCE HAS THE HIGHEST MELTING POINT?

The metal with the highest melting point is tungsten, which melts at 6177°F. In 2015, scientists found a new substance which they believe might have a higher melting point—over 7000°F!

ICE, WATER, AND STEAM •

At this hot spring in Iceland, water is in three states: solid, liquid, and gas.

> WHAT IS SNOW?

Snow is composed of small ice particles. The particles are formed when water droplets in a cloud get so cold they freeze. The ice particles start to stick together, forming snowflakes. Once the flakes are heavy enough, they fall.

WHEN DO THINGS FREEZE?

Things freeze from liquid to solid when they reach the freezing point. Most substances get smaller when they freeze as the particles pack closer together. But water gets bigger as it turns to ice.

WHEN DO THINGS MELT?

Things melt from solid to liquid on reaching a temperature called the melting point. Each substance has its own melting point. Water's is 32°F; lead's is 621.5°F.

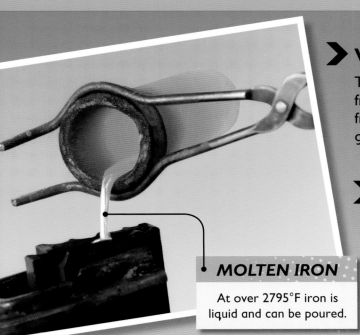

MOLTEN IRON

At over 2795°F iron is liquid and can be poured.

WHICH SUBSTANCE HAS THE LOWEST FREEZING POINT?

Mercury has the lowest freezing point of any metal, at -37.9°F. Helium has the lowest freezing point of all substances, at -452°F, which is less than 7° above absolute zero.

ICE AND WATER

When ice cubes are put into water, heat from the water makes the molecules in the ice move faster and faster until they break free of the solid—and the cubes melt.

Gases >

A gas is one of the states of matter. Gas has no definite shape or volume. Its particles are in random motion. Gases can expand and contract depending on pressure and temperature. They will grow to fill a container of any size.

> WHAT HAPPENS IN EVAPORATION AND CONDENSATION?

Evaporation happens when a liquid is warmed up and changes to a vapor. Particles at the liquid's surface vibrate so fast they escape altogether. Condensation happens when a vapor is cooled down and becomes liquid. Evaporation and condensation take place not only at boiling point, but also at much cooler temperatures.

> WHAT IS PLASMA?

A plasma is the fourth state of matter. It occurs only when a gas becomes so hot its atoms and molecules collide and electrons are ripped free. This happens inside the Sun, other stars, and lightning, and in gas neon tubes. Plasma displays, in which the plasma emits light, are used for some television screens.

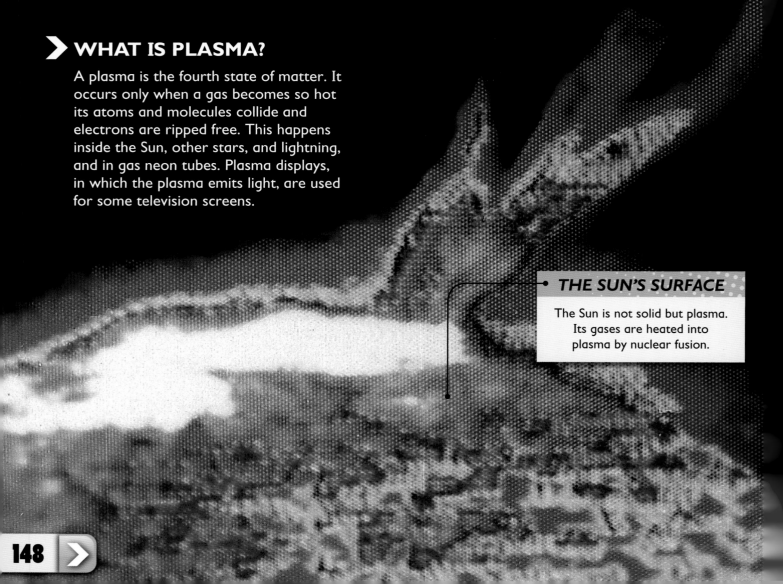

THE SUN'S SURFACE

The Sun is not solid but plasma. Its gases are heated into plasma by nuclear fusion.

› WHEN DO THINGS BOIL?

Things boil from liquid to gas when they reach boiling point, which is the maximum temperature a liquid can reach. For water this is 212°F.

› HOW DOES PRESSURE CHANGE?

If you squeeze a gas into half the space, the pressure doubles (as long as the temperature stays the same). This is Boyle's Law. If you warm up a gas, the pressure rises in proportion (as long as you keep it the same volume). This is the Pressure Law.

› WHAT ARE CLOUDS?

Clouds form when warm air is heated by the Sun and rises. As it rises, the warm air cools, eventually becoming cold enough for the water vapor it contains to condense into water droplets, which we can see as clouds.

WHAT IS PRESSURE?

Pressure is the amount of force pressing on something. Air pressure is the force with which air presses. The force comes from the bombardment of the moving air particles.

BAROMETER

A barometer measures air pressure, which rises and falls depending on the weather.

Mixing chemicals

The elements do not always exist alone. Often, elements react chemically with each other, forming compounds of two or more elements joined together. Elements may also dissolve in, or mix with, other elements without becoming joined as a compound.

WHAT ARE COMPOUNDS?

They are substances made from two or more elements joined together. Every molecule in a compound is the same combination of atoms. Sodium chloride, for instance, is one atom of sodium joined to one of chlorine. Compounds have different properties from the elements that make them up. Sodium, for instance, spits when put in water; chlorine is a gas. Yet sodium chloride is table salt!

HOW DO CHEMICALS REACT?

When substances react chemically, their atoms, ions, and molecules interact to form new combinations, separating elements from compounds or joining them together to form different compounds. Nearly all chemical reactions involve a change in energy, usually heat, as the bonds between particles are broken and formed.

SUGAR

Sugar is a compound of the elements carbon, hydrogen, and oxygen.

SALT DEPOSITS

The Dead Sea is the world's saltiest body of water. In the shallows, the water evaporates in the sunshine, leaving salt deposits.

> WHAT IS A MIXTURE?

Mixtures are substances that contain several chemical elements or compounds mixed in together but not chemically joined. The chemicals intermingle but do not react with each other, and with the right technique can often be separated.

> WHAT IS AN ION?

An ion is an atom that has either lost one or a few electrons, making it positively charged (cation), or gained a few, making it negatively charged (anion). Ions usually form when substances dissolve in a liquid.

HOW DO THINGS DISSOLVE?

When solids dissolve in liquid, it may look as if the solid disappears. Its atoms, ions, or molecules are, in fact, still intact—but are separated and evenly dispersed throughout the liquid.

DISSOLVING INK

When dropped in water, ink disperses until the water is evenly colored.

> WHAT IS THE SEA MADE OF?

The sea is water with oxygen, carbon dioxide, nitrogen, and various salts dissolved in it. The most abundant salt is common salt (sodium chloride). Others include Epsom salt (magnesium sulfate), magnesium chloride, potassium chloride, potassium bromide, and potassium iodide.

Chemical reactions >

We are constantly surrounded by chemical reactions—and many of them are essential to our daily lives. What would we do without the chemical reactions involved in fire, batteries, and cooking?

> WHAT IS FIRE?

Fire is a chemical reaction in which a substance gets so hot that it combines with oxygen in the air. The flames we see are the heat and light energy created by the reaction.

FIRE

A fire will go on burning as long as there is still oxygen and fuel to make the chemical reaction.

> WHAT IS ELECTROLYSIS?

Electrolysis is a means of separating compounds by passing an electric current through them. It makes positive ions move to the negative terminal and negative ions to the positive. For example, electrolysis can make hydrogen from water.

> WHAT IS A CHEMICAL FORMULA?

A chemical formula is a shorthand way of describing an atom, an ion, or a molecule. Initial letters (sometimes plus an extra letter) usually identify the atom or ion; a little number indicates how many atoms are involved. The formula for water is H_2O, because each molecule consists of two hydrogen atoms and one oxygen atom.

AIR COMPOSITION

The air in the Earth's atmosphere is a mixture of different gases.

> IS AIR A COMPOUND?

No. Air is a mixture of elements and compounds but not a compound itself. Air contains 78% nitrogen and 21% oxygen with traces of argon, carbon dioxide, helium, neon, krypton, xenon, and radon.

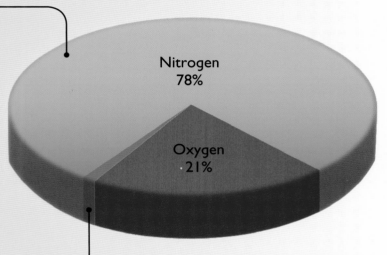

Nitrogen
78%

Oxygen
21%

Other gases less than 1%

BAKING BREAD

A chemical reaction takes place between yeast and sugar to make bread rise.

> HOW DOES BREAD RISE?

Bakers add yeast, a type of fungus, to dough before they put it in the oven. The yeast reacts with the sugar in the dough to make carbon dioxide. This gas forms pockets in the bread, making it rise.

> HOW DO BATTERIES WORK?

Batteries create electric currents from the reaction between two chemicals, one forming a positive electrode, or conductor of electricity, and the other a negative. The reaction creates an excess of electrons on the negative electrode, producing a current.

Radioactivity

Radioactivity is when the nucleus of an atom is unstable and breaks down, emitting radiation in the form of alpha, beta, and gamma rays. These high-energy rays can be dangerous in large doses, causing burns and an increased risk of cancer.

WHAT CAUSES RADIOACTIVITY?

The atoms of an element may come in several different forms, or isotopes. Each form has a different number of neutrons in the nucleus, indicated in the name, as in carbon-12 and carbon-14. The nuclei of some of these isotopes—the ones scientists call radioisotopes—are unstable, and they decay (break up), releasing radiation.

WHAT IS HALF-LIFE?

No one can predict when an atomic nucleus will decay. But scientists can predict how long it will take for half the atoms in a quantity of a radioactive element to decay. This is its half-life. Francium-223 has a half-life of 22 minutes. Uranium-238 has a half-life of 4.5 billion years.

WHICH ELEMENTS ARE VERY RADIOACTIVE?

The actinides are a group of 15 elements at the bottom of the periodic table that take their name from actinium. They include plutonium and uranium, and are radioactive.

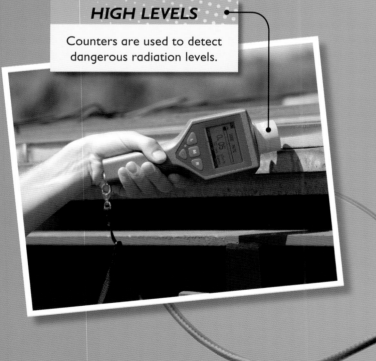

HIGH LEVELS

Counters are used to detect dangerous radiation levels.

GEIGER COUNTER

A Geiger counter measures radioactivity by detecting alpha, beta, and gamma rays.

WHAT IS THE TURIN SHROUD?

The Turin Shroud (seen in a false-color image below) is a cloth that many Christians believe bears the imprint of Christ's face after the Crucifixion. Carbon dating has been carried out to determine if the cloth is the right age for this to be true, but the results showed that the cloth is not old enough.

WHAT IS URANIUM?

Uranium is a radioactive metallic element. It can have between 141 and 146 neutrons in its nucleus. Uranium is mined from uranium-bearing minerals such as cuprosklodowskite (above).

HOW CAN RADIOACTIVITY BE USED TO INDICATE AGE?

Radioactive decay happens at a steady rate. So by measuring how much of a substance has decayed radioactively, you can tell its age. With once-living things, the best radioactive isotope to measure is carbon-14. This is called carbon dating.

Nuclear power >

The energy that binds together an atomic nucleus is enormous, even though the nucleus is tiny. By harnessing this energy, nuclear power stations can generate huge amounts of power with just a few tons of nuclear fuel.

POWER STATION

Cooling towers release waste steam into the air.

❶ FISSION

A nucleus splits when it is hit by a neutron.

> WHAT IS NUCLEAR FISSION?

Nuclear fission releases nuclear energy by splitting big atomic nuclei, usually those of uranium. Neutrons are fired at the nuclei. As the neutrons smash into the nuclei, they split off more neutrons, which bombard other nuclei, setting off a chain reaction.

❷ COLLISION

> HOW DO NUCLEAR POWER STATIONS WORK?

A nuclear reactor houses fuel rods made from uranium dioxide. A nuclear fission chain reaction is set up in the fuel rods. The resulting energy is used to heat water, which produces steam to drive the turbines, or wheels, that generate electricity.

❸ CHAIN REACTION

Further collisions result in smaller and smaller nuclei.

NEUTRON

The collisions split off more neutrons.

HOW MUCH ELECTRICITY IS MADE BY NUCLEAR POWER?

Nuclear power produces about 11% of the world's electricity. Some people oppose any further increase in it because its used fuel is very radioactive and hard to dispose of safely.

WHAT IS AN ATOMIC BOMB?

An atomic bomb is one of the two main kinds of nuclear bomb. It relies on the explosive nuclear fission of uranium-235 or plutonium-239. Hydrogen bombs, also called H-bombs, rely on the fusion of hydrogen atoms to create explosions a thousand times more powerful.

WHO INVENTED THE ATOMIC BOMB?

The first atomic bombs were developed in the United States towards the end of World War II by a team of scientists led by Robert Oppenheimer (1904–1967).

TOP ? QUESTION

WHAT IS NUCLEAR FUSION?

Nuclear energy is released by fusing, or joining together, small atoms like those of a form of hydrogen called deuterium, often in a reactor (right). Nuclear fusion is the reaction that provides energy for H-bombs. Scientists hope to find a way of harnessing nuclear fusion for power generation.

Water

The properties of water make it extraordinarily useful. In fact, water is essential to life: without water, plants and animals could not survive. Water can also be harnessed to transport loads and even to generate electricity.

> WHY IS WATER ESSENTIAL FOR LIFE?

Water is chemically neutral, yet dissolves many substances, which is why it is so important for life. Water is found in every cell of the human body. Plants need water for building cells and also for transporting nutrients from the roots to the leaves.

SAILING BOAT

A yacht floats because it is lighter than the water it displaces.

> WHAT'S SO SPECIAL ABOUT WATER?

Water is found naturally as solid ice, liquid water, and gaseous water vapor. This is unusual and happens because of the strong bonds between its two hydrogen atoms and one oxygen atom. When cooled, most substances with similar-sized atoms to water do not freeze until -22°F. But water freezes at 32°F.

DAM

Hydroelectric power depends on the fact that water is drawn downward by gravity.

> WHY DO THINGS FLOAT?

When an object is immersed in water, its weight pushes it down. But the water around it pushes it back up with a force equal to the weight of water displaced (pushed out of the way). So an object will float if it is lighter than, or weighs the same as, the water it displaces.

> WHY DO ICEBERGS FLOAT IN THE SEA?

Water is unique in that it expands when it freezes, because the special bonds between its hydrogen atoms begin to break down. This means that ice is lighter (less dense) than water, so icebergs can float.

CAN YOU SQUASH WATER?

Fluids like water cannot be squashed. So if you push fluid through a pipe, it will push out the other end. Hydraulic power, such as in a forklift truck, uses fluid-filled pipes working like this to lift loads. Hydraulic means "water," but most hydraulic systems use oil to avoid rust problems.

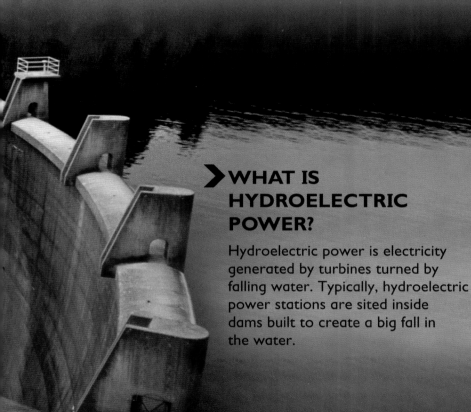

> WHAT IS HYDROELECTRIC POWER?

Hydroelectric power is electricity generated by turbines turned by falling water. Typically, hydroelectric power stations are sited inside dams built to create a big fall in the water.

The chemistry of life >

Compounds of carbon atoms form the basis of almost all life processes, from the DNA in our cells to the carbohydrates that we eat for energy. The study of carbon compounds is a vital branch of chemistry.

> WHAT IS ORGANIC CHEMISTRY?

Organic chemistry is the chemistry of carbon and its compounds. Carbon's unique atomic structure means it links atoms together in long chains, rings, or other shapes to form thousands of different compounds. These include complex molecules, such as DNA, that are the basis of life.

DNA CHAIN

The "ropes" of a DNA molecule are made of sugars and phosphates.

> WHAT IS DNA?

DNA is deoxyribonucleic acid. This is the amazing long double-spiral molecule that is found inside every living cell. It is made up of long chains of sugars and phosphates linked by pairs of chemical "bases"—adenine, cytosine, guanine, and thymine. The order in which these bases recur provides in code form the instructions for all the cell's activities, and for the life plan of the entire organism.

> WHO DISCOVERED THE SHAPE OF DNA?

The discovery in 1953 that every molecule of DNA is shaped like a twisted rope ladder, or "double helix," was one of the great scientific breakthroughs of the 20th century. Maurice Wilkins and Rosalind Franklin did the groundwork for the discovery. Francis Crick and James Watson, two young researchers at Cambridge University, UK, had the inspiration and won the Nobel Prize.

> WHAT ARE CARBOHYDRATES?

Carbohydrates are chemicals made only of carbon, hydrogen, and oxygen atoms, including sugars, starches, and cellulose. Most animals rely on carbohydrate sugars such as glucose and sucrose for energy.

WHAT ARE BUCKYBALLS?

Before 1990, carbon was known in two main forms or allotropes: diamond and graphite. In 1990, a third allotrope was created. Its molecule looks like a soccer ball or the domed stadium roofs created by architect Buckminster Fuller, so this allotrope is called, after him, a buckyball. Buckyballs are so newly discovered that research into their uses is ongoing.

BUCKYBALL

One buckyball contains dozens of carbon atoms.

SYNTHETIC SKIN

Scientists can now manufacture synthetic skin using polymers, to help people with burns or injuries.

WHAT IS A POLYMER?

Polymers are substances made from long chains of thousands of small carbon-based molecules, called monomers, strung together. Some polymers occur naturally, such as wool and cotton, but plastics such as nylon and polyethylene are human-made polymers.

161

More chemistry of life >

Carbon compounds are important ingredients in a wide range of products that we depend on every day, from plastics and paints to food and medicines. These compounds also contain other elements, such as hydrogen, nitrogen, and oxygen.

CARBON CYCLE
Cows form part of the carbon cycle by eating grass.

> WHAT ARE OILS?

Oils are thick liquids that won't mix with water. Mineral oils used for motor fuel are hydrocarbons—that is, complex organic chemicals made from hydrogen and carbon.

> WHAT IS THE CARBON CYCLE?

Carbon circulates like this: animals breathe out carbon as carbon dioxide. Plants take in carbon dioxide from the air and convert it into carbohydrates. When animals eat plants, they take in carbon again.

> HOW IS NATURAL OIL MADE?

Oil is formed from tiny plants and animals that lived in warm seas millions of years ago. As they died, they were slowly buried beneath the seabed. As the seabed sediments hardened into rock, the remains of the organisms were turned to oil and squeezed into cavities in the rock.

OIL RIG
Oil is drilled from the seabed by the workers and machinery housed in an oil rig.

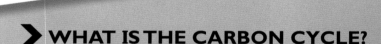

❯ WHAT IS CELLULOSE?

Cellulose is a natural fiber found in the walls of all plant cells. It is a polymer, made of long chains of sugar molecules. These long chains make it tough and stringy, which is why we can't digest it when we eat plants. It passes through our bodies largely intact.

PLANT CELLS

This image shows the enlarged cellulose-walled cells of a buttercup root.

❯ HOW IS PLASTIC MADE?

Most plastics are made from ethene, one of the products of oil that has been heated under pressure, or cracked. During the process, the ethene molecules join in chains 30,000 or more long. These molecules get tangled like spaghetti. If the strands are held tightly together, the plastic is stiff. If the strands can slip easily over each other, the plastic is bendy, like polyethylene.

❯ WHAT IS A CARBON CHAIN?

Carbon atoms often link together like the links of a chain to form very long, thin molecules, as in the molecule of propane, which consists of three carbon atoms in a row, with hydrogen atoms attached. Propane is commonly used as a fuel for engines and barbecues.

Forces and energy

Forces, energy, and power ⟩

A force is what makes an object move. An important force is gravity, which causes objects to fall to Earth. Energy is the ability to do work. For example, chemical energy fuels a space rocket and allows it to overcome the force of gravity and fly into space.

BLAST OFF

A space rocket overcomes the force of gravity.

⟩ WHAT IS A FORCE?

A force makes something move, by pushing or pulling it. Gravity is an invisible force. Other forces, such as a kick, we can see. Forces work in pairs. For every force pushing in one direction, there is an equal and opposite force pushing in the opposite direction.

⟩ WHAT IS ENERGY?

Energy takes many forms. Heat energy boils water, keeps us warm, and drives engines. Chemical energy fuels cars. Electrical energy drives machines and keeps lights glowing. Light itself is a form of energy (see pp.176–179). Almost every form of energy can be converted into other forms. But whatever form it is in, energy is essentially the capacity for making something happen, or "doing work."

⟩ WHAT IS POWER?

Power is the rate at which work is done. A high-powered engine is an engine that can move a great deal of weight very quickly. Power is also the rate at which energy is transferred. A large amount of electric power might be needed to heat a large quantity of water.

BRAKE PADS

Brake pads convert a bicycle's movement into heat energy.

TOP QUESTION

WHAT IS FRICTION?

Friction is the force between two things rubbing together, which may be brake pads on a bicycle wheel (above) or air molecules against an airplane. Friction slows things down, making them hot as their momentum, or movement, is converted into heat.

❯ WHAT IS ENERGY EFFICIENCY?

Some machines waste a great deal of energy, while others waste very little. The energy efficiency of a machine is measured by the proportion of energy it wastes. Waste energy is usually lost as heat.

❯ WHERE DOES ENERGY COME FROM?

Nearly all our energy comes from the Sun. We get some directly by using solar power cells to trap the Sun's heat. Most comes indirectly via fossil fuels (coal and oil), which got their energy from the fossilized plants of which they are made. The plants got their energy from the Sun by a process called photosynthesis (see p.244).

ANTHRACITE COAL

About 40% of the world's electricity comes from burning coal. Coal's energy is from the Sun.

On the move >

A force, such as a kick or a pull, will set an object in motion. Once an object is moving, it is said to have momentum. Momentum means that an object will always continue moving, unless another force makes it stop.

KICKING A BALL

A ball is given momentum by the force of a kick. It falls to the ground because of the force of gravity.

ROUND AND ROUND

The wind exerts force on the turbine's blades, which exert force on the rest of the windmill so that it turns on its axis.

> HOW DO THINGS GET MOVING?

Things only move if forced to move. So when something starts moving, there must be a force involved, whether it is visible, like someone pushing, or gravity, which makes things fall. But once they are moving, things will carry on moving at the same speed and in the same direction until another force is applied, typically friction.

> WHAT IS UNIFORM MOTION?

Uniform motion is when an object carries on traveling at the same speed in the same direction. This is how a space probe travels, when it is not being acted on by gravity or other forces.

➤ WHAT IS A TURNING FORCE?

When something fixed in one place, called a fulcrum, is pushed or pulled elsewhere, it turns around the fulcrum. When you push a door shut, that push is the turning force, and the hinge is the fulcrum.

➤ WHAT'S THE DIFFERENCE BETWEEN VELOCITY AND SPEED?

Speed is how fast something is going. Velocity is how fast something is going and in which direction. Speed is called a scalar quantity; velocity is a vector.

➤ WHY DO THINGS GO AROUND?

If only one force is involved, things will always move in a straight line. This is called linear motion. Things go around when there is more than one force involved. A wheel goes round on its axle because there is one force trying to make it carry on in a straight line and another keeping it the same distance from the axle.

WHAT IS A KNOCK-ON EFFECT?

When two objects collide, their combined momentum remains the same if nothing else interferes. So if one object loses momentum, this momentum must be passed on to the other object, making it move. This is a knock-on effect. Knock-on effects can be seen in action with a toy called a Newton's cradle (below).

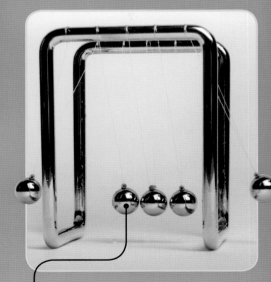

NEWTON'S CRADLE

The balls can be swung so that they knock into each other and pass on their momentum.

Keep moving >

Motion is measured according to its velocity, acceleration, distance traveled, and time taken. Some of the world's greatest scientific minds, including Sir Isaac Newton in the 17th century and Albert Einstein in the 20th century, have considered key questions about motion.

> WHO WAS EINSTEIN?

Albert Einstein (1879–1955; right) was the genius who transformed science with his two big theories—Special Relativity (1905) and General Relativity (1915).

SIR ISAAC NEWTON

Newton's studies of motion revolutionized science.

TOP ? QUESTION

WHAT WAS NEWTON'S BREAKTHROUGH?

Sir Isaac Newton's breakthrough in 1687 was to realize that all movement in the Universe is governed by three simple rules, which we now call Newton's Laws of Motion (see the opposite page).

> WHAT IS SPECIAL RELATIVITY?

The theory of Special Relativity shows how space and time can be measured only relatively, that is, in comparison to something else. This means that time can speed up or slow down, depending on how fast you are moving!

CRASH TEST

When a car brakes, momentum carries its passengers forwards.

➤ WHAT IS ACCELERATION?

Acceleration is how fast something gains speed. The larger the force and the lighter the object, the greater the acceleration. This is Newton's Second Law of Motion.

➤ WHAT IS THE DIFFERENCE BETWEEN INERTIA AND MOMENTUM?

Inertia is the tendency of things to stay still unless they are forced to move. Momentum is the tendency for things to keep going once they are moving, unless forced to stop or slow. This is the First Law of Motion.

➤ WHAT HAPPENS WITH EVERY ACTION?

This is Newton's Third Law of Motion—for every action, there is an equal and opposite reaction. This means that, whenever something moves, there is a balance of forces pushing in opposite directions. When you push your legs against water to swim, for instance, the water pushes back on your legs equally hard.

SKIING

As a skier moves downhill they gain momentum. This causes them to accelerate quickly.

Gravity >

Gravity is an invisible force. It is the force of attraction between every bit of matter in the Universe, such as between the Earth and the Sun. Gravity's strength depends on the mass of the objects involved and their distance apart.

> HOW DOES GRAVITY HOLD YOU DOWN?

The mutual gravitational attraction between the mass of your body and the mass of the Earth pulls them together. If you jump off a wall, the Earth pulls you toward the ground. You also pull the Earth toward you, but because you are tiny and the Earth is huge, you move a lot and the Earth barely moves at all.

HOW FAST DOES A STONE FALL?

At first the stone falls faster and faster at a rate of 32.1 feet per second at every second. But as the stone's speed accelerates, air resistance increases until it becomes so great that the stone cannot fall any faster. It now continues to fall at the same velocity, called the terminal velocity.

> WHAT'S THE DIFFERENCE BETWEEN MASS AND WEIGHT?

Mass is the amount of matter in an object. It is the same wherever you measure it, even on the Moon. Weight is a measure of the force of gravity on an object. It varies according to where you measure it.

> WHY DO SATELLITES GO AROUND THE EARTH?

Satellites are whizzing through space at exactly the right height for their speed. The Earth's gravity tries to pull them down to Earth, but they are traveling so fast that they go on zooming around the Earth just as fast as the Earth pulls them in.

SATELLITE

A satellite is in uniform motion around the Earth.

> DOES GRAVITY VARY?

An object's gravitational pull varies with its mass and its distance. In fact, gravity diminishes precisely in proportion to its distance away, squared. You can work out the force of gravity between two objects by multiplying their masses and dividing by the square of the distance between them. This sum works all over the Universe.

> WHY CAN WE JUMP HIGHER ON THE MOON?

The Moon is much smaller than the Earth, so its gravity is much weaker. Astronauts weigh six times less on the Moon than they do on Earth, and can jump much higher!

FREE-FALLING

A skydiver falls toward the Earth, before opening a parachute to use air resistance to slow her fall.

SPACE WALK

Far from the gravitational pull of planets, an astronaut experiences weightlessness.

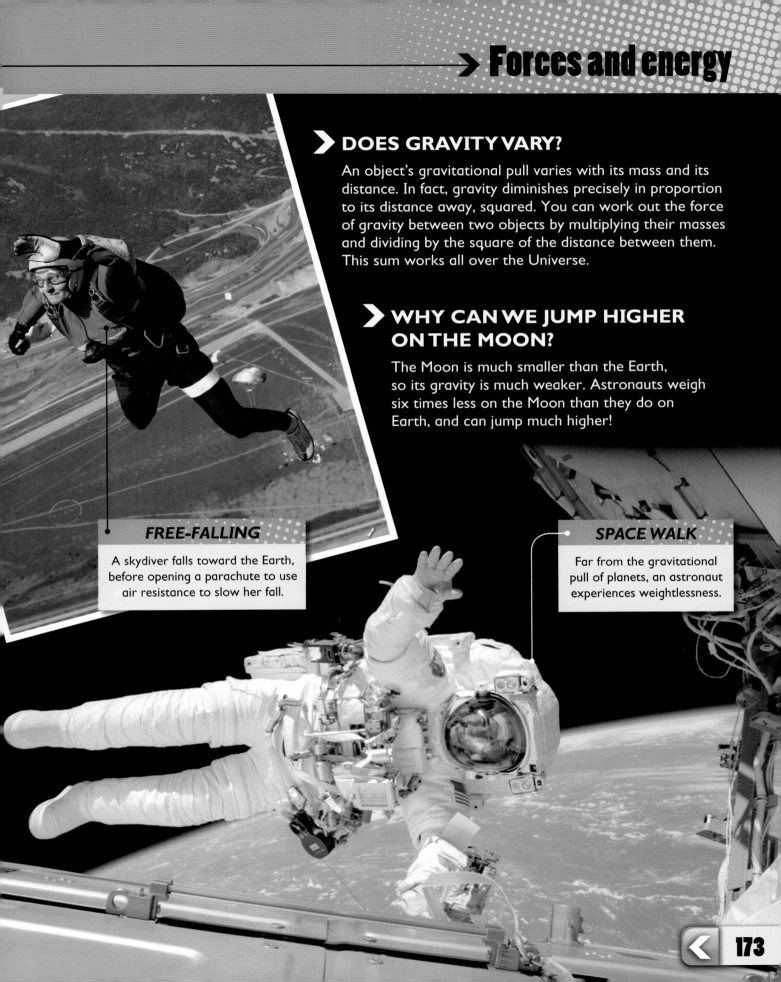

Heat >

Heat is a form of energy. It is caused by the movement of molecules. Heat is created by chemical reactions, such as fire; nuclear reactions, such as in the Sun; and when other forms of energy, such as electrical or mechanical, are converted into heat, as in friction.

> HOW IS TEMPERATURE MEASURED?

Temperature is usually measured with a thermometer. Some thermometers have a metal strip that bends according to how hot it is. But most contain a liquid, such as mercury, in a tube. As it gets warmer, the liquid expands, and its level rises in the tube. The level of the liquid indicates the temperature.

> WHAT IS THE DIFFERENCE BETWEEN HEAT AND TEMPERATURE?

Heat is molecules moving. It is a form of energy, the combined energy of all the moving molecules. Temperature, on the other hand, is simply a measure of how fast all the molecules are moving.

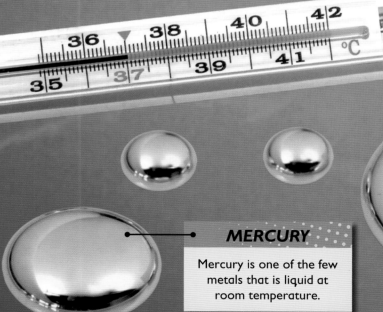

THERMOMETER
As it gets warmer, the molecules of the mercury in the tube move faster and the mercury expands.

MERCURY
Mercury is one of the few metals that is liquid at room temperature.

→ WHAT IS ABSOLUTE ZERO?

Absolute zero is the coldest possible temperature, the temperature at which atoms stop moving altogether. This happens at -459.7°F, or 0 on the Kelvin scale.

RADIATION

The Sun generates heat by nuclear fusion and radiates it in waves, which we see and feel as sunlight.

→ WHAT IS THE HIGHEST TEMPERATURE EVER RECORDED?

The highest temperature ever measured is 3.6 billion°F. It happened in a nuclear fusion experiment in a science lab. The highest air temperature ever recorded is 134°F in Death Valley, United States. Earth's lowest air temperature ever measured was -128°F. It was recorded in Antarctica. And the lowest temperature ever measured was half a billionth of a degree above absolute zero.

→ HOW DO YOU CONVERT FAHRENHEIT TO CELSIUS?

You can convert from Fahrenheit to Celsius by subtracting 32 then dividing by nine and multiplying by five. You can convert from Celsius to Fahrenheit by dividing by five, multiplying by nine and adding 32.

WHAT IS CONDUCTION?

Conduction is one of the three ways in which heat moves. It involves heat spreading from hot areas to cold areas as moving particles knock into one another. The other ways are convection, in which warm air or water rises, and radiation, which is rays of light.

CONDUCTION

A hot baking tray conducts heat and can only be touched safely with gloves.

What is light? ➤

There are many sources of light, including the Sun, light bulbs, and flames. Light is a form of energy that can be emitted, or radiated, by atoms. Visible light contains all the colors of the rainbow.

➤ WHAT IS WAVELENGTH?

Light travels in a wavelike manner. Wavelength is the distance between the top of one wave and the next. The different colors of light have different wavelengths. This is shown by a prism, which refracts (bends) light. The longer the wavelength of light, the more it is refracted, so long-wavelength colors emerge from the prism at a different point from short-wavelength colors.

PRISM

A prism splits light into its different wavelengths.

SPECTRUM

The longest waves of light that we can see are red. The shortest waves of visible light are violet.

› WHAT'S THE FASTEST THING IN THE UNIVERSE?

Light, which travels at 186,000 miles per second. This is the one speed in the Universe that is constant—that is, it is always the same no matter how fast you are going when you measure it.

› WHAT ARE PHOTONS?

Photons are almost infinitesimally small particles of light. They have no mass and there are billions of them in a single beam of light.

RAINBOW

Rainbows occur when the Sun shines through rain.

TOP QUESTION

WHEN IS THE SUN RED?

The Sun is only red at sunrise and sunset, when the Sun is low in the sky and sunlight reaches us only after passing a long way through the dense lower layers of the atmosphere. Particles in the air absorb shorter, bluer wavelengths of light or reflect them away from us, leaving just the red.

› WHAT ARE THE COLORS OF THE RAINBOW?

The colors of the rainbow are all the colors contained in white light. When white light hits raindrops in the air, it is split up in the same manner as when it passes through a prism. The colors of the rainbow appear in this order: red, orange, yellow, green, blue, indigo, violet.

› WHY IS THE SKY BLUE?

The sky appears to be blue because air molecules scatter—reflect in all directions—more blue from sunlight toward our eyes than the other colors of visible light.

How does light work?

When light hits an object, it can be reflected, absorbed, or bent. The study of light, known as optics, has allowed scientists to discover how we see things. It is light's ability to be reflected that allows us to see.

> HOW IS LIGHT BENT?

Light rays are bent when they are refracted. This happens when they strike a transparent material like glass or water, at an angle. The different materials slow the light waves down so that they slew around, like car wheels driving on to sand.

COLORS

A red ball absorbs all the colors except red.

> HOW DO OBJECTS ABSORB LIGHT?

When light rays hit a surface, some bounce off, but others are absorbed by atoms in the surface. Each kind of atom absorbs particular wavelengths, or colors, of light. You see a leaf as green because it has soaked up all colors except green, and you see only the reflected green light.

> HOW DO YOUR EYES SEE THINGS?

Light sources such as the Sun and electric light shine light rays straight into your eyes. Everything else you see only by reflected light, that is, by light rays that bounce off things. So you can see things only if there is a light source throwing light on to them. Otherwise, they just look black.

REFRACTION

Water refracts the light, making a straw appear split.

➤ DOES LIGHT TRAVEL IN WAVES?

In the last century, most scientists believed light travels in tiny waves rather than bulletlike particles. Now they agree it can be both, and it is probably best to think of light as vibrating packets of energy.

HOW DO MIRRORS WORK?

FIBER-OPTIC CABLES

The cables are widely used in telecommunications to carry messages across long distances.

Most mirrors are made of ordinary glass, but the back is silvered—coated with a shiny metal that perfectly reflects all the light that hits it—at exactly the same angle. The image in a mirror is not, in fact, back-to-front. Left is on the left, and right is on the right—which is the opposite of how we look to someone who is facing us.

➤ HOW DO FIBER-OPTIC CABLES WORK?

These cables don't bend light, but reflect it around corners. Inside a cable are lots of bundles of glass fibers. Light rays zigzag along the inside of each fiber, reflecting first off one side, then the other. In this way, light can be transmitted through the cable no matter what route it takes.

REAR VIEW

A side-view mirror allows us to watch the road behind.

Electromagnetic spectrum >

Light is just a small part of the wide range of radiation emitted by atoms—the only part we can see. This range of radiation is called the electromagnetic spectrum and ranges from long waves, such as radio waves, to short rays, such as gamma rays.

> WHO MADE THE FIRST RADIO BROADCAST?

Italian inventor Guglielmo Marconi first sent radio signals about a mile in 1895. In 1899, he sent a message in Morse code across the English Channel. (Morse code uses rhythms of short and long sounds to represent letters and numerals.) In 1901, he sent a radio message across the Atlantic Ocean.

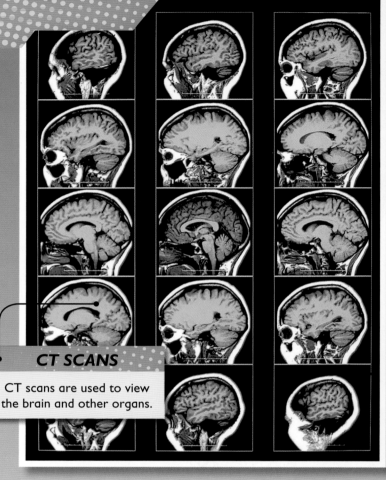

CT SCANS
CT scans are used to view the brain and other organs.

> HOW DO CT SCANS WORK?

CT (computed tomography) scans run X-ray beams right around the body, and pick up how much is absorbed with special sensors. A computer analyses the data to create a complete "slice" through the body.

VISIBLE LIGHT
Visible light has wavelengths of 400 to 700 nanometers (billionths of a meter).

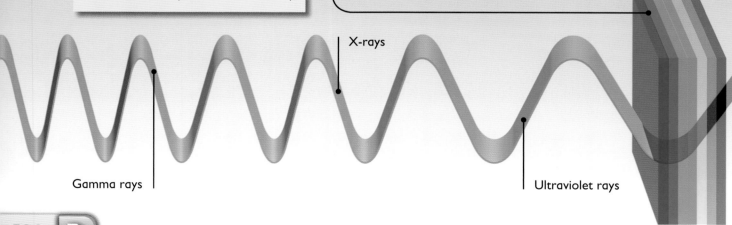

X-rays

Gamma rays

Ultraviolet rays

HOW DO TV SIGNALS TRAVEL?

TV signals travel in one of three ways. Terrestrial broadcasts are beamed out from transmitters (right) as radio waves to be picked up by TV aerials. Satellite broadcasts are sent up to satellites as microwaves, then picked up by satellite dishes. Cable broadcasts travel as electrical or light signals along underground cables, straight to the TV set.

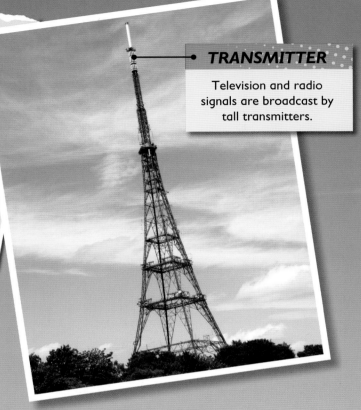

TRANSMITTER
Television and radio signals are broadcast by tall transmitters.

➤ WHAT IS INFRARED?

Infrared is light with wavelengths too long for the human eye to register. But you can often feel infrared light as warmth.

➤ HOW DO X-RAYS PASS THROUGH YOU?

X-rays are stopped only by the bones and especially dense bits of the body. They pass through the soft bits to hit a photographic plate on the far side of the body, where they leave a silhouette of the skeleton.

➤ WHY CAN'T YOU SEE ULTRAVIOLET?

Ultraviolet light is light with wavelengths too short for the human eye to register.

Infrared rays

Microwaves

WAVELENGTHS
Wavelengths range from thousands of meters to smaller than an atom.

Radio waves

Electricity

Electricity is the presence of electric charge. This charge is carried by electrons and protons in atoms. Electrons have a negative charge and protons a positive one. Electricity can be created naturally, as in lightning, or be man-made, as with a battery.

WHAT MAKES LIGHTNING FLASH?

Lightning flashes produce 100 million volts of static electricity. Lightning is created when raindrops and ice crystals inside a thundercloud become electrically charged as they are flung together, losing or gaining electrons from each other. Negatively charged particles build up at the cloud's base, then discharge as lightning.

WHAT IS AN ELECTRIC CURRENT?

A current is a continuous stream of electrical charge. It happens only when there is a complete, unbroken "circuit" for the current to flow through, typically a loop of copper wire.

LIGHTNING

Lightning flashes to the positively charged ground to discharge its negative electrical charge.

LIGHT SWITCH

Turning on a light switch completes the circuit and allows current to flow to a bulb.

HOW DO ELECTRIC CURRENTS FLOW?

The charge in an electric current is electrons that have broken free from their atoms. None of them moves very far, but the current is passed on as they bang into each other like rows of marbles.

CHARGE

An electrical charge builds at the base of a thundercloud.

WHAT IS A VOLT?

Electrical current flows as long as there is a difference in charge between two points in the circuit. This difference is called a potential and is measured in terms of volts. The bigger the difference, the bigger the voltage.

WHAT IS RESISTANCE?

Not all substances conduct electric currents equally well. Resistance is a substance's ability to block a flow of electric current. Insulators, such as the plastic around electrical wires, are used for this reason.

TOP QUESTION

WHAT MAKES YOUR HAIR STAND ON END?

When you comb dry hair, electrons are knocked off the atoms in the comb. Your hair is coated with these negative electrical charges and is attracted to anything positively charged. The same effect occurs if you rub against plastic (right).

Using electricity ➤

In the late 19th century, scientists discovered how to harness electricity to use it as a source of energy. Today, electricity is used to power lighting, industry, transportation, heating, communications, and computers. In the past century, the world has come to rely on electricity to a greater and greater extent.

➤ WHAT IS A SEMICONDUCTOR?

Semiconductors are materials such as silicon or germanium, which are partly resistant to electric current and partly conducting. They can be set up so that the conductivity is switched on or off, creating a tiny electrical switch. They are used to make silicon chips, and so are essential to electronics.

➤ WHAT ARE THE BEST CONDUCTORS?

The best conductors are metals like copper and silver. Water is also a good conductor. Superconductors are materials like aluminum, which is cooled until it transmits electricity almost without resistance.

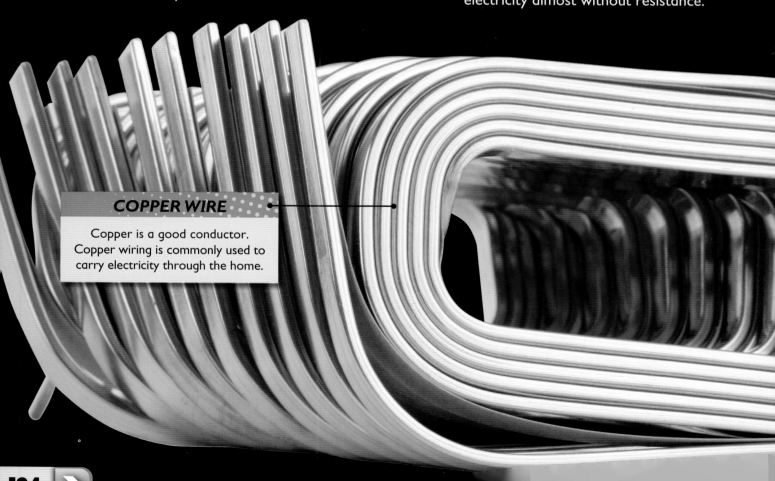

COPPER WIRE

Copper is a good conductor. Copper wiring is commonly used to carry electricity through the home.

LIGHT BULB

Thomas Edison invented the first practical bulb in 1879.

TOP QUESTION ?

WHAT IS A SILICON CHIP?

A silicon chip (below) is an electronic circuit implanted in a small crystal of semiconducting silicon, in such a way that it can be manufactured in huge numbers. This was the predecessor to the microprocessors that make computers work.

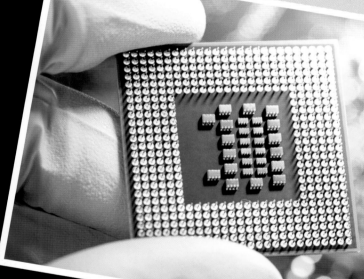

❯ HOW DOES A LIGHT BULB WORK?

An electric bulb has a very thin filament of tungsten wire inside a glass bulb filled with argon or nitrogen gas. When current flows through such a thin wire, the resistance is so great that the wire heats up and glows brightly.

❯ HOW DOES A GENERATOR WORK?

An electricity generator uses mechanical energy to create electrical energy. Many generators use electromagnetic induction, in which a coil of conducting wire, such as copper wire, is spun around inside a magnet. This causes electrons in the wire

❯ WHAT IS "AC"?

"AC" means alternating current. Electricity in the home is alternating current, which means it continually swaps direction as the generator's coil spins around past its electrodes.

Magnetism >

Magnetism is a force that both draws together and pushes apart materials. Certain metals can be strongly magnetic. The electrons in every atom act like tiny magnets, attracting and repelling other electrons. Magnetism occurs when the electrons in an object are all aligned in the same direction.

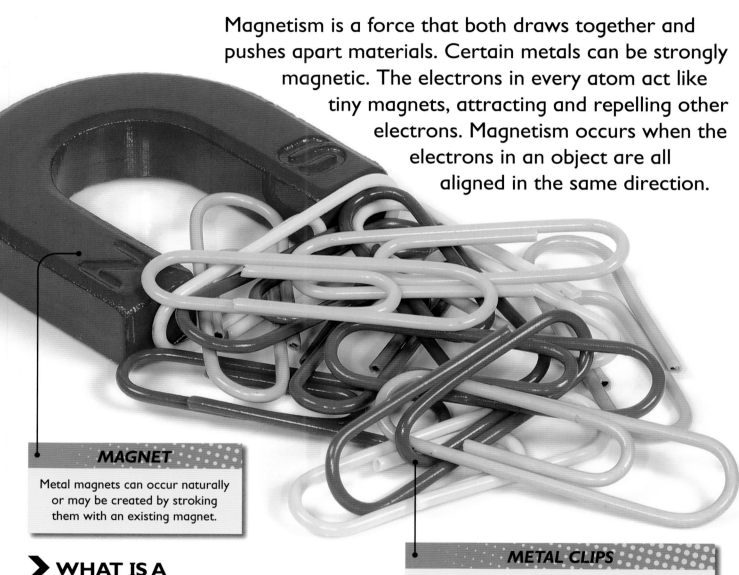

MAGNET
Metal magnets can occur naturally or may be created by stroking them with an existing magnet.

METAL CLIPS
Metal clips are drawn to a magnet. While they are in its magnetic field, the clips become magnetic, too.

> WHAT IS A MAGNETIC POLE?

Metals such as iron and nickel can exert particularly powerful magnetism. This force is especially strong at each end of the magnet. These two powerful ends are called poles. One is called the north (or north-seeking) pole, because if the magnet is suspended freely this pole swings around until it points north.

> WHAT IS A LODESTONE?

Thousands of years before people learned how to make steel magnets, they found that lumps of certain types of rock can attract or repel each other, or bits of iron. These rocks are called lodestones. They contain iron oxide, which makes them naturally magnetic.

➤ WHY IS THE EARTH LIKE A MAGNET?

As the Earth spins, the swirling of its iron core turns the core into a giant magnet. It is a little like the way a bicycle generator produces an electric current. Like smaller magnets, the Earth's magnet has two poles, a north and a south. It is because Earth is a magnet that small magnets always point in the same direction if allowed to swivel freely.

➤ HOW BIG IS THE EARTH'S MAGNETIC FIELD?

The Earth's magnetic field is called the magnetosphere and extends about 40,000 miles toward the Sun.

COMPASS

A magnetized needle always points to the North Pole.

TOP ? QUESTION

WHAT IS A MAGNETIC FIELD?

The magnetic field is the area around the magnet in which its effects are felt. It gets gradually weaker farther away from the magnet. The strength of a magnetic field is measured in teslas, named after the scientist Nikola Tesla.

➤ WHICH MATERIALS MAKE THE STRONGEST MAGNETS?

Due to the arrangement of their electrons, metals such as iron, nickel, and cobalt make strong magnets. These metals are also highly attracted to magnets.

MAGNETIC FIELD

A field can be seen when paper is scattered with iron filings.

Sound >

Every sound is created by vibration, whether it is an elastic band twanging or a loudspeaker cone shaking to and fro. Sound reaches your ears as a vibration that travels through the air in waves.

VIOLIN BOW

Drawing a bow across a violin's strings makes them vibrate, creating sound waves.

> HOW DOES SOUND TRAVEL?

When a sound source vibrates to and fro, it pushes the air around it to and fro. The sound travels through the air as it is pushed to and fro in bursts. This moving stretch and squeeze of air is called a sound wave.

> WHAT IS RESONANCE?

An object always tends to vibrate freely at the same rate. This is its natural frequency. You can make it vibrate faster or slower by jogging it at particular intervals. But if you can jog it at just the same rate as its natural frequency, it vibrates in sympathy and the vibrations become stronger. This is resonance.

RESONANCE

The sound made by a violin depends on the resonance of its strings.

➤ WHAT IS SOUND FREQUENCY?

Some sounds, like a whistle, are high-pitched. Others, like a drum, are low-pitched. What makes them different is the frequency of the sound waves. If the sound waves follow rapidly after each other, they are high frequency and make a high sound. If the waves are far apart, they are low frequency and make a low sound.

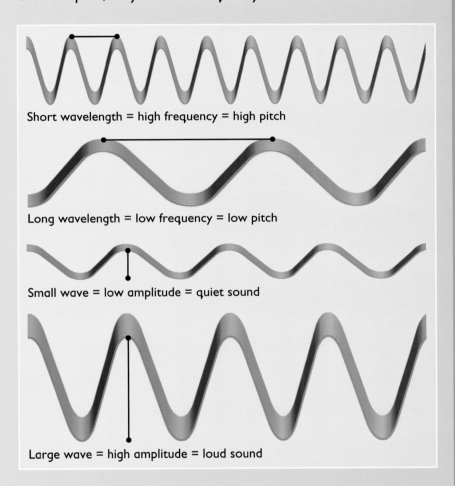

Short wavelength = high frequency = high pitch

Long wavelength = low frequency = low pitch

Small wave = low amplitude = quiet sound

Large wave = high amplitude = loud sound

HOW DO BATS LOCATE THEIR PREY?

Most bats—and some other animals, including whales—locate their prey using echolocation. The bats send out calls, then use the echoes to locate and identify objects. Echolocation is also used for navigating in complete darkness.

BAT CALLS

A bat's echolocation calls are very high frequency.

➤ WHAT IS VOLUME?

The volume of a sound is also called its amplitude. This is the amount of pressure exerted by a sound source on air molecules. The higher the pressure, the harder the molecules will collide and the farther they will travel.

➤ WHAT IS AN ECHO?

An example of an echo is when you shout in a tunnel and you hear the noise bouncing back at you a moment later as the sound waves rebound. Echoes only bounce back clearly off smooth, hard surfaces in confined spaces.

Life on the land

Rodents

Rodents are mammals, which means they have backbones, they are hairy, and they produce milk to feed their young. Rodents are distinguished by having continuously growing incisor teeth. Squirrels, hamsters, beavers, rats, and mice are all rodents.

WHY DO RODENTS GET LONG IN THE TOOTH?

The two sharp teeth, called incisors, at the front of the rodent's jaw are the ones it uses for gnawing. A rodent's incisors get worn down as it gnaws tough food, but they keep on growing throughout its life.

COYPU TEETH

The coypu, which lives in wetlands, has huge orange incisor teeth.

TOP ? QUESTION

WHY DO BEAVERS BUILD DAMS?

Beavers build their homes, or lodges, in streams or rivers. But first they need to build a dam to make an area of still water, or the current would wash the lodge away. With their huge front teeth, the beavers cut down trees to build the dam. They plaster the sides with mud and fill gaps with stones and sticks.

➤ WHICH IS THE BIGGEST RODENT?

The largest rodent in the world is the capybara, which lives in South America. It can measure more than 4 feet long and weigh up to 145 pounds. One of the smallest rodents is the pygmy mouse of North America. It is only about 4 inches long, including its tail, and weighs just 0.25 ounces.

CAPYBARA

The capybara lives in marshy places and feeds on grasses.

➤ WHEN IS A DOG REALLY A RAT?

A prairie dog is actually not a dog at all. It is a type of rodent, and lives in North America. Prairie dogs live in family groups of one adult male and several females and their young. A group of families makes a vast burrow of connecting chambers and tunnels called a colony.

➤ CAN FLYING SQUIRRELS REALLY FLY?

No, but they can glide from tree to tree. When the flying squirrel leaps into the air, it stretches out the skin flaps at the sides of its body, which act like a parachute, enabling it to glide gently between branches.

BEAVER LODGE

A beaver lodge is built of sticks behind a dam and has an underwater entrance.

Bears >

There are eight species of bear. They range in size from the sun bear, which can weigh about 100 pounds, to huge polar bears and brown bears. Bears have a large body, stocky legs, a long snout, shaggy hair, and sharp claws.

> WHICH IS THE BIGGEST BEAR?

The polar bear of the Arctic is one of the largest bears. Fully grown males are up to 8 feet long. Polar bears are meat-eaters and hunt seals, young walruses, and birds.

POLAR BEAR

The polar bear is the world's largest land-living predator.

> CAN POLAR BEARS SWIM?

Polar bears swim well and spend long periods in the freezing Arctic water. They are well equipped to survive the cold. They have a dense layer of underfur as well as a thin layer of stiff, shiny outer coat. Under the skin is a thick layer of fat to give further protection.

> HOW BIG IS A BABY BEAR?

Although adult bears are large, they have tiny babies. A huge polar bear, weighing more than several people, gives birth to cubs of only about 2 pounds, far smaller than most human babies. Baby pandas weigh as little as 3 ounces.

> IS THE GIANT PANDA A BEAR?

For years experts argued about whether this animal should be grouped with bears or raccoons or classed in a family of its own. Genetic evidence now suggests that the panda is a member of the bear family.

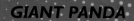

GIANT PANDA

Giant pandas live in bamboo forest reserves in west and central China.

➤ WHAT DO GIANT PANDAS EAT?

The main food of the giant panda is bamboo. An adult panda eats up to 40 pounds of bamboo leaves and stems a day.

TOP QUESTION ?

DO BEARS SLEEP THROUGH WINTER?

Brown bears (below), polar bears, and black bears that live in the far north sleep for much of the winter. Food supplies are poor, so the bears hide away in warm dens and live off their own fat reserves. Before their sleep, the bears eat as much food as they can.

TREE CLIMBER

Like all bears, giant pandas are excellent climbers. They often take shelter in hollow trees and rock crevices.

Wolves and dogs ›

The canid family of mammals includes dogs, wolves, foxes, coyotes, dingoes, and jackals. Canids are meat-eaters and have long legs for chasing their prey. Their sharp claws and teeth are perfect for slicing flesh.

› HOW MANY KINDS OF DOG AND FOX ARE THERE?

There are about 35 species in the canid family, split between the "true dogs" and the "foxes." True dogs include wolves, jackals, and wild dogs.

DINGO

Dingoes hunt alone, returning to their pack every few days to socialize.

› WHAT IS A DINGO?

Dingoes are Australian wild dogs. They are probably descended from dogs introduced 5,000 to 8,000 years ago by Aborigines. Nowadays, they hunt mainly sheep and rabbits. A fence of over 3,000 miles has been built across southeastern Australia to keep dingoes out of sheep-grazing lands.

➤ WHAT DO FOXES EAT?

Foxes, such as the red fox, are hunting animals. They kill and eat small creatures, including rats, mice, and rabbits. But foxes are very adaptable and will eat more or less anything that comes their way, such as birds and birds' eggs, insects, and even fruit and berries. More and more foxes in cities are feasting on our discarded food from trash bins and compost heaps.

HOW BIG IS A WOLF PACK?

In areas where there are plenty of large animals to catch, a pack may contain up to 30 wolves. Hunting in a pack means that the wolves can kill prey much larger than themselves, such as moose. A wolf pack has a territory, which it defends against other wolves.

RED FOX PUP

Red fox pups are taken care of by their parents until they reach 8–10 months old.

➤ WHAT IS A COYOTE?

The coyote looks similar to a wolf, with large ears and long legs for running. It lives in North and Central America, where it hunts small mammals such as squirrels and mice. Coyotes form a small pack but hunt with just one partner.

Cats >

There are about 36 species of wild cat, ranging from the tiger to the African wild cat, which is closely related to the domestic cat. Wild cats live in every sort of habitat, from tropical rain forest to desert. There are no wild cats in Antarctica, Australia, or New Zealand.

> WHAT DO LIONS DO ALL DAY?

Like domestic cats, lions are actually asleep for a surprisingly large part of the day. As many as 20 hours a day are spent resting and grooming. The rest of the time is taken up with looking for prey, hunting, and feeding. Lionesses do most of the hunting, then share the catch with the rest of the pride.

TIGER

The pattern of stripes on a tiger's fur is unique. No two tigers have quite the same pattern.

HUNTING LIONS

Lionesses develop a carefully coordinated group strategy to bring down their prey.

TOP QUESTION ?

WHY DO TIGERS HAVE STRIPES?

A tiger's stripes help it hide among grasses and leaves so it can surprise its prey. Tigers cannot run fast for long distances, so they depend on being able to get close to their prey before making the final pounce. The stripes help to break up their outline and make them hard for prey to see.

➤ WHICH IS THE BIGGEST CAT?

Tigers are the biggest of the big cats. They can measure 10 feet long, including the tail, and weigh 550 pounds or more. Tigers are becoming very rare. They live in parts of Asia, from snowy Siberia in the north to the tropical rain forests of Sumatra, Indonesia.

➤ WHICH IS THE FASTEST CAT?

The cheetah is the fastest-running cat and one of the speediest of all animals over short distances. It has been timed running at 64 miles an hour over a distance of 200 meters—more than twice as fast as humans.

SNOW LEOPARD
This big cat hunts alone, sometimes killing animals three times its size.

➤ WHERE DO JAGUARS LIVE?

Jaguars live in the forests of Central and South America. The jaguar is a good climber and often clambers up a tree to watch for prey. It hunts other forest mammals such as peccaries and capybaras, as well as birds and turtles.

➤ WHAT IS A SNOW LEOPARD?

The snow leopard is a big cat that lives in the mountains of Central Asia. Its beautiful pale coat with dark markings has made it the target of fur poachers. Killing snow leopards for their fur is now illegal, but poaching still goes on.

Elephants >

Elephants are the largest land animals. There are probably three species: the African bush elephant, African forest elephant, and Asian elephant. Elephants have tusks, long trunks, flapping ears, and very thick skin.

> HOW LONG ARE AN ELEPHANT'S TUSKS?

An elephant's tusks grow throughout its life, so the oldest elephants have the longest tusks. One tusk in the British Museum measures nearly 12 feet.

> WHY ARE BIG EARS USEFUL?

Elephants live in hot climates, so they flap their ears to create a breeze. This breeze cools their surface blood vessels, and the cooler blood is circulated to the rest of the elephant's body.

> HOW MUCH DO ELEPHANTS EAT?

A fully grown elephant eats 150 to 330 pounds of plant food a day. Its diet includes grass, twigs, branches, leaves, flowers, and fruits.

AFRICAN ELEPHANT

An elephant uses its tusks to dig for water, tree pulp, or roots, and to clear its path of trees and branches.

> WHAT DO ELEPHANTS DO WITH THEIR TRUNKS?

Without its trunk, an elephant could not reach the ground to feed because its neck is so short. The trunk is also used for taking food from high in trees. The elephant can smell with its trunk, pick up objects, and caress its young. It drinks by sucking up water into its trunk and squirting it into its mouth. It also sprays itself with water or dust to clean its skin.

> HOW BIG IS A BABY ELEPHANT?

A newborn African baby elephant weighs up to 260 pounds and stands up to 3 feet high. It sometimes feeds on its mother's milk for five years, by which time it may weigh more than a ton.

ASIAN ELEPHANT

The Asian elephant has smaller ears and a more humped back than the African.

> HOW CAN YOU TELL AN AFRICAN ELEPHANT FROM AN ASIAN ELEPHANT?

The African elephant is bigger and has larger ears and longer tusks. The head and body of the African elephant measures up to 25 feet long. The Asian elephant measures up to 22 feet and has a more humped back. There is another difference at the end of the long trunk. The African elephant's trunk has two flexible fingerlike lips, whereas the Asian animal's trunk has only one.

Large animals >

After the elephant, the largest land animals are the rhinoceros, hippopotamus, and giraffe. All three live in Africa, while the rhino also lives in Asia. These mammals are plant eaters known as ungulates, which are distinguished by their hoofed feet.

> HOW MANY BONES ARE THERE IN A GIRAFFE'S NECK?

A giraffe has seven bones in its neck, just like other mammals, including humans. But the giraffe's neck bones are much longer than those of other animals, and have more flexible joints between them.

> HOW TALL IS A GIRAFFE?

A male giraffe stands up to 18 feet tall to the tips of its horns. It has a very long neck, and front legs that are longer than its back legs so that the body slopes down toward the tail. The long neck allows it to feed on leaves that other animals cannot reach.

GIRAFFES

A giraffe's height allows it to watch out constantly for predators. It needs to sleep for only two hours a day.

❯ CAN HIPPOS SWIM?

The hippo spends most of its day in or near water and comes out on to land at night to feed on plants. It is a powerful swimmer and walks on the bottom of the river at surprisingly fast speeds.

HIPPO

Hippos wallow to stay cool in the hot African sun.

❯ WHAT IS AN OKAPI?

An okapi is a relative of the giraffe that lives in the African rain forest. It was unknown until 1900. The male has small horns on its head and a long tongue like a giraffe's, but it does not have a long neck.

❯ IS THE RHINO ENDANGERED?

All five species of rhinoceros are endangered. The Javan rhino is the most vulnerable: only about 60 animals remain. Rhinoceroses have been overhunted for their horns, which are valuable in traditional medicine.

WHITE RHINO

The white rhino is actually grayish. It is also known as the square-lipped rhino.

❯ ARE RHINOCEROSES FIERCE?

Despite their ferocious appearance and huge horns, white rhinos are usually peaceful, plant-eating animals. However, black rhinos can be ill-tempered and aggressive. If threatened, one will charge its enemy at high speed. Mothers defending their young can be particularly dangerous.

Marsupials >

Marsupials have much shorter pregnancies than other mammals. After birth, the tiny newborns often live in a pouch on their mother's belly. Many of the 334 species of marsupial live in Australia and New Guinea.

> DO ALL MARSUPIALS HAVE A POUCH?

Most female marsupials have a pouch, but not all. Some very small marsupials such as the shrew opossums of South America do not have a pouch. Others, such as the American opossums, simply have flaps of skin around the nipples that the tiny young cling on to.

> IS A KOALA REALLY A BEAR?

No, it's a marsupial and not related to bears at all. Koalas live in Australia in eucalyptus forests. They feed almost entirely on eucalyptus leaves, preferring those of only a few species. A baby koala spends its first six or seven months in the pouch and then rides on its mother's back until it is able to fend for itself. A baby measures around an inch at birth.

KOALA

The koala has strong claws to help it hold on to branches as it climbs in search of food.

HOW MUCH DOES A KOALA EAT?

A koala eats just over a pound of eucalyptus leaves every day, which it chews down to a fine pulp with its broad teeth.

PLATYPUS

This unusual mammal hunts in rivers and lakes using its sensitive bill. It feeds on insects, frogs, and shrimp.

WHAT IS THE SMALLEST MARSUPIAL?

The smallest marsupials are the mouselike ningauis, which live in Australia. They are only about 2 inches long.

WOMBAT

Wombats eat grasses, roots, bark, and herbs.

IS A PLATYPUS A MARSUPIAL?

No, the platypus is not a marsupial, but it is an unusual animal that lives in Australia. Unlike most mammals, which give birth to live young, the platypus lays eggs. When they hatch, the young suck milk from the mother from special patches of fur.

WHAT IS A WOMBAT?

A wombat is a small bear-like marsupial with a heavy body and short, strong legs. It digs burrows to shelter in, using its strong teeth and claws. Its pouch opens to the rear so that it does not fill up with earth when the wombat is burrowing.

More marsupials >

More than 140 species of marsupial live in Australia and surrounding islands. There are also over 100 marsupial species in the Americas. Most of these live in South and Central America, with just the Virginia opossum native to North America.

> DO ANY MARSUPIALS SWIM?

The water opossum of South America is an excellent swimmer and has webbed back feet. Strong muscles keep its pouch closed when the opossum is in water.

> WHAT ARE BANDICOOTS?

Bandicoots are a group of small marsupials that live in Australia and New Guinea. Most have short legs, a rounded body, and a long pointed nose. They have strong claws, which they use to dig for insects and other small creatures in the ground.

BANDICOOT

The bilbie bandicoot has extremely large ears to hear its insect prey.

> HOW FAST DO KANGAROOS MOVE?

A kangaroo bounds along on its strong back legs at up to 30 miles an hour. It can cover 45 feet in one giant bound.

TOP QUESTION ?

WHAT IS A TASMANIAN DEVIL?

The Tasmanian devil (right) is the largest of the carnivore, or flesh-eating, marsupials. It is about 3 feet long, including its tail, and has sharp teeth and strong jaws. The devil feeds mostly on carrion—the flesh of animals that are already dead—but it does also kill prey such as birds.

WHY DOES A KANGAROO HAVE A POUCH?

At birth, kangaroos are very tiny and poorly developed. A kangaroo is only about an inch long when it is born. The female kangaroo has a pouch so that its young can complete their development in safety. The tiny newborn, called a joey, crawls up to the pouch by itself and starts to suckle on one of the nipples inside the pouch.

WHAT DO KANGAROOS EAT?

Kangaroos eat grass and the leaves of low-growing plants, just as deer and antelopes do in the northern hemisphere.

RED KANGAROO

The largest kangaroo of all, an adult red kangaroo weighs 200 pounds.

JOEY

Joeys stay in the pouch until they weigh 20 pounds.

Monkeys >

Monkeys are members of the primate group, which also contains tarsiers, lemurs, aye-ayes, lorids, galagos, apes, and humans. Primates have large brains, hands that can form a good grip, and a tendency to walk on two legs.

> HOW MANY KINDS OF MONKEY ARE THERE?

About 260 species in two main groups. One group lives in Africa and Asia. The other group lives in Central and South America.

> WHICH MONKEY MAKES THE LOUDEST NOISE?

Howler monkeys shout louder than other monkeys and are among the noisiest of all animals. Their voices carry for more than 2 miles.

HOWLER MONKEY •—

The howler monkey spends most of its time in trees, feeding on leaves and fruit.

MACAQUES

Japanese macaques often bathe in hot springs.

➤ CAN MONKEYS LIVE IN COLD PLACES?

Most monkeys are found in warm areas near to the equator, but some macaque monkeys live in cooler places. The rhesus macaque lives in the Himalayas as well as in parts of China and India, and the Japanese macaque survives freezing winters with the help of its thick coat.

➤ WHICH IS THE BIGGEST MONKEY?

The mandrill is the largest monkey, as it can grow to be more than 3 feet long. It lives in the tropical rain forests of Central Africa, where it hunts for insects, plants, and small animals. The smallest monkey is the pygmy marmoset of the South American rain forests. It is about 9 inches long, plus tail, and it weighs only between 3 and 5 ounces.

GRIPPING TAIL

A prehensile tail is almost as useful as having a fifth limb.

TOP QUESTION ?

WHY DOES A MONKEY HAVE A LONG TAIL?

To help it balance and control its movements as it leaps from branch to branch in the rain forest. The tails of some South American monkeys are prehensile—they have special muscles that the monkey can use to twine around branches.

Apes >

Apes are probably the most intelligent animals in the primate group. There are three families of apes. One includes all the gibbons. The second contains the gorilla, chimpanzee, and orangutan. And the third has only one species—humans.

> WHAT DO GORILLAS EAT?

Gorillas eat plant food, such as leaves, buds, stems, and fruit. Because their diet is juicy, gorillas rarely need to drink.

FEMALE GORILLA

Closely related to humans, gorillas are very intelligent.

> WHICH IS THE BIGGEST APE?

The gorilla. A fully grown male stands almost 6 feet tall and weighs as much as 500 pounds. Gorillas live in the forests of West and Central Africa. A family group contains one or two adult males, several females, and a number of young of different ages. The male, known as a silverback because of the white hair on his back, leads the group.

➤ DO CHIMPANZEES USE TOOLS?

Yes. The chimpanzee can get food by poking a stick into an ants' nest. It pulls out the stick and licks off the ants. It also uses stones to crack nuts, and it makes sponges from chewed leaves to mop up water or wipe its body.

➤ DO CHIMPS HUNT PREY?

Yes, they do. Although fruit is the main food of chimps, they also eat insects and hunt young animals, including monkeys. They hunt alone or in a group. Groups work together, some driving a couple of animals out of the group and toward other chimps, who make the kill.

CHIMPANZEE

Chimpanzees show love toward each other and even mourn when a relative dies.

➤ WHERE DO CHIMPANZEES LIVE?

Chimpanzees live in forest and grasslands in equatorial Africa. There is another less familiar chimpanzee species called the pygmy chimpanzee, or bonobo, which lives in rain forests in Congo in Africa. It has longer limbs than the common chimpanzee and spends more of its time in trees.

WHERE DO ORANGUTANS LIVE?

Orangutans live in Southeast Asia in the rain forests of Sumatra and Borneo. This ape has long, reddish fur and spends most of its life in the trees. Fruit is its main food, but the orangutan also eats leaves, insects, and even eggs and small animals. The orangutan is active during the day. At night it sleeps on the ground or in a nest of branches in the trees.

Lizards >

Lizards are reptiles, which means that they need to breathe air and they have skin that is covered in scales. Most lizards have four limbs and a tail. Many lizards can shed their tail to escape a predator.

KOMODO DRAGON

No predators in its habitat are large enough to take on the fearsome adult Komodo dragon.

> WHICH IS THE LARGEST LIZARD?

The Komodo dragon, which lives on some Southeast Asian islands. It grows up to 10 feet long and hunts animals such as wild pigs and small deer.

> HOW MANY KINDS OF LIZARD ARE THERE?

There are probably over 5,000 species of lizard. These belong to different groups, such as geckos, iguanas, skinks, and chameleons. Lizards mostly live in warm parts of the world.

> ARE THERE ANY VENOMOUS LIZARDS?

There are only two venomous lizards in the world, the Gila monster (right) and the Mexican beaded lizard. Both of these live in southwestern North America. The venom is made in glands in the lower jaw. When the lizard seizes its prey and starts to chew, venom flows into the wound and the victim soon stops struggling.

➤ WHERE DO CHAMELEONS LIVE?

There are about 171 different sorts of chameleon and most of these live in Africa and Madagascar. There are also a few Asian species, and one kind of chameleon lives in parts of southern Europe.

➤ WHY DOES A CHAMELEON CHANGE COLOR?

Changing color helps the chameleon get near to its prey without being seen and allows it to hide from its enemies. The color change is controlled by the chameleon's nervous system. Nerves cause areas of color in the skin to be spread out or to become concentrated in tiny dots. Chameleons go darker when they are cold and lighter when they are hot.

➤ WHICH LIZARD SWIMS THROUGH SAND?

The sand skink lives in the sandhills of the southeastern United States. It spends most of its time below the surface, pulling itself through the sand as a swimmer moves through water.

GIVING SIGNALS

Chameleons change color not just as camouflage but as a means of communication.

CHAMELEON

The veiled chameleon can turn bright blue when it is on vivid flowers.

Snakes ▶

Like other reptiles, snakes are covered in scales. All snakes are carnivorous, which means that they feed on other animals. There are more than 3,000 species of snake. They live on every continent except Antarctica, but there are no snakes in Ireland, Iceland, or New Zealand.

▶ HOW FAST DO SNAKES MOVE?

The fastest-moving snake on land is thought to be the black mamba, which lives in Africa. It can wriggle along at up to 7 miles an hour.

▶ WHICH IS THE BIGGEST SNAKE?

The world's longest snake is the reticulated python, which lives in parts of Southeast Asia. It grows to an amazing 33 feet long. The anaconda, which lives in South American rain forests, is heavier than the python but not quite as long. Pythons and anacondas are not venomous snakes. They kill by crushing prey to death. A python wraps the victim in the powerful coils of its body until it is suffocated.

RATTLESNAKE

If the rattle breaks, a new ring will be added when the snake moults.

▶ WHICH IS THE MOST DANGEROUS SNAKE?

The saw-scaled carpet viper is probably the world's most dangerous snake. It is extremely aggressive and its venom can kill humans. Saw-scaled carpet vipers live in Africa and Asia.

WHY DO SNAKES SHED THEIR SKIN?

Snakes shed their skin, or molt, to allow for growth and because their skin gets worn and damaged. Some snakes, even as adults, shed their skin every 20 days.

➤ ARE ALL SNAKES VENOMOUS?

Only about a third of all snakes are venomous and fewer still have venom strong enough to harm humans. Nonvenomous snakes either crush their prey to death or simply swallow it whole.

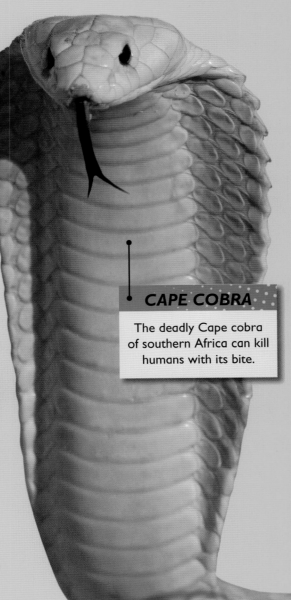

CAPE COBRA

The deadly Cape cobra of southern Africa can kill humans with its bite.

SNAKESKIN

Snakes wriggle out of their skin by rubbing against rough surfaces.

➤ WHY DOES A RATTLESNAKE RATTLE?

Rattlesnakes make their rattling noise to warn their enemies to stay well away. The rattle is made by a number of hard rings of skin at the end of the tail that make a noise when shaken. Each ring was once the tip of the tail. A new one is added every time the snake grows and sheds its skin.

Life in the water and air

Marine mammals →

Not all mammals live on land. Seals, sea lions, and walruses are just some of the mammals that depend on the oceans for food. Marine mammals need to breathe air, so they have to come to the water's surface regularly. They have a thick layer of blubber, or fat, which keeps them warm in the water.

› HOW FAST CAN SEALS AND SEA LIONS SWIM?

Sea lions can reach swimming speeds of 25 miles an hour. On land, the crabeater seal can reach 15 miles an hour.

› HOW CAN YOU TELL A SEAL FROM A SEA LION?

With practice! Seals and sea lions both have streamlined bodies and flippers instead of limbs. But sea lions have small ear flaps, whereas seals have only ear openings. Sea lions can bring their back flippers under the body to help them move on land. Seals cannot do this—they drag themselves along.

› WHICH IS THE BIGGEST SEAL?

The male elephant seal is the biggest. It is 22 feet long and weighs up to 2 tons, which is as much as a small elephant.

BASKING SEAL

Seals spend a lot of their time resting on beaches between hunting trips.

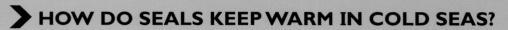

> HOW DO SEALS KEEP WARM IN COLD SEAS?

A layer of fatty blubber under the skin helps to keep seals, sea lions, and walruses warm. The blubber may be up to 4 inches thick. These animals also have a covering of fur.

SEA LION PUP

Sea lions have external ear flaps and long front flippers.

> ARE BABY SEALS AND SEA LIONS BORN IN WATER?

No, they are born on land. Seals and sea lions spend most of their lives in water, but do come out on to land to give birth. They remain on land for a number of weeks, feeding their young on their rich milk.

TOP QUESTION ?

HOW BIG IS A WALRUS?

The largest male walruses (left) are more than 10 feet long and weigh 3,700 pounds. Females are smaller, averaging 9 feet long and weighing about 1,750 pounds. The walrus' skin is up to 2.5 inches thick and helps protect the walrus from the tusks of others.

Whales >

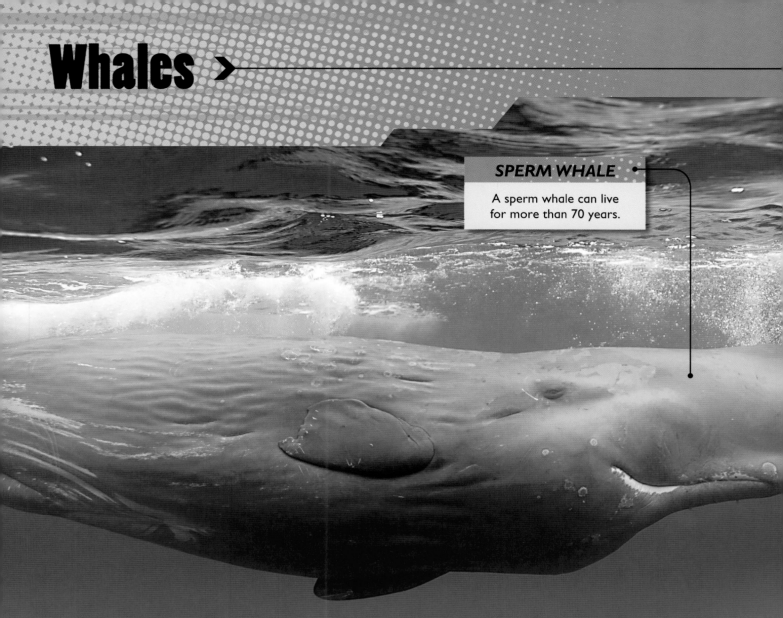

Whales, dolphins, and porpoises belong to the group of marine mammals known as cetaceans. They are highly intelligent and have large tails perfect for swimming. Cetaceans breathe air through the blowhole on the top of their head.

> WHICH IS THE BIGGEST WHALE?

The blue whale is the largest whale, and also the largest animal that has ever lived. It measures more than 100 feet long. Although it is huge, the blue whale is not a fierce hunter. It eats tiny shrimplike creatures called krill. It may gobble up as many as four million of these in a day.

> WHICH WHALE DIVES THE DEEPEST?

The sperm whale is routinely found half a mile beneath the surface of the sea.

> HOW BIG IS A BABY BLUE WHALE?

A baby blue whale is about 25 feet long at birth and is the biggest baby in the animal kingdom.

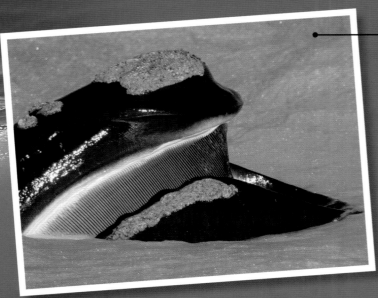

BALEEN PLATES

A right whale skims the sea for krill, showing its baleen plates.

> HOW DOES A BLUE WHALE FEED?

Hanging from the whale's upper jaw are lots of plates of a bristly material called baleen. The whale opens its mouth and water full of krill flows in. The water flows out at the sides of the mouth, leaving the krill behind on the baleen for the whale to swallow.

> WHY DO SOME WHALES MIGRATE?

Whales such as humpbacks migrate—travel seasonally —to find the best conditions for feeding and breeding. They spend much of the year feeding in the waters of the Arctic and Antarctic, where there is lots of krill to eat. When it is time to give birth, the humpbacks travel to warmer waters near the equator.

> DO HUMPBACK WHALES SING?

Yes, they do. They make a series of sounds, including high whistles and low rumbles, that may last from 5 to 35 minutes. No one knows why the humpback whale sings, but it may be to court a mate or to keep in touch with others in the group.

HUMPBACK WHALE

Whales often "breach," flinging themselves out of the water and landing with a noisy splash.

More whales →

There are two groups of whales: toothed whales and whales that catch food with baleen filters. Dolphins and porpoises are toothed, whereas blue and humpback whales are baleen whales.

> ## DO WHALES EVER COME TO LAND?

No, whales spend their whole lives in the sea. But they do breathe air and surface regularly to take breaths.

> ## IS A DOLPHIN A WHALE?

A dolphin is a small whale. Most of the 44 species of dolphin live in the sea, but there are five species that live in rivers. The biggest dolphin is the killer whale (left), which grows up to 32 feet long. Dolphins have a streamlined shape and a beaked snout containing sharp teeth.

SPYHOPPING
Dolphins often "spyhop," coming to the surface to look around.

➤ DO WHALES GIVE BIRTH IN WATER?

Yes, they do. The baby whale comes out of the mother's body tail first so that it does not drown during birth. As soon as the head emerges, the mother and the other females attending the birth help the baby swim to the surface to take its first breath.

➤ WHAT IS A PORPOISE?

A porpoise is a small whale with a rounded head, not a beaked snout like a dolphin. There are six species of porpoise. They live in coastal waters in the Atlantic, Pacific, and Indian Oceans. Like other toothed whales, the porpoise uses echolocation to find its prey. It gives off a series of high-pitched clicking sounds and the echoes tell the porpoise its prey's direction.

➤ HOW FAST DO WHALES SWIM?

Blue whales can move at speeds of up to 20 miles an hour when disturbed. Some small whales, such as pilot whales and dolphins, may swim at more than 30 miles an hour.

WHAT IS A NARWHAL?

A narwhal is a whale with a single long tusk at the front of its head. The tusk is actually a tooth, which grows out from the upper jaw. It can be as much as 10 feet long. Only male narwhals have tusks. They may use them in battles with other males.

TUSKING

These narwhals are "tusking," or rubbing their tusks together.

COMMON DOLPHIN

Dolphins are fast swimmers and catch squid and fish to eat.

Sharks and rays >

Sharks and rays belong to a group of fish that have skeletons made of cartilage rather than bone. Cartilage is softer and bendier than bone. Sharks and rays also have much larger brains than other types of fish. Sharks are the ocean's most feared predators.

> HOW MANY KINDS OF SHARK ARE THERE?

There are well over 400 different species of shark living all over the world. They range in size from dwarf dogfish measuring only 8 inches long to the giant whale shark, which can grow to 50 feet.

> ARE ALL SHARKS KILLERS?

No, two of the largest sharks, the whale shark and the basking shark, eat only tiny shrimplike creatures. They filter these from the water through sievelike structures in the mouth.

> HOW BIG IS A GREAT WHITE SHARK?

Great white sharks (right) are mostly about 20 feet long, but some can grow up to 40 feet. They live in warm seas all over the world. Great white sharks are fierce hunters and attack large fish and creatures such as sea lions and porpoises. Their main weapons are their large, jagged-edged teeth.

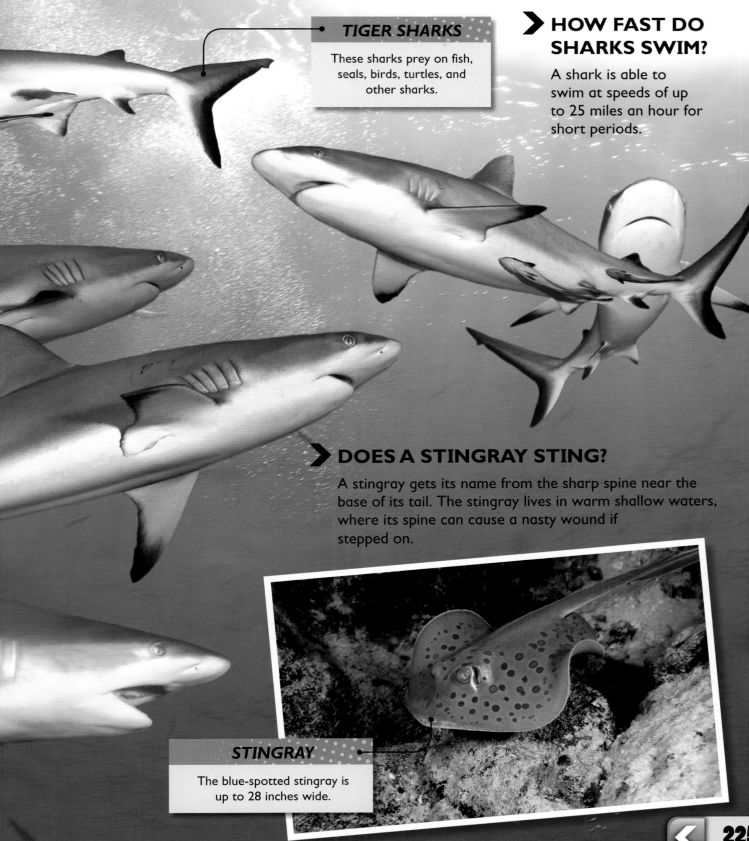

TIGER SHARKS

These sharks prey on fish, seals, birds, turtles, and other sharks.

HOW FAST DO SHARKS SWIM?

A shark is able to swim at speeds of up to 25 miles an hour for short periods.

DOES A STINGRAY STING?

A stingray gets its name from the sharp spine near the base of its tail. The stingray lives in warm shallow waters, where its spine can cause a nasty wound if stepped on.

STINGRAY

The blue-spotted stingray is up to 28 inches wide.

Fish >

Fish live in all the world's bodies of water, from mountain streams to the depths of the oceans. Fish have streamlined bodies ideal for swimming through water. Most fish are covered in scales to provide protection from predators.

> WHAT IS AN ANEMONEFISH?

Anemonefish live in sea anemones that thrive in tropical waters. Sea anemones are related to jellyfish and have a powerful sting. Anemonefish are the only fish that are immune to the poison, so they can hide from predators in their host.

> HOW FAST DO FISH SWIM?

The sailfish is one of the fastest-swimming fish. It can move at speeds of more than 65 miles an hour. Marlins and tunas are also fast swimmers. All these fish have sleek, streamlined bodies.

ANEMONEFISH

The clown anemonefish hides among anemone tentacles.

PIRANHA

Piranhas are known for their triangular-shaped teeth.

TOP QUESTION ?

WHICH IS THE FIERCEST FRESH-WATER FISH?

The piranha, which lives in rivers in tropical South America, is the fiercest of all freshwater fish. Each fish is only about 10 to 24 inches long, but a school of hundreds attacking together can kill and eat a large mammal very quickly. The piranha's weapons are its extremely sharp, flesh-ripping teeth.

ARE ELECTRIC EELS REALLY ELECTRIC?

Yes, they are. The electric eel's body contains special muscles that can release electrical charges into the water. These are powerful enough to stun its prey.

WHY DOES A FLYING FISH "FLY"?

A flying fish usually lifts itself above the water to escape from danger. It has extra-large fins, which act as "wings." After building up speed under the water, the fish lifts its fins and glides above the surface for a short distance.

PUFFER FISH

This fish puffs up its body when it is threatened.

ARE THERE ANY POISONOUS FISH IN THE SEA?

Yes, and the puffer fish is one of the most poisonous of all. It has a powerful poison in some of its internal organs, such as the liver, which can kill a human. Despite this, carefully prepared puffer fish is a delicacy in Japan.

Amphibians ➤

Unlike other land animals, most amphibians lay their eggs in water. Young amphibians live and breathe in water, before transforming into air-breathing and land-living adults.

➤ HOW CAN TREEFROGS CLIMB TREES?

Treefrogs are excellent climbers. On each of their long toes is a round sticky pad, which allows them to cling to the undersides of leaves and to run up the smoothest surfaces. Treefrogs spend most of their lives in trees, catching insects to eat, and may only come down to the ground to lay their eggs in or near water.

➤ WHY DO FROGS CROAK?

Male frogs make their croaking calls to attract females. The frog has a special sac of skin under its chin, which blows up and helps make the call louder.

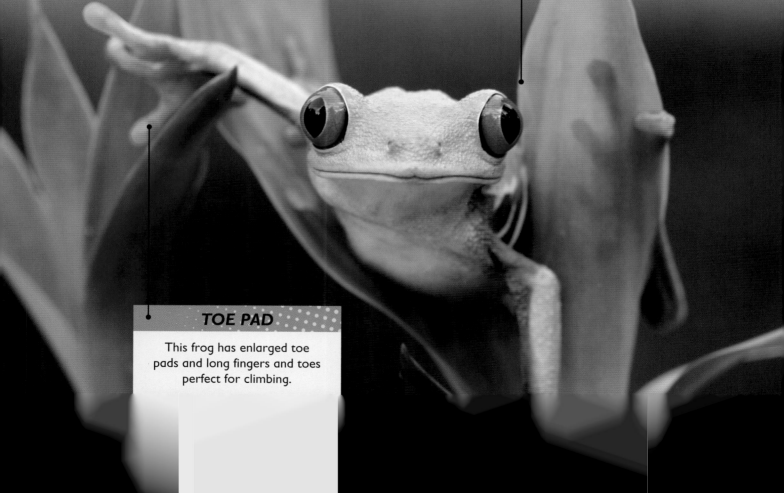

TREEFROG

Treefrogs are tiny creatures, so that their weight can be taken by delicate leaves and twigs.

TOE PAD

This frog has enlarged toe pads and long fingers and toes perfect for climbing.

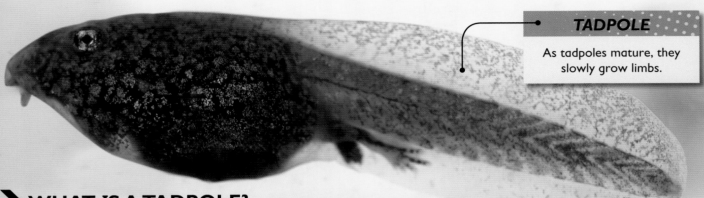

TADPOLE

As tadpoles mature, they slowly grow limbs.

❯ WHAT IS A TADPOLE?

A tadpole is the young, or larva, of an amphibian such as a frog or newt. The amphibian egg is usually laid in water and hatches out into a small, swimming creature with a long tail, called a tadpole. The tadpole feeds on water plants and gradually develops into its adult form.

❯ WHICH IS THE SMALLEST FROG?

The smallest frog, and the smallest of all amphibians, is the Cuban frog, which measures around 0.4 inches long. The tiny gold frog, which lives in Brazilian rain forests, is probably about the same size.

❯ HOW MANY TYPES OF FROG AND TOAD ARE THERE?

There may be as many as 4,000 species of frog and toad. They live on all continents except Antarctica. Most live in areas with plenty of rainfall, but some manage to live in drier lands by sheltering in burrows.

FROGSPAWN

Many frog species release thousands of eggs at a time.

❯ DO ALL FROGS LAY THEIR EGGS IN WATER?

No, some frogs have very unusual breeding habits. The male marsupial frog (and sometimes the female) carries his mate's eggs in a pouch on his back or hip. The male Darwin's frog keeps his mate's eggs in his vocal pouch until they have developed into tiny frogs.

Crocodiles and alligators ⟩

Crocodiles and alligators are water-dwelling reptiles that live in tropical climates. They have sharp teeth and very powerful jaws. These reptiles also have streamlined bodies and strong legs, so they can move very fast, in and out of water.

⟩ WHAT DO CROCODILES EAT?

Baby crocodiles start by catching insects and spiders to eat. As they grow, fish and birds form a larger part of their diet. Fully grown crocodiles prey on anything that comes their way, even large animals such as giraffes.

⟩ WHICH IS THE BIGGEST CROCODILE?

The Nile crocodile grows up to 20 feet long, but the Indo-Pacific crocodile, which lives in parts of Southeast Asia, may be even larger.

⟩ HOW MANY TYPES OF CROCODILE ARE THERE?

There are 14 species of crocodile, two species of alligator, several species of caiman, and one species of gavial. The gavial is very like the crocodile and the alligator, with a long, slender snout.

NILE CROCODILE
The crocodile is armored with rows of scales.

DO CROCODILES LAY EGGS?

Crocodiles do lay eggs and they look after them very carefully. Most female crocodiles dig a pit into which they lay 30 or more eggs. They cover them over with earth or sand. While the eggs incubate for about three months, the female crocodile stays nearby guarding the nest.

> ARE CROCODILES AN ANCIENT SPECIES?

Crocodiles have looked the same since the time of the dinosaurs. They are 200 million years old.

> HOW CAN YOU TELL A CROCODILE FROM AN ALLIGATOR?

Crocodiles and alligators are very similar, but you can recognize a crocodile because its teeth stick out when its mouth is shut! In alligators, the fourth pair of teeth on the lower jaw disappears into pits in the upper jaw, but in crocodiles, these teeth slide outside the mouth.

ALLIGATOR AGGRESSION

Adult alligators get into frequent battles to defend their territory.

Aquatic reptiles >

Crocodiles are not the only reptiles that live in oceans, rivers, and lakes. Aquatic turtles spend most of their lives in water, coming to land to lay eggs. Their bodies are protected by a hard, bony shell. They cannot breathe in water, so must come to the surface for air.

> ## HOW DO TURTLES SWIM?

Turtles "fly" through the water with the help of their strong, paddle-shaped flippers.

HAWKSBILL TURTLE

The hawksbill turtle is one of the few creatures that feeds mostly on sea sponges.

› WHICH IS THE BIGGEST TURTLE?

The leatherback is the largest of all the turtles. It grows up to 5 feet long and weighs up to 800 pounds. Leatherback turtles can usually be seen far out at sea.

› WHAT DO SEA TURTLES EAT?

Most sea turtles eat a range of underwater creatures, such as clams, shrimp, and snails, but some concentrate on certain foods. For example, the green turtle eats mainly sea grass.

WHERE DO SEA TURTLES LAY THEIR EGGS?

Female sea turtles dig a pit on a sandy beach in which to lay their eggs. They then cover the eggs with sand. When the young hatch, they dig their way out and struggle to the sea.

› ARE THERE SNAKES IN THE SEA?

Yes, there are 50 to 60 species of snake that spend their whole lives in the sea. They eat fish and other sea creatures and all are extremely poisonous. One species, the beaked sea snake, is potentially lethal.

GIANT FLIPPERS

The female hawksbill uses its flippers for swimming and for digging nests.

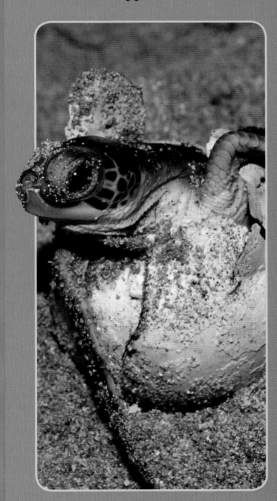

› DO TURTLES LIVE IN FRESHWATER?

Yes, there are about 200 species of freshwater turtles living throughout the world's warmer regions.

Polar birds →

Few animals are able to survive in the harsh climates of the Arctic and Antarctic. Some hardy birds travel to the polar regions to breed during the relatively warm summers. Some penguin species are able to withstand the bitter Antarctic cold.

❯ WHICH IS THE BIGGEST PENGUIN?

The emperor penguin lives in Antarctica and is the biggest penguin in the world. It stands about 45 inches tall. Like all penguins, it cannot fly, but it is an expert swimmer and diver, using its wings as paddles. It spends most of its life in the water, where it catches fish and squid to eat.

❯ DO ALL PENGUINS LIVE IN ANTARCTICA?

Most of the 17 species of penguin live in or near Antarctica, but some are found in warmer areas, such as around New Zealand. There are no penguins in the northern hemisphere.

❯ HOW FAST DO PENGUINS SWIM?

Penguins can swim at speeds of 8 miles an hour, but they may move even faster for short periods. Some penguins are able to stay under water for up to 20 minutes.

EMPEROR PENGUIN COLONY •

Emperor penguins come to land to breed. The female lays an egg that the male keeps warm on his feet for about 60 days until it hatches.

WHICH BIRD MAKES THE LONGEST MIGRATION?

The Arctic tern makes the longest migration journey of any bird. Each year it makes a round trip of 22,000 miles. The birds nest in the Arctic during the northern summer and then travel south to escape the northern winter, spending the southern summer near Antarctica, where food is plentiful.

ARCTIC TERN

These long-lived birds can survive for up to 20 years.

WHICH BIRD HAS THE LONGEST WINGS?

The wandering albatross has the longest wings of any bird. When fully spread, they measure up to 11 feet. This majestic seabird lays its eggs and cares for its young on islands near Antarctica.

TOP QUESTION ?

WHICH IS THE SMALLEST PENGUIN?

The little, or fairy, penguin is the smallest penguin. It is only about 16 inches long. It lives in waters off the coasts of New Zealand and Tasmania, Australia.

Birds >

There are around 10,000 different species of bird. They inhabit every one of the world's ecosystems, from deserts to rain forests. Birds have feathers, a beak, and wings. All birds lay hard-shelled eggs.

> HOW MANY KINDS OF GULL ARE THERE?

There are about 45 species of gull. They live in all parts of the world, but there are more species north of the equator. Gulls range in size from the little gull, which is only 11 inches long, to the great black-backed gull, a huge 26 inches long. Many gulls find food inland as well as at sea.

GANNET

Gannets are the largest seabirds in the North Atlantic Ocean, with a wingspan of more than 6 feet.

> HOW DOES A GANNET CATCH ITS FOOD?

The gannet catches fish and squid in spectacular dives into the sea. This seabird flies over the water looking for prey. When it sees something, it plunges from as high as 100 feet above the ocean, dives into the water with its wings swept back, and seizes the catch in its daggerlike beak.

PUFFIN

Puffins have black and white plumage and display a colorful beak when breeding.

> IS A PUFFIN A KIND OF PENGUIN?

No, puffins belong to a different family of birds, called auks. They live in the northern hemisphere, particularly around the Arctic. Auks are good swimmers and divers, like penguins, but can also fly, which penguins cannot do.

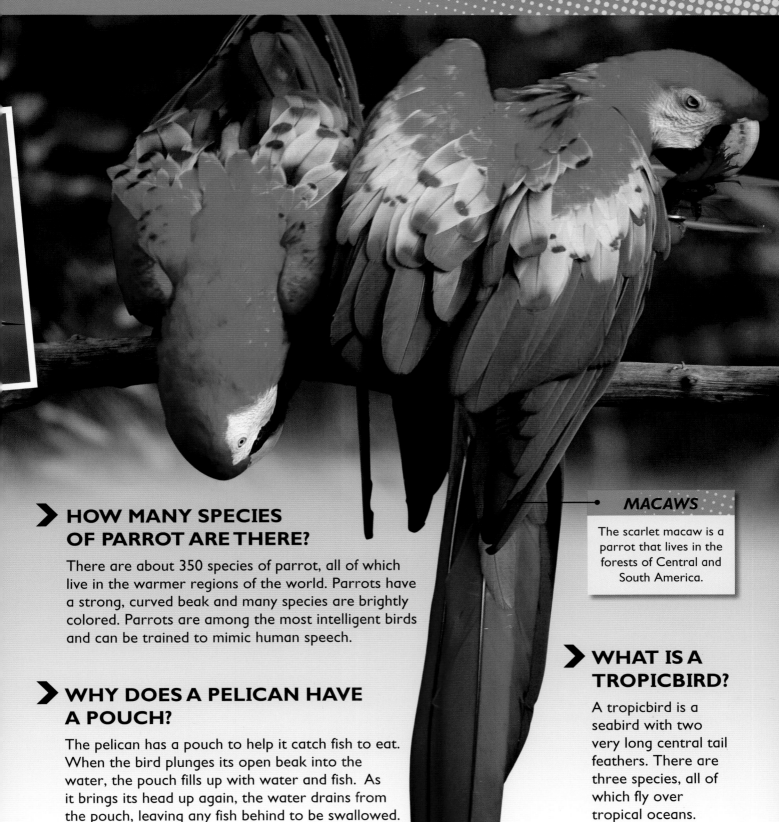

› HOW MANY SPECIES OF PARROT ARE THERE?

There are about 350 species of parrot, all of which live in the warmer regions of the world. Parrots have a strong, curved beak and many species are brightly colored. Parrots are among the most intelligent birds and can be trained to mimic human speech.

› WHY DOES A PELICAN HAVE A POUCH?

The pelican has a pouch to help it catch fish to eat. When the bird plunges its open beak into the water, the pouch fills up with water and fish. As it brings its head up again, the water drains from the pouch, leaving any fish behind to be swallowed.

MACAWS

The scarlet macaw is a parrot that lives in the forests of Central and South America.

› WHAT IS A TROPICBIRD?

A tropicbird is a seabird with two very long central tail feathers. There are three species, all of which fly over tropical oceans.

Birds of prey >

Birds of prey are hunters, feeding on small animals from insects to fish and mammals. They often make use of keen eyesight and sharp hearing, while their strong beaks and claws are ideal for tearing into flesh.

> DO EAGLES CATCH SNAKES?

Yes, snake eagles feed on snakes and lizards. The rough surface of the eagle's toes helps it hold on to wriggly snakes.

GRIFFON VULTURE

The vulture's bald head is ideal for feeding in messy carcasses.

> DO VULTURES HUNT AND KILL PREY?

Vultures do not usually kill their prey. They are scavengers, feeding on animals that are already dead or have been killed by hunters such as lions. They have strong claws and beaks, and their bald head allows them to plunge into carcasses without matting their feathers.

> WHICH VULTURE IS A BONE-CRACKER?

The bearded vulture picks up bones and drops them from a great height on to rocks. This smashes them open, so the bird can feed on the marrow inside.

PEREGRINE FALCON

This falcon likes to feed on birds, plus small mammals and reptiles.

> WHICH IS THE FASTEST BIRD?

As it dives to catch other birds in the air, the peregrine falcon may move at about 200 miles an hour, faster than any other bird. The falcon circles above its victim before making its fast dive and killing the prey on impact.

> HOW CAN OWLS HUNT AT NIGHT?

Owls have excellent sight, even in low light, and very sharp hearing. Owls also have special soft-edged wing feathers that make very little noise as they beat their wings, swooping down on their unsuspecting prey.

HOW MANY KINDS OF OWL ARE THERE?

There are 145 species of owl in two families. The barn owl family contains about 10 species and the true owl family about 135 species. Owls live in most parts of the world, except a few islands. They usually hunt at night, catching small mammals, birds, frogs, lizards, insects, and even fish.

More birds of prey >

There are about 500 species of birds of prey, including eagles, hawks, buzzards, harriers, kites, falcons, and vultures. All these birds hunt during the day and rest at night. The only nocturnal birds of prey are the owls.

OSPREYS

Ospreys share a small fish in their nest, which is made of a heap of sticks and seaweed.

> WHICH IS THE SMALLEST BIRD OF PREY?

The black-legged falconet and the Bornean falconet, of Southeast Asia, both have an average length of 6 inches. They feed on small birds and insects.

> WHAT DOES AN OSPREY EAT?

The osprey feeds mostly on fish. When it sees something near the surface, it dives down toward the water and seizes the fish in its feet. The soles of its feet are covered with small spines to help it hold on to the slippery fish.

> WHICH IS THE BIGGEST EAGLE?

The biggest eagle in the world is Steller's sea eagle, which weighs 10 to 20 pounds and has a wingspan of up to 8 feet. Although it breeds mainly in Russia it is also found in Korea and Japan, and preys on fish and water birds.

WHICH IS THE BIGGEST BIRD OF PREY?

The Andean condor is the biggest bird of prey in the world. It measures up to 44 inches long and weighs up to 25 pounds. Its huge wingspan is over 10 feet across.

TOP QUESTION ?

DO EAGLES BUILD NESTS?

Yes, and the nest, called an eyrie (above), made by the bald eagle is the biggest made by any bird, at up to 18 feet deep. They are used again and again, with the eagles adding more nesting material each year.

ANDEAN CONDOR

The Andean condor's face is nearly featherless but it has a ruff of white feathers around its neck.

HOW DO EAGLES KILL THEIR PREY?

An eagle kills with the four long, curved claws on each of its feet. It drops down on to its prey, seizes it in its long talons, and crushes it to death. The eagle then tears the flesh apart with its strong hooked beak.

Plants

Growing in the sun >

GREEN LEAVES

Plants reduce carbon dioxide and produce vital oxygen through photosynthesis.

There are 350,000 named species of plants, although many more are believed to exist. These range from trees, bushes, and herbs to grasses, ferns, and mosses. Most plants get their energy for growing from sunlight, using a process called photosynthesis.

> HOW DO GREEN PLANTS FEED?

Green plants make their own food in a process called photosynthesis. Chlorophyll helps to trap energy from the Sun. Plants use this energy to convert water and carbon dioxide into sugars and starch.

> WHY ARE MOST PLANTS GREEN?

Most plants are green because they contain the green pigment chlorophyll in their stems and leaves. Sometimes the green pigment is masked by other colors, such as red. This means that not all plants that contain chlorophyll look green.

❯ HOW DOES A FLOWER FORM SO QUICKLY?

When a flower opens out from a bud, it may appear in just a few hours. This is possible because the flower is already formed in miniature inside the bud, just waiting to open out. The bud opens as its cells take in water and grow.

BLOSSOMING

Buds open in the warm and sunny weather of spring.

❯ HOW MUCH SUGAR DOES PHOTOSYNTHESIS MAKE IN A YEAR?

Plants turn the sugar they make by photosynthesis into other chemical compounds that they need for growth and development. They also use sugar to make energy. Some scientists have estimated that the total mass of green plants alive in the entire world makes more than 180 billion tons of sugar every year by photosynthesis.

❯ WHAT MAKES A SEED GROW?

To grow, a seed needs moisture, warmth, and air. Some seeds can only germinate (begin to grow) if they have first been in the low temperatures of winter. The seeds of some plants can lie dormant (inactive) for years before germinating.

WHY DO SHOOTS GROW UPWARD?

Most shoots grow upward, toward the sunlight. The growing tip of the shoot can detect the direction of the light, and chemicals are released that make it grow more on the lower or darker side, thus turning the shoot upward.

SHOOTING UP

Like most plants, a bean shoot relies on the soil for water and support.

Feeding

Plants need water, mineral salts, and foods such as carbohydrates in order to grow. Green plants make their own food, while other plants may take in food from decaying plants or animals, or direct from other living plants.

HOW DOES A PARASITIC PLANT FEED?

Parasitic plants do not need to make their own food, and many are not green. Instead, they grow into the tissues of another plant, called the host, and tap into its food and water transport system, taking all the nourishment they need.

ROOTS

Roots anchor the plant while taking in water and mineral salts.

HOW DOES A VENUS FLYTRAP CATCH ITS PREY?

The flytrap is a carnivorous (meat-eating) plant that catches insects and other small animals. The trap is a flattened, hinged pad at the end of each leaf, fringed with bristles. When an insect lands on the pad and touches one of the sensitive hairs growing there, the trap is sprung and closes over the insect.

TOP QUESTION

WHY DO ROOTS GROW DOWNWARD?

Roots grow down because the root responds to gravity by releasing chemicals that prevent growth on the lower side, thus turning the root downward.

HOW DOES MISTLETOE FEED?

Mistletoe is a hemiparasitic plant, which means that it takes some of its nutrients from a host plant and some from its own photosynthesis. It can attach itself to the branches of many different trees and shrubs.

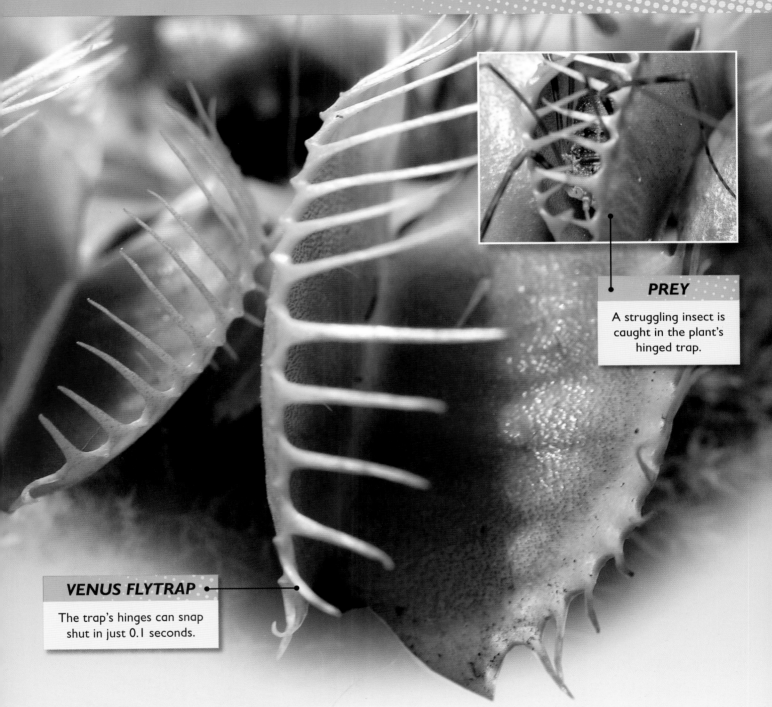

PREY

A struggling insect is caught in the plant's hinged trap.

VENUS FLYTRAP

The trap's hinges can snap shut in just 0.1 seconds.

❯ HOW DO PLANTS TAKE IN WATER?

Plants use their extensive root systems to take in water from the ground. Each root branches into a network of rootlets, which in turn bear root hairs. Water passes into the root across the cell walls of millions of tiny root hairs.

❯ HOW FAST DOES SAP FLOW THROUGH A TREE?

Sap is the fluid that transports water and food through plants. Sap may flow through a tree as fast as 3 feet every hour.

Many plants reproduce by pollination. The pollen, containing the male cells, fertilizes the female ovules, which then produce seeds. The pollen can be taken to its destination by insects, birds, the wind, or water.

> WHAT HAPPENS IN A FLOWER AFTER POLLINATION?

After pollination, the pollen that has landed on the stigma of another flower of the same species will begin to germinate, if conditions are right. It sends a tube down into the ovary of the flower, which it enters to fertilize an ovule. Each ovule can now become a seed.

> WHICH FLOWERS LAST FOR JUST ONE DAY?

The flowers of morning glory and day lilies open each morning and shrivel and die toward evening.

MORNING GLORY

The flowers are pollinated by bees, hummingbirds, butterflies, and moths.

> CAN PLANTS REPRODUCE WITHOUT SEEDS?

Some plants, such as mosses, liverworts, and ferns, do not produce seeds. Instead, they spread by dispersing spores, which can produce a new plant without the need for pollination. Other plants can reproduce by sending out runners or splitting off from bulbs, or swollen stems.

HOW ARE FLOWERS POLLINATED?

Many flowers have evolved their colors and scent to attract insects. The animal lands on the flower, gets showered with pollen, then moves to the next flower, transporting the pollen.

SOWING SEEDS

Seeds must be dispersed, or spread around, so that some will find suitable places to germinate. Seeds contained in berries and fruit are spread in bird droppings.

POLLINATION

Bees, wasps, and butterflies like to feed from flowers' nectar.

❯ WHICH FLOWERS ARE POLLINATED BY MAMMALS?

The flowers of the African baobab tree are pollinated by bushbabies and bats.

❯ HOW ARE SEEDS DISPERSED?

Many seeds are dispersed by animals. Birds eat berries and pass out the tougher seeds unharmed in their droppings. Some fruit capsules have hooks that catch in animal fur and are transported that way. Many seeds can be carried by the wind. The maple has "helicopter" wings to carry it along.

Plants and the environment →

Plants are vital to the environment. In fact, without plants, there would be no life on our planet. Plants are key producers of oxygen, which most animals need to survive. Many animals, including humans, rely on plants for shelter, water, food, and oxygen.

CATERPILLAR

A tree's leaves may provide food for caterpillars.

❯ WHAT IS THE NITROGEN CYCLE?

Bacteria in the soil use nitrogen from the air and turn it into a form that plants can use. Plants then use the nitrogen in their cells to make complex compounds, such as proteins. When animals eat plants, the nitrogen returns to the soil in their droppings. It also returns when plant and animal bodies decay and rot.

❯ HOW DO PLANTS RECYCLE WATER?

Plants help to return water to the air through the process of transpiration. This is when water evaporates from the stems and leaves of plants. Water enters the plant through its roots. A column of water moves up through the plant, from the roots right through the trunk or stem, into the leaves.

TOP QUESTION

?

WHAT LIVES IN A TREE?

Many species of beetle lay their eggs in a tree's bark. Birds select a fork in a branch to build a nest, or use a natural hole in the trunk, and wild bees may also choose to nest inside a hollow tree. Many mammals are tree dwellers, including squirrels, monkeys, sloths, bats, and koalas.

> **HOW ARE PLANTS USED TO CLEAN UP SEWAGE?**

Sewage works use tiny algae and other microscopic organisms in their filter beds. These algae and other organisms feed on the pollutants in the water and help to make it clean.

HERBIVORE

Caterpillars are the larvae of moths and butterflies. They only eat plant matter.

> **HOW DO FORESTS HELP IMPROVE THE AIR?**

Forests do this by releasing huge quantities of water vapor and oxygen into the atmosphere. Plants also absorb carbon dioxide, and help prevent this gas from building up to damaging levels.

Plants and the soil →

Plants take water and nutrients from the soil, only to return them in a never-ending, finely balanced cycle. But this cycle can be destroyed by humans, if we forget to care for our vital forests and fields.

❯ WHAT HAPPENS TO ALL THE LEAVES THAT FALL?

Huge quantities of leaves fall from forest trees, but they do not build up on the woodland floor from year to year. The dead leaves are attacked, for example by fungi and bacteria, and break down, becoming part of the soil. The leaves are also eaten by animals, including worms and insects.

❯ HOW DO PLANTS MAKE SOIL MORE FERTILE?

When plants die, they decompose, releasing the chemicals in their tissues into the surrounding soil. The mixture of rotting leaves and other plant material in the soil is called humus, and this makes the soil more fertile.

LEAF FOOD

Fallen leaves provide food for animals and fertilize the soil.

➤ WHAT IS OVERGRAZING?

It is when livestock such as cows and sheep are allowed to eat the grasses and other plants in one area for too long. The plants are not able to recover and, in dry areas, the land may become eroded or turn into desert.

➤ HOW DO PLANTS COLONIZE BARE GROUND?

Some plants can quickly colonize bare soil by germinating rapidly from lightweight, wind-blown seeds. Some colonizing plants spread by putting out runners, which split off, becoming new plants.

• *DANDELION*

A dandelion's seeds are carried by "parachutes" to take root on bare ground.

HOW DO PLANTS HELP US RECLAIM LAND?

Several types of grass, including marram, can be planted on coastal dunes. Their roots anchor the sand and help to stop it blowing away. Plants can even begin to reclaim land contaminated by industrial poisons. Some species have evolved forms that can tolerate toxic substances. They gradually improve the fertility and build up the soil so that other plants can grow there too.

➤ HOW CAN PLANTS BE USED TO HELP STOP EROSION?

Erosion is when soil is loosened and removed by the action of natural forces such as wind and water. This can often be reduced or prevented by using plants. The roots of the plants trap the loose soil and stop it being blown away. This can be useful on steep slopes or the edges of deserts.

Plants as food >

About 7,000 species of plant are known to have been used by people as food, and about 150 of these are in regular cultivation. Human cultivation of plants is part of agriculture, alongside raising animals. Without agriculture, there would be no human civilization.

> WHAT ARE THE MOST IMPORTANT FOOD CROPS?

The most important crops are the cereals, such as wheat, rice, and corn. These form the basis of many people's diet. Tuber crops, such as potatoes, are also widely grown. All these foods provide carbohydrates, while pulses, such as peas, beans, and lentils, are rich in protein.

PEACHES

Peaches grow well in warm climates such as in the Mediterranean and the southern USA.

> WHICH FRUITS ARE GROWN FOR FOOD?

Fruits of the temperate regions include apples, pears, and strawberries. In warmer regions, there are citrus fruits such as oranges and lemons, and other fruits such as papayas, pineapples, and melons. Some fruits have a savory flavour, such as avocados and peppers.

SUGAR MAPLE

Maple syrup is often used as a sweetener with pancakes.

❯ WHAT TREES GIVE US A SWEET, SUGARY SYRUP?

The sugar maple has a sweet sap, which is harvested to make maple syrup. Most maple syrup comes from the province of Quebec, in Canada.

❯ WHAT IS THE AMAZON COW TREE?

The Amazon cow tree is a tropical fig. It takes its name from the fact that it produces a milklike sap, or latex, which can be drunk just like cow's milk.

SUNFLOWER

Sunflower oil is commonly used for frying food and contains essential vitamin E.

❯ WHICH PLANTS GIVE US OIL?

The seeds of many plants are rich in oil, which they store as a source of food and energy. We extract oil from several of these plants, including olive, sunflower, corn, soybean, peanuts, oil-seed rape, sesame, and African oil palm.

❯ WHAT PLANTS ARE USED TO MAKE SUGAR?

The main source of sugar is the sweet stems of sugarcane, a tall grass that grows in tropical countries. In some temperate areas, including Europe, there are large crops of sugar beet. This plant stores sugar in its thickened roots. In some parts of the tropics, the sap of the sugar palm is made into sugar.

Harvesting the land

It is not just our staple crops, such as cereals and potatoes, that are provided by plants. Drinks such as tea, coffee, wine, and beer are made from plants. Sometimes we do not even notice the plants on our plate, such as the pectin from plant cells that stiffens preserves.

❯ WHAT IS BREADFRUIT?

Breadfruit is a tree native to the Malay Archipelago. It grows to about 65 feet and has large edible fruits which are eaten as a vegetable. The related jackfruit, from India and Malaysia, also has edible fruits—up to 2 feet long.

EAR OF WHEAT

Wheat is used to make flour for bread, cookies, cakes, pasta, noodles, and couscous.

❯ WHERE DID WHEAT COME FROM?

Wheat is one of the oldest known crops. It was probably first cultivated over 6,000 years ago in Mesopotamia (present-day Iraq). Many useful crop plants have their origins in the Middle East. Other examples are barley, oats and rye, peas and lentils, onions, olives, figs, apples, and pears.

TOP QUESTION ?

HOW IS TEA MADE?

Tea comes from the leaves of a camellia grown on hillsides in India, Sri Lanka, Indonesia, Japan, and China. The young leaf tips are harvested, dried, and then crushed to make tea.

TEA PICKING

After water, tea is the world's most consumed drink.

❯ HOW IS CHOCOLATE MADE?

The cacao tree comes originally from the lowland rain forests of the Amazon and Orinoco. The fruits, called pods, develop on the sides of the trunk, and each pod contains about 20 to 60 seeds—the cocoa "beans." The beans must be fermented, roasted, and ground before they become cocoa powder, the raw material for making chocolate.

❯ WHERE DOES COFFEE COME FROM?

The coffee plant is a large shrub, and its berries are used to make coffee. The ripe berries are harvested, then dried to remove the flesh from the hard stones inside. These are the coffee "beans," which are then often roasted.

❯ WHERE WERE POTATOES FIRST GROWN?

Potatoes grow wild in the Andes Mountains of South America and were first gathered as food by the native people of that region. All the many varieties grown today derive from that wild source.

COCOA POD

Today cocoa is a highly valuable crop in West Africa and the Caribbean.

Plants as medicine >

ROSY PERIWINKLE

Extracts from this plant, vinblastine and vincristine, are used by many international drugs companies.

Plants have been used as medicine for at least 100,000 years. In much of the world, especially in China and India, herbal remedies are used more than any other kind of medicine. Today, scientists are still researching the valuable healing properties of plants for use in conventional medicines.

> CAN PLANTS HELP FIGHT CANCER?

Several plants are effective against cancer tumors. One of the most famous is the rosy periwinkle. One of its extracts, vincristine, is very effective against some types of leukemia, a cancer of the blood.

> WHICH PLANTS AID DIGESTION?

Many plants, including the herbs and spices used in cooking, help digestion. In Europe, the bitter extract of wild gentians provides a good remedy for digestive problems.

➤ WHAT IS GINSENG?

Ginseng is a plant related to ivy, and has been used in herbal medicine for centuries. It is claimed—but not proved—to help many conditions, including fatigue and depression, kidney disease, heart problems, and headaches.

➤ WHICH PLANT HELPS COMBAT MALARIA?

Quinine, from the bark of the quinine tree, which grows in the South American Andes, can cure or prevent malaria. Before the widespread use of quinine, malaria used to kill 2 million people each year.

GINSENG

Ginseng root is often taken in dried form.

➤ WHICH PLANT IS BELIEVED TO HELP ASTHMA?

Lungwort is a herb with purple flowers and spotted leaves that are said to look like lungs. For this reason, it is sometimes used to treat asthma. There is no definite proof that it works.

LUNGWORT

The lungwort herb gets its name from the belief that it helps the lungs.

➤ CAN WILLOWS HELP PAIN?

Willow twigs were once chewed to give pain relief. A compound similar to the drug aspirin was once extracted from willows and the herb meadowsweet, known as spiraea—giving aspirin its name.

Materials from plants >

Plant materials are an essential part of our lives, keeping us warm, dry, safe, and even—in the case of musical instruments—entertained. From wood to leaves, plants supply many of our raw materials.

> WHAT TYPES OF THINGS CAN BE MADE FROM PLANTS?

We make all kinds of things from plant materials. Wood alone is used to make countless objects, big and small, from construction timbers to toys. All kinds of cloth are also made from plants—and so is the paper you are looking at!

TOP QUESTION ?

HOW MANY THINGS CAN BE MADE FROM BAMBOO?

Bamboo is one of the world's most useful plant products. It is used for scaffolding and building houses, and for making paper, furniture, pipes, canes, and (when split) for mats, hats, umbrellas, baskets, blinds, fans, and brushes. Some bamboos have young shoots that are delicious to eat.

> WHAT IS JOJOBA?

Jojoba is a bush found in Mexico. The fruits have a high-grade oily wax. It is used as a lubricant, in printing inks, and in body lotions and shampoo.

> WHAT ARE VIOLINS MADE OF?

The body of a violin is usually made from finely carved spruce and maple woods, creating its beautiful sound.

THATCHED COTTAGE
Traditional British cottages have a wooden frame and roofs of thatched straw or reeds.

➤ WHAT IS BALSA?

Balsa is the world's lightest timber—it floats high in water. Balsa trees grow in tropical Central and South America. Balsa wood is used for making models such as airplanes, and also for rafts, life preservers, and insulation.

➤ WHAT IS RAFFIA?

Raffia is a natural fiber made from the young leaves of the raphia palm, which grows in tropical Africa. Raffia is used in handicrafts such as basketry.

RAFFIA BAGS

Dyeing and weaving raffia is a traditional handicraft.

BAMBOO CAFÉ

Giant bamboo plants shade bamboo furniture in China.

Plant products >

Plant products are chosen for different uses depending on their natural properties. The softness of cotton makes it ideal for clothing. The springiness of rubber makes it perfect for products from rubber bands to rubber gloves.

> HOW IS CORK PRODUCED?

Cork comes from a tree called the cork oak. The cork is the thick, spongy bark. It is stripped away from the lower trunk, then left to grow back for up to 10 years before the next harvest. Cork is used to make many things, from bottle corks and pinboards to floor tiles.

CORK OAK

Cork oaks grow wild around the Mediterranean Sea and have been cultivated in Portugal and Spain.

> WHAT IS KAPOK?

Kapok is similar to cotton. It comes from the kapok tree, which is cultivated in Asia and can be as tall as 160 feet. The fluffy seed fibers are used to stuff mattresses, jackets, quilts, and sleeping bags.

COTTON

Cotton plants grow in the Americas, India, and Africa.

➤ HOW IS COTTON TURNED INTO CLOTH?

Cotton is a soft fiber that grows naturally around the seeds of the cotton plant, forming "bolls." These are "ginned" to remove the seeds; spun, or twisted, into thread; and then woven to make cloth.

➤ WHAT IS RUBBER?

Rubber is the sap of some plants, particularly the para rubber tree. The trees are pierced, or tapped, and the sap drips slowly into a waiting container.

➤ WHAT WOOD MAKES THE BEST CRICKET BAT?

The best bats are made in India, from the timber of the cricket-bat willow, a white willow. The blade (the part the ball strikes) is made from willow, and the handle from a different wood or cane.

WILLOW BAT

Willow is lightweight but will not splinter when hit by a ball.

➤ CAN PLANTS PRODUCE FUEL TO RUN CARS?

The copaiba tree of the Amazon rain forest yields an oil similar to diesel that can be used to run engines. Oil-seed rape, soybean, and the petroleum nut tree of Southeast Asia can also be used to produce biofuels, or plant fuels. As crude oil reserves are used up, biofuels may become more important.

Extreme plants >

The many species of plants are all competing for resources. They have evolved countless extreme survival strategies, from great height to immense roots. They have adapted to hostile environments, from deserts to mountains, so that they can find a place to grow and thrive.

DUCKWEED

These simple plants just consist of a platelike structure that floats on the water surface.

> ## WHICH IS THE LARGEST SEED?

The coco de mer of the Seychelles has the largest seeds, each weighing up to 50 pounds. They are produced inside a big fruit that takes six years to grow.

> ## WHAT IS THE SMALLEST FLOWERING PLANT?

A tiny tropical floating duckweed is the world's smallest flowering plant. Some species measure less than 0.02 inches across, even when fully grown.

BANYAN TREE

This single banyan looks as if it is a whole grove of trees.

WHAT IS THE OLDEST PLANT?

The oldest known plant is a grove of quaking aspens in Utah. The trees are all part of a single organism which could be over 80,000 years old. The bristlecone pine, which grows mainly in the southwestern USA, notably in the White Mountains of California, is also very long-lived. The oldest is about 4900 years old.

WHAT PLANT CAN SPREAD ACROSS THE WIDEST AREA?

The banyan of India and Pakistan often starts life as an epiphyte—a small plant growing on another tree. As it grows, it sends down woody roots that come to resemble tree trunks. Eventually it can seem like a grove of separate trees. One 200-year-old banyan had 100 "trunks."

AGED PINE

Although the original branches die, bristlecone pines can live for 5,000 years.

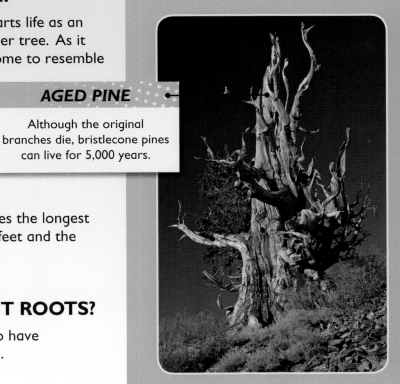

WHICH PLANT HAS THE LONGEST LEAF?

The raphia palm of tropical Africa produces the longest known leaves. The stalk can be nearly 13 feet and the leaf-blade more than 60 feet long.

HOW DEEP ARE THE DEEPEST ROOTS?

Roots of a South African fig were found to have penetrated 400 feet below the dry surface.

Plant records

Tall conifers tower above other plants in their forest, while giant flowers feed among roots on the ground. In the oceans and lakes, seaweeds and waterlilies grow huge to absorb nutrients and sunlight.

WHAT IS THE LARGEST FLOWER?

It's the rafflesia, which grows in Southeast Asia. It is a parasite, growing on the stems of lianas in the forest. Flowers can measure 3 feet—and they stink, mimicking the aroma of rotting flesh to attract flies to pollinate the flower.

> WHICH PLANT GROWS THE SLOWEST?

The record for the slowest-growing plant probably goes to the dioon plant. The dioon grows in Mexico, and one specimen was recorded to have an average growth rate of 0.03 inches per year.

> WHICH PLANT GROWS THE FASTEST?

The giant bamboo of Burma grows at up to a foot per day, making it one of the fastest growing of all plants. However, another species from India, the spiny bamboo, holds the record for growth in a greenhouse—it achieved 36 inches in a day.

> WHAT IS THE WORLD'S LONGEST SEAWEED?

Giant kelp is a huge seaweed that forms underwater forests in the coastal waters of California. Its fronds can be up to 215 feet long, making it one of the tallest plants known.

GIANT KELP

Kelp forests are vital ecosystems that are home to many animals, from fish and starfish to sea urchins.

> WHICH IS THE TALLEST TREE?

The California redwood, which grows along the North American Pacific coast, is the tallest tree in the world, reaching 367 feet. Some Australian eucalyptus trees can grow to 300 feet.

> WHICH PLANT HAS THE LARGEST FLOATING LEAVES?

The giant waterlily of the Amazon region has huge leaves. They grow up to 8.7 feet across, and can support the weight of a child.

GIANT WATERLILY

These lilies, which grow in still lakes and swamps, have stalks up to 23 feet long.

Ecosystems

Desert

A desert is an area that receives very little rain and so is unable to support much plant growth. Although many deserts are in hot regions, some of the world's deserts can be extremely cold.

> WHICH IS THE DRIEST DESERT?

Most areas of the Sahara Desert have around 3 inches of rainfall in an average year, making this one of the driest deserts. Parts of the Atacama Desert in Chile are also very dry. Some years may pass between rainfalls there.

SAHARA DESERT

The dry central region of the Sahara Desert is covered by vast sand dunes.

> WHICH IS THE HOTTEST DESERT?

Parts of the Sahara, in North Africa, and the Mojave Desert, in California, experience extremely high temperatures. The average summer temperature may be over 100°F. In Death Valley in the Mojave Desert, temperatures of 134°F have been recorded.

> WHICH IS THE BIGGEST DESERT?

The Sahara in North Africa covers an area of about 3,563,000 square miles. This is nearly as big as the United States of America.

➤ WHAT IS A RAIN SHADOW?

A rain shadow is a dry region of land that lies close to a mountain range. The mountains block the passage of rain-bringing clouds, casting a "shadow" of dryness. The Gobi Desert (above), in Central Asia, is in the shadow of the Himalayan Mountains.

➤ WHY ARE SOME DESERTS EXPANDING?

The Sahara is growing larger each year, partly because the climate is getting gradually warmer, but mainly because the plant life on the edges of the desert has been destroyed by grazing animals.

WHICH IS THE COLDEST DESERT?

Antarctica is sometimes called a cold desert, and is in fact extremely dry, because all its water is locked up as ice. The deserts of Central Asia—in Mongolia and western China—are chilled in winter by cold air from the Arctic. Even in summer, when the days are hot, the temperature can drop to below freezing at night.

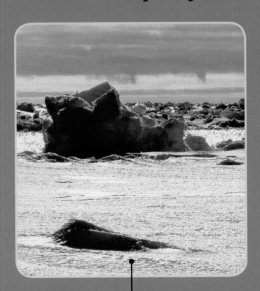

ANTARCTIC DESERT

The continent is too dry and cold to support much plant life: only moss, lichen, and algae can grow.

Desert plants

The key problem faced by desert plants is lack of water. Plants must survive months—or even years—of drought. Some desert plants store water in their leaves, roots, and stems.

WHAT IS AN OASIS?

An oasis is a place in the desert where water is in plentiful supply, such as at a pool permanently fed by a spring. Many plants can grow at an oasis, even in the heat of the desert. Date palms are commonly planted at oases, both for shade and to provide fruit.

WHAT LIVES IN A LARGE CACTUS?

Cacti are home to a variety of wildlife. Their flowers are visited by butterflies, moths, and hummingbirds. Holes in cactus stems provide nest sites for desert rodents and for birds like the tiny elf owl.

HOW DOES A CACTUS SURVIVE IN THE DESERT?

Cacti have generally leafless, swollen stems that store water. Since they lack leaves, they do not lose much water through evaporation. Most cacti are spiny, which probably protects them from being eaten by hungry and thirsty desert animals.

DESERT OASIS

An oasis is a source of vital water, where trees, bushes, grasses, and water plants can grow.

➤ WHAT IS A YUCCA PLANT?

Yucca plants are succulents. This means that they are adapted to very dry conditions and can store water in their leaves. Other succulents are cacti, aloes, and agaves. Some species make popular house plants as they are easy to keep.

➤ WHAT IS A JOSHUA TREE?

The Joshua tree grows in the Mojave Desert in California. It grows only about 4 inches a year. The fibers inside the tree's leaves can be used to make paper.

HOW BIG IS THE LARGEST CACTUS?

The largest of all cacti is the giant cactus, or saguaro, of the southwestern USA and Mexico. A 125-year-old saguaro can measure up to 50 feet tall and weigh as much as 6 tons.

JOSHUA TREE
Each of the tree's long and spiky leaves can survive for up to 20 years.

SAGUARO CACTUS
Cacti grow slowly in the dry desert. It may take 75 years to grow one side arm.

More desert plants

Desert plants have adapted to dry conditions in a variety of ways. As well as the ability to store water, some plants have very long roots to search out underground water. Others can lie dormant, waiting for rain in order to grow.

DESERT BLOOMS

The North American deserts can flower after rainfall.

WHAT ARE LIVING STONES?

Living stones are special desert plants from southern Africa. They have swollen leaves and grow low down among the sand and gravel of the desert surface, looking very much like small pebbles or rocks. It is only when they flower that they reveal their true nature.

❯ HOW DO DESERT FLOWERS SURVIVE DROUGHTS?

Many desert flowers live for only a short time, but survive as seeds in the desert soil. When the next rains fall, they trigger the seeds to germinate.

> ## HOW DO "RESURRECTION" PLANTS SURVIVE DROUGHTS?

When conditions get very dry, the leaves of these plants shrivel up and turn brown. This cuts down the loss of water. When it rains, they turn green again.

> ## WHAT IS A PRICKLY PEAR?

A prickly pear is a type of cactus. The fruits of prickly pears are commonly called cactus figs and are tasty to eat, as long as their small spines are removed.

> ## HOW DEEP DO THE ROOTS OF DESERT PLANTS GO?

Some desert plants have very long roots that can tap into deep underground water sources. Mesquite roots often grow as deep as 65 feet in search of water.

WELWITSCHIA

The plant's two leaves can grow to 13 feet long and split into several strands.

> ## WHICH IS THE STRANGEST DESERT PLANT?

Welwitschia is probably the strangest desert plant of all. It lives for centuries, growing very slowly and producing just two twisted leathery leaves. It lives in the coastal deserts of southwest Africa and gets its water mainly from sea fog.

Grassland >

In temperate regions—lying between the polar areas and the tropics—that have warm summers and cold winters, grassland develops in areas that do not have enough rainfall for trees and woods to grow. Many types of grasses thrive in these habitats.

> WHERE ARE GRASSLANDS FOUND?

There are grasslands in Central Asia, North America, Argentina, and southern Africa. The Asian grasslands are called the steppes, and the North American grasslands are the prairies. In Argentina they are called pampas, and in southern Africa the veld. The steppes are the largest area, stretching from Hungary to Mongolia.

TOP QUESTION ?

HOW DO GRASSLAND FIRES START?

Fires can start quite naturally, for example when lightning strikes dead or dying grass. If a wind is blowing and the weather is dry, the sparks can quickly turn into a fire that spreads.

STEPPES

Very few trees break the monotony of the Central Asian steppes.

➤ HOW DO GRASSLAND PLANTS SURVIVE FIRE?

Some grassland plants survive fires by persisting as thickened roots, and sprouting again after the fire has passed. Others may die, but germinate again later, from seeds left behind in the soil.

➤ WHY DON'T TREES TAKE OVER THE GRASSLAND?

Trees cannot survive easily in natural grassland areas, mainly because the rainfall is too low to support their growth. But in areas where the rainfall is higher, trees will gradually invade, unless they are chopped down or eaten by grazing animals.

➤ WHICH ANIMALS LIVE ON THE PRAIRIES?

The original prairie animals include buffalo, deer, and prairie dogs. The wild buffalo once numbered some 40 million, but it was almost wiped out by settlers.

ZEBRA ON THE VELD

The zebra's stripes act as camouflage in the dappled light and shade of long grass.

➤ WHAT ARE GRASSLANDS USED FOR?

Grasslands have long been used for grazing herds of domestic animals, such as cows. But because the soils are so fertile, much of the original grassland has now been plowed up and planted with crops, such as wheat and corn.

Mountains

Conditions get harsher the higher you go up a mountain, and the plant life reflects this. Fir or pine forest on the upper slopes gives way to shrubs then grassland, followed by snow and rock.

> WHICH IS THE WORLD'S HIGHEST MOUNTAIN RANGE?

The Himalayas, in Asia. It contains 96 of the world's 109 peaks that are more than 24,000 feet above sea level. One of these peaks is Mount Everest, the world's highest mountain.

TOP QUESTION

WHAT IS THE TIMBERLINE?

Trees cannot grow all the way up a mountain, and the highest level for them is known as the timberline. This varies according to the local climate of the region, but is about 11,000 feet in the Rockies. Trees at this level grow slowly and are often short.

TIMBERLINE

Trees give way to grasses and higher rocky slopes.

➤ WHY IS IT COLDER IN THE MOUNTAINS?

The Sun heats the ground and this heat is trapped close to the ground by the Earth's atmosphere. As you go up a mountain, and rise above the zone in which the heat is held, the atmosphere becomes thinner and the air gets colder. It falls about 2°F for every 500 feet you ascend in height.

➤ WHAT ARE CONIFEROUS FORESTS?

Coniferous forests often grow on mountain slopes, as well as in many other regions. Coniferous trees are conifers such as pines and firs. These trees are evergreen, which means they do not lose their leaves in winter. The trees cope well with weather extremes, such as cold and drought.

➤ WHY IS IT DAMAGING TO CUT DOWN MOUNTAIN FORESTS?

On mountain slopes, forests do more than provide homes and food for animals. Tree roots anchor the soil, preventing it being washed away by rain running down the slopes. Without trees to prevent them, dangerous landslides can occur.

➤ HOW DO PLANT-EATING ANIMALS FIND FOOD IN THE MOUNTAINS?

Many mountain mammals burrow under the snow and continue to feed on mountain plants even at high altitudes. Others, such as marmots, store fat in their bodies and hibernate during the winter.

MOUNT EVEREST

The mountain's peak, at 29,029 feet, is bare of plants. Flowering plants grow up to 20,000 feet.

MARMOT

Marmots eat mountain grasses, berries, mosses, roots, and flowers.

Mountain plants ›

On mountainsides, plants must survive colder and windier weather than on the valley floor below. They must grow in thinner soil and on uneven or rocky ground. Yet many plants thrive in these exposed conditions.

› WHY DO DIFFERENT PLANTS GROW ON DIFFERENT SIDES OF A MOUNTAIN?

Different sides of a mountain have different climates, or average weather conditions. On the south side (or north side in the southern hemisphere), there is more sunshine and conditions are warmer, while on the other side, the snow stays on the ground much longer.

ALPINE MEADOW

Dandelions and cuckoo flowers grow in grassland high in the European Alps.

› HOW DO PLANTS SURVIVE THE COLD?

Some plants grow close to the ground in cushionlike shapes, which keeps them out of the wind. Some have thick, waxy, or hairy leaves to help insulate them from the cold.

EDELWEISS

Edelweiss is a European mountain plant that thrives on rocky slopes.

➤ HOW DO PLANTS SURVIVE THE SNOW AND ICE?

Few plants can survive being completely frozen, but many can thrive under the snow. Snow acts like a blanket to keep the freezing ice and wind at bay, and saves the plants from being killed. Alpine grasses stay alive and green under the snow, ready to grow again as soon as it melts.

➤ WHY ARE ALPINE PLANTS POPULAR IN GARDENS?

Alpine plants are those that survive above the timberline. Many are popular because they have bright flowers and tend to grow well in poor conditions.

➤ HOW DO SOME MOUNTAIN PLANTS REPRODUCE WITHOUT FLOWERS?

Many mountain plants have dispensed with flowers because of the lack of insects to pollinate them. Instead, for example, some grasses grow miniature plants where the flowers should be. These drop off and grow into new plants.

GENTIAN

Many mountain plants, like this vivid blue gentian, have showy flowers to attract insects.

➤ HOW DO MOUNTAIN PLANTS ATTRACT POLLINATORS?

Many mountain plants have large, colorful flowers to attract the few insects that live there. Some, such as mountain avens, track the Sun to warm their flowers, which encourages insects to sunbathe there.

Tundra >

Tundra is an area where the temperatures are too cold for trees to grow. Tundra normally occurs close to the polar regions. The dominant plants are grasses, mosses, lichens, and shrubs such as heathers.

> WHERE IS THE TUNDRA?

Tundra lies north of the coniferous forest belt, in a band following the Arctic Circle. It covers about 9.5 million square miles, from Alaska, through Canada, Greenland, Iceland, and Scandinavia into Siberia. Only a small area of the Antarctic has similar conditions, on the northern tip nearest South America. Most of Antarctica is covered with snow and ice all year.

TOP QUESTION

WHAT IS THE MOST NORTHERLY FLOWER?

The Arctic poppy has been found growing farther north than any other flower, at 83°N, or on a level with the north of Greenland.

SIBERIAN TUNDRA

The snow melts in summer, leaving behind marshy puddles.

❯ WHAT IS PERMAFROST?

Even where the surface soil in the Arctic thaws in the summer, farther down it is permanently frozen. This icy layer is known as the permafrost.

❯ WHY ARE MANY ARCTIC SHRUBS EVERGREEN?

Many Arctic shrubs keep some of their leaves through the winter. Leaves formed in late summer stay on the plant, often protected by dead leaves formed earlier. As soon as spring returns, the green leaves begin to photosynthesize, losing no time to make their food over the short summer months.

❯ WHAT PLANTS DO CARIBOU EAT?

Caribou survive the Arctic winter by foraging for food. They dig beneath the snow with their hooves and antlers, seeking out mosses and grasses.

❯ WHY ARE MANY TUNDRA FLOWERS WHITE OR YELLOW?

Most tundra flowers are pollinated by insects. However, there are relatively few bees this far north, and the main pollinators are flies. Flies cannot distinguish colors as bees can, so the flowers do not need to be so colorful.

CARIBOU

The caribou, also known as the reindeer, is common in tundra regions.

Temperate forest →

There are two main types of forest in the world's temperate regions: the deciduous forest and the evergreen coniferous forest. Deciduous forests are characterized by trees that lose their leaves in the winter. Evergreen trees keep their leaves year-round.

› WHAT IS TEMPERATE DECIDUOUS FOREST LIKE IN SUMMER?

In summer the forests hum with life—birds call from the trees and mice rustle in the undergrowth. The leaf canopy is fully developed, cutting out much of the sunlight from the forest floor. Nevertheless, shrubs such as roses and hazel, and flowers such as woodsorrel, grow among the trees.

› WHAT IS TEMPERATE DECIDUOUS FOREST LIKE IN WINTER?

In winter, the tall trees forming the woodland canopy have lost all their leaves. Most of the flowers have died back. Evergreen species such as holly, ivy, and yew stand out at this time of year, and provide valuable cover for forest animals.

› ARE TEMPERATE FORESTS QUIETER IN WINTER?

Yes! Many of the birds heard in temperate forests are summer visitors and migrate south in winter. Many chirping forest insects die or hibernate during the cold winters.

SUMMER WOODLAND

Beneath the canopy of trees, layers of shrubs and herbs grow closer to the ground.

➤ HOW ARE TEMPERATE FORESTS HARVESTED FOR WOOD?

Many forests are not natural, but have been managed for centuries to provide timber. This involves removing only a portion of the trees at a time, which lets the forest regenerate. Sometimes branches are cut from trees, and the trees can then resprout from the base, to provide another crop of branches later. This is called coppicing.

➤ WHAT ELSE DO WE GET FROM TEMPERATE FORESTS?

Lots of things! Charcoal is made by slowly burning certain kinds of wood. In the past, people depended upon woodland animals such as wild boar and deer for food and skins. Many edible fungi, including chanterelle and truffles, grow in temperate woods, while woodland brambles and wild strawberries have edible fruits.

TOP QUESTION ?

WHAT LIVES ON THE FOREST FLOOR?

Invertebrates thrive in the dead leaves and roots of the woodland floor. Beetles, wood lice (above), worms, slugs, snails, and ants, to name but a few, help break down the organic material, as well as providing food for mice and voles.

MUSHROOM

A mushroom is the fleshy body of a fungus.

Temperate forest plants ›

Temperate forests are found in parts of Europe, North America, eastern Asia, South America, and Australasia. The most common plants are trees, but shrubs and low-growing plants also thrive.

› WHY DO SOME TREES LOSE THEIR LEAVES IN THE FALL?

Deciduous trees and other plants that lose their leaves usually do so in the fall, and remain bare through winter. In this way they shut down their main life processes—photosynthesis and transpiration (through which water and nutrients flow through the plant)—remaining dormant until spring.

FALL LEAF

A leaf's green pigment decreases as winter nears.

› WHY DO MOST WOODLAND FLOWERS APPEAR IN SPRING?

By developing early, they can benefit from the sunlight before it is shut out by the trees. Insects, which help to pollinate flowers, may also find it easier to spot them before the rest of the vegetation grows.

BLUEBELLS

Bluebells are a common sight in springtime woods.

› WHICH ARE THE MOST COMMON TREES?

The most common trees in deciduous forests are oaks, beeches, maples, and birches. Common coniferous trees are pines, firs, and spruces.

➤ WHICH FOREST TREE CAN BE TRACKED DOWN BY ITS SOUND?

The leaves of the aspen tree move from side to side in the wind and rustle against each other, even in the lightest breeze. So the practiced ear can easily track down an aspen.

➤ WHICH CONIFER IS DECIDUOUS?

Larch is a coniferous tree—it bears cones and has needle-like leaves. But unlike most conifers, larch loses its leaves all at once, in the fall, so it is also deciduous. In fact, there are also broadleaved trees that are evergreen, such as the oaks of the Mediterranean regions.

➤ HOW OLD CAN FOREST TREES GET?

Many forest trees reach a great age, notably oaks, which live between 200 and 400 years. Most elms live to about 150 years.

LARCH CONE

When fertilized by pollen, a cone produces seeds.

Rain forest

Tropical rain forests occur in the Earth's hotter regions where rainfall is very high. The rain forests help preserve the planet's atmosphere, by releasing huge quantities of water vapor and oxygen and absorbing carbon dioxide.

HOW MUCH RAIN FALLS IN THE RAIN FOREST?

The tropical rain forests are warm and wet. In many, the rainfall is more than 6 feet per year. It may rain at any time of the day, but there are often storms in the afternoon.

WHERE ARE THE RAIN FORESTS?

The world's largest rain forest is around Brazil's Amazon River and the foothills of the Andes Mountains. The world's main areas of tropical rain forest are in South and Central America, West and Central Africa, Southeast Asia, and north Australia.

RAIN FOREST

Just one acre of tropical rain forest can contain nearly 100 species of trees.

WHAT DO WE GET FROM RAIN FORESTS?

We get many things from rain forests, including timber, Brazil nuts, fruit such as bananas and mangoes, rubber, rattan (a kind of palm from which furniture is made), cosmetics, and medicines.

> WHY ARE RAIN FORESTS BEING CUT DOWN?

Many rain forests are destroyed so the land can be used for crops, or for grazing. Tropical forest soils are fertile, and many crops, such as cocoa and sugarcane, can be grown after the trees have been felled. However, the fertility of the soil is short-lived.

RAIN FOREST FRUIT

Pineapple and urucum (above right) grow in tropical forests.

> HOW FAST ARE RAIN FORESTS BEING DESTROYED?

Every year an area of rain forest the size of the state of Wisconsin is lost. When the forest is cleared, the fertile topsoil is soon washed away by tropical rainstorms, making the ground useless for crops.

> ARE RAIN FORESTS VITAL?

Yes! Rain forests are home to two-thirds of the world's animal and plant species. And without rain forests to regulate the Earth's atmosphere, climate change would speed up.

Rain forest plants ➤

The rain forest is in four basic layers. At the top are the very tallest trees. Below is the canopy, a dense cover of foliage made by the bulk of the trees. The understory is the layer of shrubs, while the forest floor below is dimly lit and relatively bare of plants.

➤ ## HOW TALL ARE THE BIGGEST RAIN FOREST TREES?

The main canopy of the rain forest develops at around 100 feet, with occasional taller trees (known as emergents) rising above to about 150 feet or more.

➤ ## WHAT STOPS THE TALL TREES FROM BEING BLOWN OVER?

Many of the taller forest trees have special supporting flanges near the base of their trunks, called stilts or buttresses. These make the tree less liable to be pushed over in a storm.

TOP QUESTION

WHICH PLANTS CAN TRAP THEIR OWN RAINWATER?

It rains very often in the tropical rain forest, and many plants trap the water before it reaches the ground. Bromeliads have special leaves that form a waterproof cup for this purpose.

BROMELIAD

The plant's colored leaves form a rosette to trap vital water.

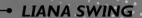

LIANA SWING

An orangutan uses a liana as a swing in Borneo, Southeast Asia.

> WHAT IS AN AIR PLANT?

An air plant grows without anchoring itself to the ground. Air plants are common in some tropical forests. They get the moisture they need direct from the damp air.

> WHAT ARE LIANAS?

Lianas, or lianes, are plants that clamber over and dangle from rain forest trees. They grow very long, and animals such as monkeys and squirrels use lianas to help them move through the branches.

ORCHID

Many orchids are air plants, with roots that cling on to other plants for support.

> WHAT'S A STRANGLER FIG?

The strangler starts out as a seed high in a tree, carried there by a monkey or bird that has eaten the fig's fruit. The seedling sends down long roots to the ground, from where it starts to surround the host tree, slowly suffocating it.

Wetland

Wetlands include swamps, bogs, and marshes. Wetland plants are adapted to living in water-soaked soil. Bulrushes, water lilies, and mangroves are just some of the common wetland species.

WHY DO MOST WATER PLANTS GROW ONLY IN SHALLOW WATER?

Most plants need to root themselves in the soil, even if they live mainly submerged in the water. In deep water there is not enough sunlight for plants to grow successfully.

HOW ARE WETLANDS DAMAGED?

When soil is drained, or too much water is pumped from the land nearby, wetlands suffer as the water-table is lowered. They are also easily damaged by pollution: chemicals released from factories find their way into streams, upsetting the natural balance.

WHAT IS THE WATER HYACINTH?

Water hyacinth is a floating plant with beautiful mauve flowers. However, it is also a fast-growing weed and can spread rapidly to choke waterways.

WATER HYACINTH

Water hyacinths flourish on Lake Naivasha in Kenya, eastern Africa.

➤ HOW DO WATER PLANTS GET THEIR FLOWERS POLLINATED?

Most water plants hold their flowers above the water, for pollination by the wind or by insects. Some, like the water starwort, have water-resistant floating pollen that drifts to the female flowers.

DRAGONFLY

Dragonflies live around wetlands because they lay eggs in or near water.

➤ WHAT FOOD PLANTS COME FROM WETLANDS?

The most important wetland crop is rice, which is grown in many parts of the world, notably India and China. It grows best in flooded fields called paddies. Another aquatic grass crop is wild rice, a traditional food of Native Americans, and now a popular specialty.

HOW DO WATER PLANTS STAY AFLOAT?

Some water plants stay afloat because their tissues contain chambers of air, making their stems and leaves buoyant. Others, such as water lilies, have flat, rounded leaves that sit boatlike on the water's surface. They may also have waxy leaves, which repel the water and help to keep the leaves afloat, or upcurved rims to the leaves.

Planet Earth

Earth's history

HOW IS THE EARTH'S HISTORY DIVIDED?

Scientists divide the last 590 million years into three eras: the Paleozoic (meaning old life), Mesozoic (middle life), and Cenozoic (new life). Earth's history before the Paleozoic era is divided into three eons: the Hadean, Archean, and Proterozoic (see diagram below).

WHAT ARE PERIODS AND EPOCHS?

The geological eras are subdivided into periods, such as the Jurassic. Periods are divided into epochs, such as the Pleistocene.

OUR PLANET'S BIRTH

The Earth formed 4.6 billion years ago, but conditions were not ready for life until 800 million years later.

Humans have only been on the Earth for about 100,000 years. But scientists can form a picture of our planet's history before humans existed by studying the Earth's rocks and fossils. We have discovered when the earliest life forms emerged and what the first animals looked like.

TIMELINE

This timeline shows the Earth's history.

HADEAN	ARCHEAN				PROTEROZOIC								
	Eoarchean	Paleo-archean	Meso-archean	Neo-archean	Paleoproterozoic				Mesoproterozoic			Neoproterozoic		
					Siderian	Rhyacian	Orosirian	Statherian	Calymmian	Ectasian	Stenian	Tonian	Cryogenian	Ediacaran

4600 3800 3600 3200 2800 2500 2300 2050 1800 1600 1400 1200 1000 850 630 542

Millions of years ago

❯ WHAT DID EARLY ANIMALS LOOK LIKE?

By around 500 million years ago, bacteria in the oceans had evolved into the earliest fish. These strange creatures had no jaws—they had funnel-like sucking mouths.

EARLY LIFE

Stromatolites form when bacteria builds up solid mats of calcium carbonate, also known as lime.

TOP ? QUESTION

WHAT ARE STROMATOLITES?

Primitive life forms may have first appeared on Earth about 3.8 billion years ago. These bacteria lived in the oceans and formed deposits called stromatolites. Today, modern stromatolites can be seen in shallow seas (left).

❯ WHY WASN'T THERE LIFE ON EARTH STRAIGHT AWAY?

The Earth's surface was probably molten for many millions of years after its formation. Life first began in the oceans, and these did not exist for the first 400–800 million years.

❯ WHEN DID PLANTS START TO GROW ON LAND?

The first land plants appeared in the Silurian period. These simple plants reproduced by releasing spores. Plants produced oxygen and provided food for the first land animals—amphibians. Amphibians first developed in the Devonian period from fish whose fins had evolved into limbs.

PHANEROZOIC															
Paleozoic						Mesozoic			Cenozoic						
Cambrian	Ordovician	Silurian	Devonian	Carboniferous	Permian	Triassic	Jurassic	Cretaceous	Paleogene			Neogene		Quaternary	
									Paleocene	Eocene	Oligocene	Miocene	Pliocene	Pleisto-cene	Holo-cene
542	488.3	443.7	416	359.2	299	251	199.6	145.5	65.5	55.8	33.9	23	5.3	1.8	0.01 0

Millions of years ago

Evolving life >

Humans are descended from the bacteria that were Earth's earliest life forms. Evolution is the process of how life forms change over the course of generations. When an animal develops a successful new feature—such as the ability to walk on two legs—this trait is passed down to future generations.

> WHY DID DINOSAURS BECOME EXTINCT?

The dinosaurs died out at the end of the Cretaceous period, 65 million years ago. Many experts believe that this happened when an enormous asteroid struck the Earth. The impact threw up a huge cloud of dust, which blocked out the sunlight for a long time. Land plants died and so the dinosaurs starved to death.

FOSSIL FISH

This fish, with a visible backbone, lived in Devonian times.

> WHAT WERE THE FIRST ANIMALS WITH BACKBONES?

Jawless fish were the first animals with backbones. They appeared during the Ordovician period. Fish with skeletons of cartilage, such as sharks, first appeared in the Devonian period.

> WHY IS THE CAMBRIAN PERIOD IMPORTANT?

Before the Cambrian period, most living creatures were soft-bodied and left few fossils. During the Cambrian period, many creatures had hard parts, which were preserved as fossils in layers of rock—ready for scientists to study later!

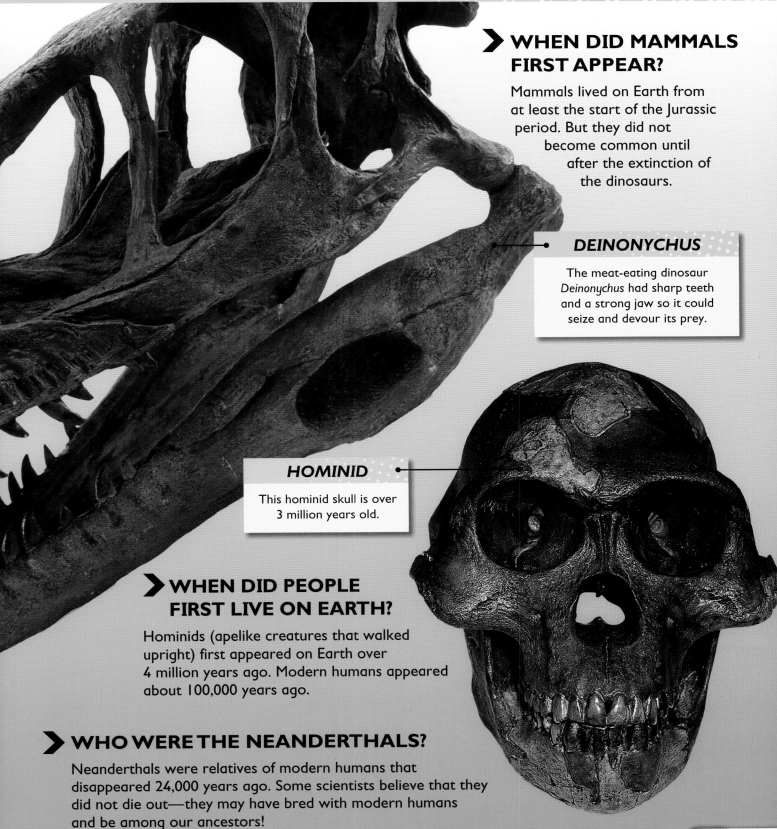

❯ WHEN DID MAMMALS FIRST APPEAR?

Mammals lived on Earth from at least the start of the Jurassic period. But they did not become common until after the extinction of the dinosaurs.

DEINONYCHUS

The meat-eating dinosaur *Deinonychus* had sharp teeth and a strong jaw so it could seize and devour its prey.

HOMINID

This hominid skull is over 3 million years old.

❯ WHEN DID PEOPLE FIRST LIVE ON EARTH?

Hominids (apelike creatures that walked upright) first appeared on Earth over 4 million years ago. Modern humans appeared about 100,000 years ago.

❯ WHO WERE THE NEANDERTHALS?

Neanderthals were relatives of modern humans that disappeared 24,000 years ago. Some scientists believe that they did not die out—they may have bred with modern humans and be among our ancestors!

The Earth's plates >

The surface of the Earth may appear solid but it is actually like a giant jigsaw puzzle. Earth's outer layers are divided into plates that float on a partly molten layer of rock. Currents in the molten rock slowly move the plates around. Over millions of years, the movement of these plates can create huge mountain ranges.

> WHAT IS THE EARTH'S MANTLE?

The mantle is a partly molten rocky shell that is about 1,750 miles thick. It makes up 70% of the Earth's volume. The mantle surrounds the Earth's iron-rich core (see also p.11). Surrounding the mantle is the Earth's crust, on which we live. It is a thin layer of crystallized products, formed by melting and movement within the mantle.

> WHAT ARE PLATES?

The Earth's hard outer layers are divided into large blocks called plates. These consist of the Earth's crust and the top part of the mantle.

> HOW DEEP ARE PLATES?

There are about seven large plates. Their exact thickness is uncertain but it could be up to 90 miles in places.

GROWING PEAKS

The mountains continue to rise by 0.2 inches a year.

THE HIMALAYAS

The Himalayas started to form when plates collided about 50 million years ago.

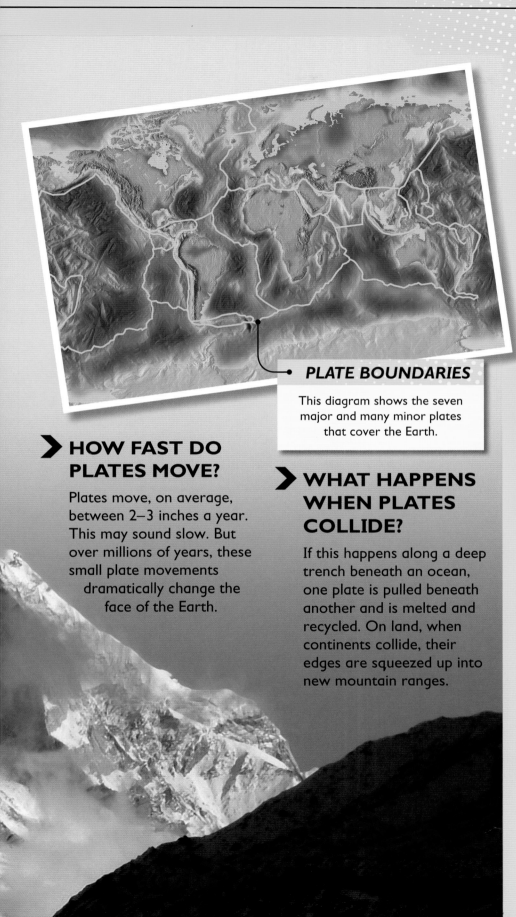

PLATE BOUNDARIES

This diagram shows the seven major and many minor plates that cover the Earth.

Yes. Plates can move apart, push against each other, or move sideways along huge cracks in the ground called transform faults.

❯ HOW FAST DO PLATES MOVE?

Plates move, on average, between 2–3 inches a year. This may sound slow. But over millions of years, these small plate movements dramatically change the face of the Earth.

❯ WHAT HAPPENS WHEN PLATES COLLIDE?

If this happens along a deep trench beneath an ocean, one plate is pulled beneath another and is melted and recycled. On land, when continents collide, their edges are squeezed up into new mountain ranges.

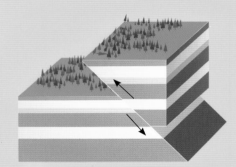

Plates push against each other

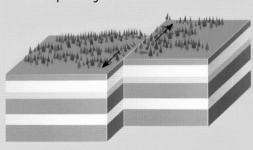

Plates move sideways (transform fault)

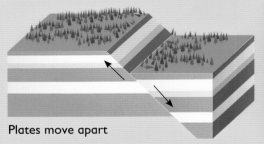

Plates move apart

Continental drift →

The continents—Europe, the Americas, Africa, Australia, Asia, and Antarctica—lie on different plates. The plates constantly move, slowly changing the face of the Earth. This movement of the continents is called continental drift.

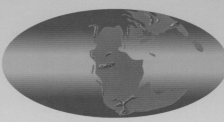

220 million years ago

› HAS EARTH ALWAYS LOOKED THE SAME?

No. If aliens had visited Earth 200 million years ago, they would have seen only one huge continent, called Pangaea, surrounded by one ocean. Around 180 million years ago, Pangaea began to break up. By 100 million years ago, plates supporting India, Australia, and Antarctica were drifting away from Africa, and North America was moving away from Europe.

155 million years ago

› ARE THE CONTINENTS STILL MOVING?

Africa is moving northward into Europe by fractions of an inch each year. The Americas are moving farther from Africa.

60 million years ago

› WHO FIRST SUGGESTED THE IDEA OF CONTINENTAL DRIFT?

In the early 1900s, an American, F.B. Taylor, and a German, Alfred Wegener, both suggested the idea of continental drift. But scientists could not explain how the plates moved until the 1960s, following studies of the ocean floor.

HAWAIIAN ISLANDS •

A volcanic cone rises behind Waikiki Beach in Hawaii.

TOP ? QUESTION

HOW IS CONTINENTAL DRIFT MEASURED?

A global network of observation stations measures the time taken for lasers to bounce back from satellites. This provides exact measurements of where the continents are and how they are moving.

› HAVE FOSSILS HELPED TO PROVE CONTINENTAL DRIFT?

Fossils of animals that could not have swum across oceans have been found in different continents. This suggests that the continents were once all joined together and that animals could walk from one continent to another.

LASER TRACKING

A laser at the McDonald Observatory in Texas tracks the drift of the continents.

› HOW WAS HAWAII FORMED?

Hawaii's existence proves that continental drift takes place! The Hawaiian islands were created as the Pacific Plate drifted to the northwest. As it moved, the plate passed over a hot spot in the mantle and a series of new volcanoes was punched up through the surface, one after another. Each of the islands in the Hawaiian chain has a volcano.

Earthquakes

Earthquakes happen when the Earth's plates move in a sudden jerk, shaking the ground. Powerful earthquakes can make buildings wobble and collapse. Earthquakes on mountains can cause landslides that sometimes destroy towns in the valleys below.

> WHERE ARE EARTHQUAKES LIKELY TO HAPPEN?

The most violent earthquakes occur around the edges of the plates that make up the Earth's outer layers. For most of the time, the plates' edges are jammed together. But gradually currents under the plates build up, increasing pressure, and the plates move in a jerk. This shakes all the rocks around them, setting off an earthquake.

> DO EARTHQUAKES AND VOLCANOES OCCUR IN THE SAME PLACES?

Yes, most active volcanoes occur near the edges of moving plates. Earthquakes are common in these regions too.

> WHAT IS A TSUNAMI?

Earthquakes on the seabed trigger waves called tsunamis. Tsunamis travel through the water at up to 500 miles an hour. As they approach land, the water piles up into deadly waves many feet high.

SAN FRANCISCO QUAKE

In 1906, half of San Francisco's buildings were destroyed by an earthquake.

TOP QUESTION ?

WHAT IS THE SAN ANDREAS FAULT?

The San Andreas fault is a long transform fault (see p.301) in California. Movements along this plate edge have caused huge earthquakes in the cities of San Francisco and Los Angeles.

SICHUAN QUAKE

In 2008 an earthquake hit
Sichuan province in China,
leaving more than
90,000 people dead.

❯ CAN SCIENTISTS PREDICT EARTHQUAKES?

In 1975, Chinese scientists correctly predicted an
earthquake using a seismograph (left) to measure plate
movements. They saved the lives of many people.
But scientists have not yet found an absolutely
certain way of forecasting earthquakes, so
fatalities and injuries regularly occur as a
result of quakes around the world.

Volcanoes

Volcanoes erupt when hot molten rock from deep down in the Earth's mantle rises through the Earth's hard outer layers and reaches the surface. The molten rock is called magma, but when it reaches the surface it is called lava. Most volcanoes occur near the edges of plates.

WHAT ARE HOT SPOTS?

Some volcanoes lie far from plate edges. They form over "hot spots"—areas of great heat in the Earth's mantle. Hawaii in the Pacific Ocean is over a hot spot (see also p.303).

DO ALL VOLCANOES ERUPT IN THE SAME WAY?

Volcanoes can explode upward or sideways, or erupt "quietly." Trapped inside the magma in explosive volcanoes are gases and water vapor. These gases splatter the magma and hurl columns of volcanic ash and dust into the air. Sometimes, clouds of ash and gas are shot sideways out of volcanoes. In "quietly" erupting volcanoes, magma emerges as runny lava and flows downhill.

LAVA BURST

Lava erupts from a central vent and burns everything in its path as it flows downhill.

WHAT ARE HOT SPRINGS AND GEYSERS?

These are places where underground water, heated by magma inside the Earth, breaks through to the surface. Warm water bubbles up at hot springs. Geysers hurl boiling water and steam into the air.

➤ WHAT IS AN EXTINCT VOLCANO?

Volcanoes that have not erupted in recorded history are said to be "extinct." This means that scientists consider they will not erupt again.

➤ WHAT IS A DORMANT VOLCANO?

Some active volcanoes erupt only now and then. When they are not erupting, they are said to be dormant, or sleeping.

➤ DO VOLCANOES DO ANY GOOD?

Volcanic eruptions cause tremendous damage, but soil formed from volcanic ash is extremely fertile. Volcanic rocks are also used in building and chemical industries.

GEYSER

Eruptions at the Lady Knox geyser in New Zealand create a water jet 60 feet high.

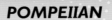

POMPEIIAN

The volcano Vesuvius erupted in AD 79, burying the town of Pompeii in volcanic ash. This victim was buried before he or she could escape.

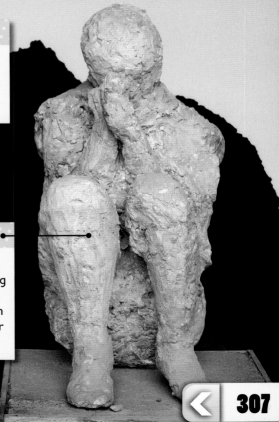

Rocks and minerals >

Minerals are solids that are formed naturally in the Earth. A common mineral is quartz. Like all minerals, it has a crystal structure— a symmetrical shape like that of a snowflake. Rocks are made of a mixture of minerals. Sandstone and limestone both contain quartz.

> WHAT ARE ELEMENTS AND MINERALS?

Earth's crust contains 92 elements. The two most common elements are oxygen and silicon. Some minerals, such as gold, occur in a pure state. But most minerals are chemical combinations of elements. For example, minerals made of oxygen and silicon—such as quartz—are called silicates.

> WHAT ARE THE THREE MAIN KINDS OF ROCK?

There are igneous, sedimentary, and metamorphic rocks. Igneous rocks, such as basalt and granite, are formed from cooled magma. Many sedimentary rocks are made from worn fragments of other rocks. For example, sandstone is formed from sand. Sand consists mainly of quartz, a mineral found in granite. Metamorphic rocks are changed by heat and pressure. For example, great heat turns limestone into marble.

> WHAT ARE THE MOST COMMON ROCKS?

Sedimentary rocks cover 75% of the Earth's land surface. But igneous rocks make up 95% of the rocks in the top 10 miles of the Earth's crust.

CHALK CLIFFS

England's White Cliffs of Dover are formed of the sedimentary rock chalk.

❯ WHAT ARE THE MOST VALUABLE MINERALS?

Gemstones such as diamonds, rubies, sapphires, and emeralds are valuable minerals. Gold and silver are regarded as minerals too, although they occur as pure elements.

GOLD NUGGETS

Precious gold nuggets and grains appear in rocks and soil.

❯ WHAT IS PUDDING-STONE?

It's a stone that looks rather like a plum pudding. It is a sedimentary rock made of a mixture of different-sized pebbles cemented together by sand. It is formed in river channels over thousands of years.

COAL MINE

Coal is often mined deep under the ground and is burned as fuel around the world.

TOP QUESTION ?

IS COAL A ROCK?

No. Although coal is sometimes called an organic rock, it is not a proper rock as rocks are inorganic (lifeless). Coal, like oil and natural gas, was formed millions of years ago from the remains of once-living things. That is why coal, oil, and gas are called fossil fuels.

More rocks and minerals

People have been making use of rocks and minerals for millennia. Rock is used for building, from the sandstone of the Egyptian pyramids to the limestone of New York's Empire State building. Minerals are needed everywhere from jewelry to industry, where diamonds are used to cut other materials.

CAN MINERALS MAKE YOU INVISIBLE?

No, although in the Middle Ages people thought that you would become invisible if you wore an opal wrapped in a bay leaf.

WHAT ARE BIRTHSTONES?

Birthstones are minerals that symbolize the month of a person's birth. For example, garnet is the birthstone for January, while ruby is the stone for people born in July.

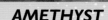

AMETHYST

Amethyst is the birthstone for people born in February.

WHAT IS THE HARDEST MINERAL?

Diamond, a pure but rare form of carbon, is formed under great pressure deep inside the Earth. It is the hardest natural substance.

MINING

Diamonds are mined around the globe, but about half the world's diamonds come from Africa.

❯ WHAT COMMON ROCKS ARE USED FOR BUILDINGS?

Two sedimentary rocks, limestone and sandstone, and the igneous rock granite are all good building stones. The metamorphic rock marble is often used to decorate buildings.

MARBLE
The Acropolis in Athens is constructed from marble.

❯ ARE SOME MINERALS MORE PLENTIFUL THAN OTHERS?

Many useful minerals are abundant. Other important minerals are in short supply and are often recycled from scrap. Recycling saves energy, which has to be used to heat and filter metal ores such as iron to get the pure metal.

CARYATIDS
Marble is ideal for carvings, such as these 5th-century BC female figures, or caryatids.

❯ WHICH IS THE WORLD'S LARGEST GEMSTONE?

Many jewels compete for this title. It may be an emerald that is 50 inches long and weighs 1,183 pounds—that's the weight of about seven men!

DIAMONDS
Gems are measured in carats, which are equal to 0.2 grams. A 1-carat diamond may cost up to $40,000.

Fossils →

Fossils are the impressions of ancient life preserved in rocks. When creatures die, their remains are often slowly buried in sand or soil. Their soft parts usually rot, but the hard parts—such as bones, teeth, and shells—can be preserved as minerals or molds in the rock.

> WHAT ARE TRACE FOSSILS?

Trace fossils give information about animals that lived in ancient times. Animal burrows are sometimes preserved, giving scientists clues about the creatures that made them. Other trace fossils include footprints.

> HOW ARE FOSSILS TURNED TO STONE?

When tree trunks or bones are buried, minerals deposited from water sometimes replace the original material. The wood or bone is then petrified, or turned to stone.

> WHAT IS AN AMMONITE?

Ammonites were sea-dwelling mollusks, related to squid. Fossils of ammonites are common in rocks of the Mesozoic era.

DINOSAUR PRINTS •

Footprints can be preserved when the mud in which they are made quickly hardens and then is buried under more mud.

TRILOBITES

Trilobites were very common in the seas of the Paleozoic era.

➤ HAS FLESH EVER BEEN PRESERVED AS A FOSSIL?

In Siberia, woolly mammoths, which lived more than 40,000 years ago, sank in swampy ground. When the soil froze, their complete bodies were preserved in the icy subsoil.

➤ WHAT IS THE OLDEST FOSSIL INSECT EVER FOUND?

This is a 400-million-year-old creature known as *Rhyniognatha hirsti*. It was found in Scotland in 1919. The insect is believed to have had wings, making it one of the earliest known creatures to take to the air.

TOP QUESTION ?

WHAT IS AMBER?

Amber is a hard substance formed from the sticky resin of trees. Tiny animals were sometimes trapped in the resin. Their bodies were preserved when the resin hardened.

SPEED AND SIZE

Studying dinosaur tracks can tell scientists about the length of the animal's legs and the speed at which it was moving.

FOSSIL FLIES

These flies were trapped in sticky resin millions of years ago.

More fossils >

Paleontologists study fossils to discover what prehistoric animals looked like and how they might have survived. Examining the fossils of plants has allowed scientists to build up a picture of how the world may have looked millions of years ago.

> HOW ARE FOSSILS DATED?

Sometimes, dead creatures are found buried under volcanic ash. The ash sometimes contains radioactive substances that scientists can date. In this way, they can work out the time when the animals lived.

> WHAT IS CARBONIZATION?

Leaves usually rot after plants die. But sometimes they are buried by mud on lake beds. Sediments around the leaf are gradually compressed into rock. Over time, bacteria change the chemistry of the leaf until only the carbon it contains remains. The shape of the leaf is preserved in the rock as a carbon smear.

FOSSIL LEAVES

The imprints of these leaves have been carbonized.

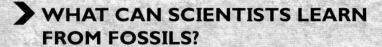

> WHAT CAN SCIENTISTS LEARN FROM FOSSILS?

From the study of fossils—known as paleontology—scientists can learn about how living things evolved on Earth. Fossils can also help paleontologists to date rocks. This is because some species lived for only a short period on Earth. So, if the fossils of these creatures are found in rocks in different places, the rocks must have been formed at the same time. Such fossils are called index fossils.

BITE SIZE

Prehistoric sharks' teeth, such as those of *Auriculatus*, *Megalodon*, and *Otodus obliquus*, tell scientists what sharks might have eaten.

> WHAT IS EOHIPPUS?

Eohippus is the name of the dog-sized ancestor of the horse, which lived about 55 million years ago. Fossil studies of Eohippus and its successors have shown how the modern horse evolved.

> WHAT IS A PETRIFIED LOG?

Petrified logs were formed when water replaced the molecules in buried logs with minerals. Slowly, stone replicas of the logs were produced.

PILTDOWN MAN

The identity of the famous Piltdown hoaxer remains unknown to this day.

> WHAT WAS PILTDOWN MAN?

Some bones, thought to be fossils of an early human ancestor, were discovered at Piltdown Common, England, between 1910 and 1912. But Piltdown Man was a fake. The skull was human, but the jawbone came from an orangutan.

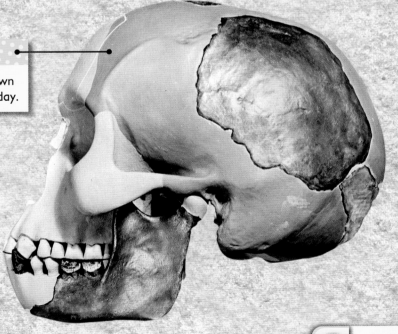

Earth extremes >

TIBETAN PLATEAU

The plateau is surrounded by mountain ranges.

Over billions of years, constant movement and heat beneath the Earth's surface has created vast mountain ranges and towering volcanoes. Oceans crash on to wide bays, while rivers snake across continents. Earth's extremes are part of what makes our planet such an extraordinary home.

> WHICH IS THE LARGEST HIGH PLATEAU?

The immense, wind-swept Tibetan Plateau in China covers about 711,000 square miles.

> WHICH IS THE LARGEST RIVER BASIN?

The Amazon river basin in South America covers about 2,708,100 square miles. The Madeira River, which flows into the Amazon, is the world's longest tributary, at 2,096 miles.

WHICH IS THE DEEPEST LAKE?

Lake Baikal, in Siberia, eastern Russia, is the world's deepest lake. The deepest spot measured so far is 5,251 feet.

VAST AREA

The plateau is about four times the size of France and has an average height of 15,000 feet.

WHICH IS THE LARGEST ISLAND?

Greenland covers 836,070 square miles. (Geographers regard Australia as a continent and not as an island.)

WHICH IS THE TALLEST VOLCANO?

It's Mauna Kea in Hawaii. It is both the world's tallest mountain and tallest volcano, but 19,000 feet of it lies under the Pacific Ocean.

WHICH IS THE LARGEST BAY?

Hudson Bay in Canada covers an area of about 475,000 square miles. It is linked to the North Atlantic Ocean by the Hudson Strait.

AMAZON BASIN

The Amazon Basin lies in six different countries.

LAKE BAIKAL

The lake holds more water than all of the five North American Great Lakes combined.

More Earth extremes >

On our amazing planet, we could climb 29,029 feet high to the summit of Mount Everest or descend 5,256 feet beneath the surface in the world's deepest cave. We could sail on the planet's widest lake or journey across the largest continent.

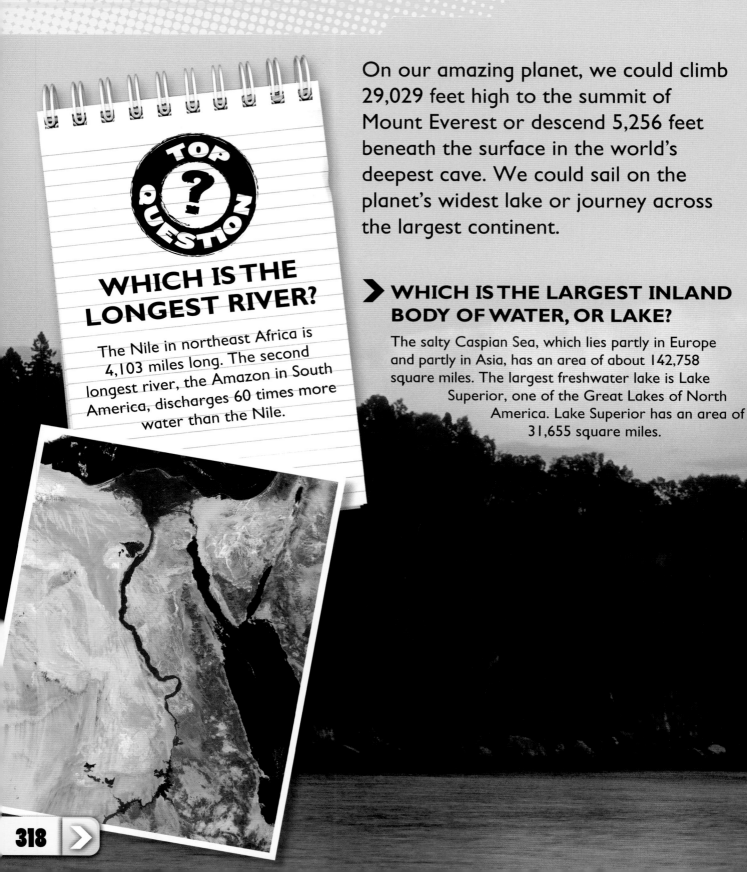

TOP QUESTION

WHICH IS THE LONGEST RIVER?

The Nile in northeast Africa is 4,103 miles long. The second longest river, the Amazon in South America, discharges 60 times more water than the Nile.

> WHICH IS THE LARGEST INLAND BODY OF WATER, OR LAKE?

The salty Caspian Sea, which lies partly in Europe and partly in Asia, has an area of about 142,758 square miles. The largest freshwater lake is Lake Superior, one of the Great Lakes of North America. Lake Superior has an area of 31,655 square miles.

THE DEAD SEA

This inland lake is nearly nine times saltier than the ocean.

> **WHICH IS THE LOWEST POINT ON LAND?**

The shoreline of the Dead Sea, between Israel and Jordan, is 1,300 feet below the sea level of the Mediterranean Sea.

> **WHICH IS THE DEEPEST CAVE?**

The Réseau Jean Bernard in France is the deepest cave network. It reaches a depth of 5,256 feet.

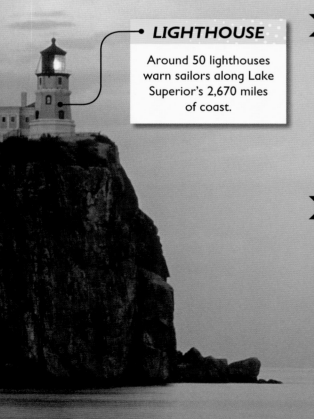

LIGHTHOUSE

Around 50 lighthouses warn sailors along Lake Superior's 2,670 miles of coast.

> **WHICH IS THE BIGGEST CONTINENT?**

Asia covers an area of 16,991,970 square miles. The other continents are Africa (11,678,046 square miles), North America (9,351,008 square miles), South America (6,884,974 square miles), Antarctica (5,405,430 square miles), Europe (4,032,065 square miles) and Australia (2,978,006 square miles).

> **WHICH IS THE BIGGEST OCEAN?**

The Pacific Ocean is the world's largest. It covers a third of the Earth's surface, with an area of 70 million square miles. The world has four other oceans, in descending order of size: Atlantic, Indian, Southern, and Arctic.

LAKE SUPERIOR

Over 200 rivers flow into the lake, which is drained by St. Mary's River.

The Earth's changing face

Weathering 1 →

There are two forms of weathering. Physical weathering is the breakdown of rocks through contact with atmospheric conditions such as heat, water, ice, and pressure. Chemical weathering is caused by chemicals naturally occurring in the atmosphere.

WEATHERING ROCK

Rocks such as limestone are chemically weathered by the action of rainwater.

❯ HOW QUICKLY IS THE LAND WORN AWAY?

An average of 1.5 inches is worn away from land areas every 1,000 years. Over millions of years, mountains can be worn down to plains.

❯ WHAT IS GROUNDWATER?

Groundwater is water that seeps slowly through rocks, such as sandstone and limestone. The top level of the water in the rocks is called the water table. Wells are dug down to the water table.

❯ HOW DOES WATER WEATHER ROCKS?

Water dissolves rock salt. It also reacts with some types of the hard rock granite, turning minerals in the rock into a clay called kaolin.

➤ CAN THE SUN CAUSE WEATHERING?

In dry regions, rocks are heated by the Sun, but they cool at night. These changes crack rock surfaces, which peel away.

TOP QUESTION

WHAT ARE SPRINGS?

Springs occur when groundwater flows to the surface. Springs are the sources of many rivers. Hot springs often occur in volcanic areas, where the ground water is heated by magma.

➤ HOW IS LIMESTONE WEATHERED?

Limestone is worn away by chemical weathering. Limestone consists mostly of calcium carbonate, which reacts with rainwater. Over time, the rainwater slowly dissolves the limestone.

LIMESTONE CLIFFS

The extraordinary limestone cliffs around Guilin in China were created by limestone weathering.

Weathering 2 >

Once weathering has broken down a rock, the materials left over can form soil, in which plants take root. Weathering also creates some of the Earth's most beautiful natural features.

> HOW DO LIVING THINGS WEATHER ROCKS?

Rocks can be exposed by burrowing animals and then weathered. Bacteria can also help to weather rocks.

> WHAT ARE STALACTITES AND STALAGMITES?

Water containing calcium carbonate drips down from the ceilings of limestone caves. The water gradually deposits calcium carbonate to form hanging, icicle-like structures called stalactites. Stalagmites are columns of calcium carbonate deposited by dripping water, but stalagmites grow upward from the floors of caves.

STALAGMITES
Stalagmites grow upward from the floors of caves, while stalactites (top) grow downward.

➤ HOW DOES FROST BREAK UP ROCKS?

At night in the mountains, people may hear sounds like gunshots. These are made by rocks being split apart by frost action (an example of physical weathering). As the water in cracks in the rocks freezes and turns into ice, it takes up nearly one-tenth as much space again, and so it exerts pressure, widening the cracks until they split apart.

➤ HOW ARE LIMESTONE CAVES FORMED?

Rainwater slowly dissolves limestone, opening up cracks in the surface and wearing out holes. Over time, the holes eventually lead down into huge caves.

➤ CAN PLANTS CHANGE THE LAND?

Plant roots can break up rock. When the seed of a tree falls into a crack in a rock, it grows roots that push downward. As the roots grow, they push against the sides of the crack until the rock splits apart.

WHAT ARE POTHOLES?

Potholes are circular holes in the ground that allow people called spelunkers (below) to climb down to explore limestone caves. They are formed when the roofs of shallow caves collapse.

TREE ROOTS

Tree roots grow into cracks in the rock, forcing it to split apart.

The work of rivers

Rivers wear away, or erode, the land. Young rivers push loose rocks down steep slopes. The rocks rub against riverbeds and deepen valleys. The rocks also rub against each other and break into finer pieces.

WHERE DO RIVERS START?

Some rivers start at springs, where groundwater reaches the surface. Others start at the ends of melting glaciers or are the outlets of lakes.

WHAT ARE TRIBUTARY RIVERS?

Tributary rivers are rivers that flow into a main river. This swells the amount of water in the main river and increases its load of worn material.

WHAT IS AN OXBOW LAKE?

In old age, rivers flow more slowly. Sometimes they change course. Cutoff bends become oxbow lakes, with a distinctive curved shape.

CANYON

Young rivers flow swiftly and can wear out deep-sided gorges.

NILE DELTA

As it meets the sea, the river moves slowly across flat plains.

TOP QUESTION

WHAT ARE DELTAS?

Deltas are areas of sediments, made up of sand, mud, and silt, that pile up around the mouths of some rivers. In many rivers, currents sweep the sediments into the sea.

HOW DO CANYONS FORM?

A fast-moving river, carrying with it large rocks, can slowly wear away the riverbed. Over time, the river may erode a steep canyon.

WHY DO WATERFALLS OCCUR?

Waterfalls can occur when rivers cross hard rocks. When softer rocks downstream are worn away, the hard rocks form a ledge over which the river plunges in a waterfall.

IGUAZÚ FALLS

On the border of Brazil and Argentina, the falls are up to 270 feet high.

The work of seas

Waves continually batter the shore. Large waves pick up sand and pebbles, and hurl them at cliffs. This can hollow out the bottom layers of the cliff until the top collapses. Waves and tides can also move beach sand and gravel.

> WHAT ARE SPITS?

Waves and currents transport sand, gravel, and pebbles along coasts. In places where the coasts change direction, the worn sand and pebbles pile up in narrow ridges called spits.

> DOES THE SEA WEAR AWAY THE LAND?

Waves wear away soft rocks to form bays, while harder rocks on either side form headlands. Parts of the coast of northeast England have been worn back by 3 miles in the last 2,000 years.

> WHAT IS A BAYMOUTH BAR?

Some spits join one headland to another. They are called baymouth bars, because they can cut off bays from the sea, turning them into enclosed lagoons.

BREAKWATERS

Breakwaters are built at many beach resorts to prevent the continual movement of sand by sea currents.

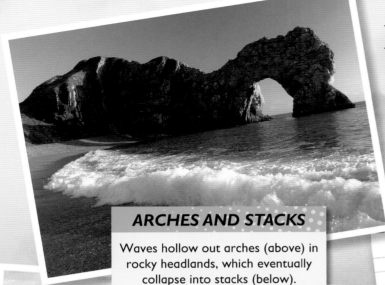

ARCHES AND STACKS

Waves hollow out arches (above) in rocky headlands, which eventually collapse into stacks (below).

> WHAT IS A BLOWHOLE?

It is a hole in the rock formed above a sea cave. When waves enter the mouth of the cave, they are funneled up into the blowhole, sometimes causing spectacular blasts of water.

TOP QUESTION ?

WHAT ARE ARCHES AND STACKS?

Waves attack headlands from both sides, wearing away caves in the cliffs. Eventually a natural arch is formed when two caves meet. When the arch collapses, all that remains is an isolated rock, called a stack.

> HOW CAN PEOPLE SLOW DOWN WAVE EROSION?

On many beaches, structures are built at right angles to the shore. These breakwaters slow down the movement of sand by waves and currents.

The work of ice >

A glacier is a slow-moving river of ice. Glaciers form in cold mountain areas, when snow compacts into ice. Eventually the ice starts to move downhill. Rocks frozen into the glaciers erode the valleys through which they flow.

> WHAT IS MORAINE?

Ice from mountaintops spills downhill to form glaciers. These carry worn rock, called moraine.

MORAINE RIDGES

Dark ridges of moraine can be seen in this glacier in Switzerland.

> WHAT IS A GLACIAL LAKE?

A melting glacier often leaves behind large patches of ice in hollows along its path. These will eventually melt to create lakes.

> WHICH IS THE LARGEST GLACIER?

The Lambert Glacier in Antarctica is the world's largest. It is 300 miles long.

GLACIAL LAKES

As it melted, the glacier left behind deposits of ice in hollows. The ice melted to form a series of lakes.

❯ HOW CAN WE TELL THAT AN AREA WAS ONCE COVERED BY ICE?

Certain features give this away. Mountain areas contain steep-sided valleys worn by glaciers. Armchair-shaped basins where glacier ice formed are called cirques. Knife-edged ridges between cirques are called arêtes. Peaks called horns were carved when three or more cirques formed back to back.

GLACIAL VALLEY

Ice-worn valleys are U-shaped, with steep sides and flat bottoms.

❯ IS GLOBAL WARMING MAKING THE GLACIERS MELT?

Rising temperatures are making glaciers shrink and disappear all over the world. Some glaciers are retreating at a rate of 50 feet every year.

❯ WHAT ARE ERRATICS?

Erratics are boulders made of a rock that is different from the rocks on which they rest. They were carried there by moving ice.

CIRQUE

A cirque is an armchair-shaped basin eroded at a glacier's head.

Ice ages

During ice ages, temperatures fall and ice sheets spread over large areas. Several ice ages have occurred in Earth's history, dramatically shaping our planet.

> WHEN WAS THE LAST ICE AGE?

The last ice age began about 1.6 million years ago and ended 10,000 years ago. The ice age included warm periods and long periods of bitter cold.

> WILL THERE BE ANOTHER ICE AGE?

Scientists think that we are living in an interglacial period, between two ice ages. The interglacial period may last for another 50,000 years or so.

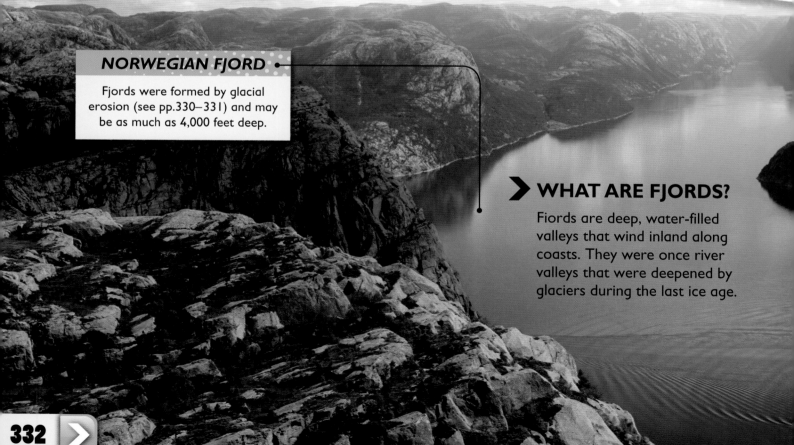

NORWEGIAN FJORD

Fjords were formed by glacial erosion (see pp.330–331) and may be as much as 4,000 feet deep.

> WHAT ARE FJORDS?

Fiords are deep, water-filled valleys that wind inland along coasts. They were once river valleys that were deepened by glaciers during the last ice age.

> HOW MUCH OF THE WORLD IS COVERED BY ICE?

Ice covers about 10% of the world's land. But during the last ice age, it spread over much of northern North America and Europe. The same ice sheet reached what are now New York City and London.

BEN BULBEN

This ridge in Ireland, called Ben Bulben, was cut by glaciers in the last ice age.

> DO ICE AGES CHANGE THE LANDSCAPE?

Yes! Northern Europe and America are marked by glacial valleys, fjords, and erratics.

WHAT ARE THE WORLD'S LARGEST BODIES OF ICE TODAY?

The largest bodies of ice are the ice sheets of Antarctica and Greenland. Smaller ice caps occur in the Arctic, while mountain glaciers are found around the world.

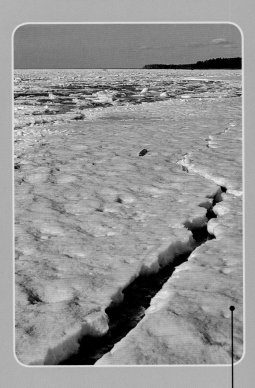

ICE SHEET

Although we are in an interglacial period, ice still covers Earth's poles.

Changing deserts ➤

In deserts, wind-blown sand is important in shaping the scenery. It acts like the sandblasters used to clean dirty city buildings. It polishes rocks, hollows out caves in cliffs, and shapes boulders.

TOP ? QUESTION

WHAT ARE DUST STORMS?

Desert winds sweep fine dust high into the air during choking dust storms. Wind from the Sahara in North Africa is often blown over southern Europe, carrying the pinkish dust with it.

➤ CAN WATER CHANGE DESERT SCENERY?

Thousands of years ago, many deserts were rainy areas, and many land features were shaped by rivers. Flash floods sometimes occur in deserts. They sweep away much worn material.

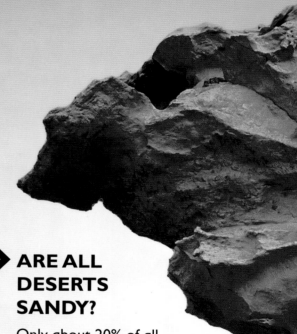

➤ ARE ALL DESERTS SANDY?

Only about 20% of all desert land is sandy. Nearly all hot deserts are plains where the wind has exposed rock, gravel, or sand. "Erg" is the name given to sandy desert. "Reg" is covered with gravel. "Hamada" is bare rock.

BARCHAN DUNE

Tall barchan dunes form in sandy deserts where the wind direction is constant.

➤ HOW ARE SAND DUNES FORMED?

The wind blowing across a desert piles the sand up in hills called dunes. Where the wind directions keep changing, the dunes have no particular shape. But when they blow mainly from one direction, crescent-shaped dunes called barchans form. Barchans may occur singly or in clusters.

➤ WHAT IS A WADI?

Wadis are dry waterways in deserts. Travelers sometimes shelter in them at night. But a freak storm can soon fill them with water and drowning can be a real danger.

MUSHROOM ROCK

The Western Desert in Egypt is the home of dramatic mushroom rocks.

➤ WHAT IS A MUSHROOM ROCK?

In the desert, winds lift grains of sand, which are then blown and bounced forward. Sand grains are heavy and seldom rise over 6 feet above ground level. Boulders whose bases have been worn by wind-blown sand are top-heavy and mushroom-shaped, perched on a narrow stem.

Changing poles →

The North Pole lies in the middle of the Arctic Ocean, which is covered by sea ice for much of the year. The South Pole lies in the freezing continent of Antarctica, which is covered by the world's largest ice sheet.

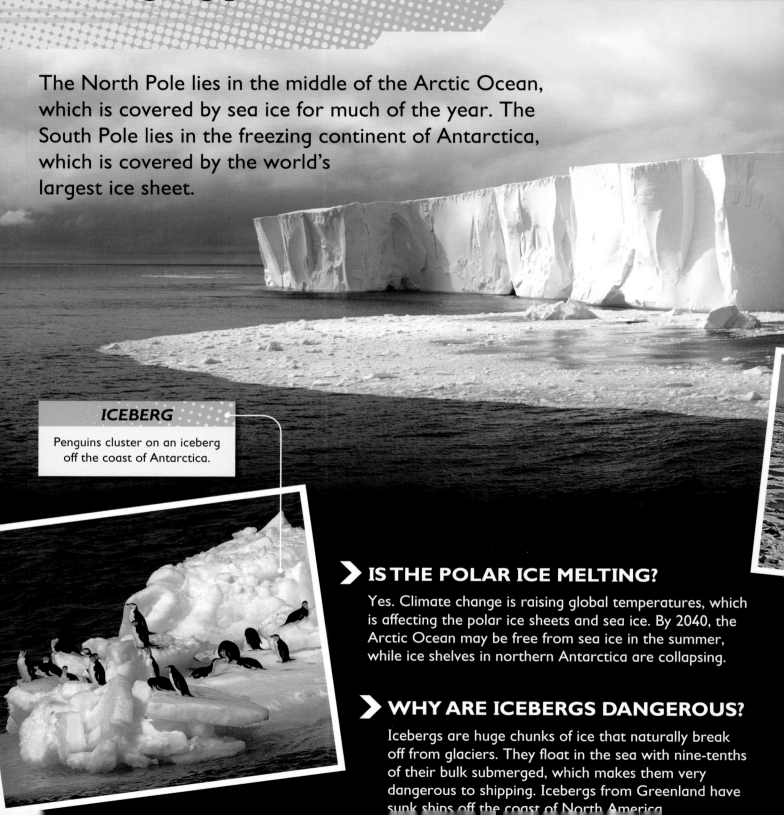

ICEBERG

Penguins cluster on an iceberg off the coast of Antarctica.

> IS THE POLAR ICE MELTING?

Yes. Climate change is raising global temperatures, which is affecting the polar ice sheets and sea ice. By 2040, the Arctic Ocean may be free from sea ice in the summer, while ice shelves in northern Antarctica are collapsing.

> WHY ARE ICEBERGS DANGEROUS?

Icebergs are huge chunks of ice that naturally break off from glaciers. They float in the sea with nine-tenths of their bulk submerged, which makes them very dangerous to shipping. Icebergs from Greenland have sunk ships off the coast of North America.

ICE SHELF

Scientists predict that Antarctic ice shelves could be at risk of collapse by 2100 due to global warming.

WHAT ARE ICE SHELVES?

Ice shelves are large blocks of ice joined to Antarctica's ice sheet, but which jut out over the sea. When chunks break away, they form flat-topped icebergs. Some of them are huge. One covered an area about the size of Maryland.

TOP QUESTION ?

WHAT IS IT LIKE AROUND THE NORTH POLE?

It is bitterly cold. The ice-covered Arctic Ocean is surrounded by northern North America, Asia, and Europe. In spring, the sea ice is about 10 feet thick in mid-ocean. The ocean contains several islands, including Greenland.

HOW THICK IS THE ICE IN ANTARCTICA?

Ice and snow cover 98% of Antarctica, with some coastal areas and high peaks being ice-free. The Antarctic ice sheet is the world's largest, and contains about seven-tenths of the world's fresh water. In places, the ice is up to 3 miles thick. The world's record lowest temperature, -128.6°F, was recorded at the Vostok research station in 1983.

IS ANTARCTICA'S ICE SHEET GETTING THINNER?

Unfortunately, parts of the ice sheet are thinning. In West Antarctica, rising temperatures are

People changing the Earth >

Since humankind first learned to cut down trees to clear land for growing crops, we have changed the face of the Earth. Today, some of these changes are threatening our environment, our health, and our future.

> WHAT IS AIR POLLUTION?

Air pollution occurs when gases such as carbon dioxide are emitted into the air by factories, homes, and offices. Vehicles also cause air pollution, which produces city smogs, acid rain, and global warming.

> WHAT IS HAPPENING TO THE WORLD'S FORESTS?

When trees are cut down without new trees being planted, deforestation takes place. Today, the tropical rain forests are particularly affected by deforestation. These forests contain more than half of the world's species and many are threatened with extinction.

DEFORESTATION
Around 32 million acres of forest are lost each year.

➤ WHAT IS DESERTIFICATION?

Human misuse of the land near deserts, caused by cutting down trees and overgrazing grasslands, may turn fertile land into desert. This is called desertification. Natural climate changes may also create deserts. This happened in the Sahara about 7,000 years ago.

➤ WHAT IS GLOBAL WARMING?

It is a rise in average worldwide temperatures. This is partly caused by activities such as deforestation and the burning of fossil fuels, such as coal. These activities release greenhouse gases, such as the carbon dioxide stored in trees. These gases trap heat in the Earth's atmosphere. Global warming is likely to cause changes in rainfall patterns, causing floods in some areas and droughts in others.

THE MALDIVES

The Maldives is a chain of coral islands that is threatened by rising sea levels.

➤ WILL GLOBAL WARMING AFFECT ANY ISLAND NATIONS?

Coral islands are low-lying. If global warming melts the world's ice, then sea levels will rise. Countries such as the Maldives and Kiribati could vanish under the waves.

CITY SMOG

Smog causes an increase in asthma and allergies. It is dangerous for people with heart and lung problems.

The human touch >

The environment is in a delicate balance. Industry, farming, and the growth of cities can destroy that balance. But not all human change is harmful, with deserts and sea being turned into farmland.

> WHAT IS THREATENING FISH IN THE SEA?

Coral reefs and mangrove swamps are breeding places for many fishes. The destruction or pollution of these areas is threatening the numbers of fish in the oceans.

> CAN THE POLLUTION OF RIVERS HARM PEOPLE?

When factories pump poisonous waste into rivers, creatures living near the rivers' mouths, such as shellfish, absorb poison into their bodies. When people eat such creatures, they, too, are poisoned.

RIVER POLLUTION

Water pollution is a major cause of death and disease. Pollution includes trash, chemicals, and sewage.

People sometimes turn useless coastal land into fertile farmland. The Netherlands is a flat country and about two-fifths of it is below sea level at high tide. The Dutch have created new land by building dikes called polders (sea walls, seen below) around areas once under the sea. Rainwater washes the salt from the soil and the polder land finally becomes fertile.

CAN DESERTS BE FARMED?

In the USA and other countries, barren deserts have been turned into farmland by irrigation. The land is watered from wells that tap groundwater, or the water is piped from faraway areas.

IRRIGATION

Circles of irrigated land can be seen in the desert of the southwestern United States.

WHAT IS SOIL EROSION?

Natural erosion, caused by running water, winds, and other forces, is a slow process. Soil erosion occurs when people cut down trees and farm the land. Soil erosion on land made bare by people is a much faster process than natural erosion.

WHAT IS A DAM?

A dam is a man-made barrier that holds back flowing water. Dams are often built to retain water in order to generate hydroelectric power or for irrigation. The construction of a dam can sometimes place large areas under water.

Natural wonders

The world's natural wonders can be found on every continent. Many of these beautiful features were created by weathering, erosion, and the work of rivers, seas, and ice.

> HOW ARE NATURAL WONDERS PROTECTED?

One important step in protecting natural wonders was made in 1872, when the world's first national park was founded at Yellowstone in the northwestern United States. Since then, national parks have been founded around the world.

GRAND CANYON

The Grand Canyon is regarded as one of the greatest natural wonders.

> WHAT ARE HOODOOS?

Hoodoos can be seen at Bryce Canyon in the United States (see pp.320–321). These rock needles are formed by water, wind, and ice erosion.

> WHICH IS THE WORLD'S LARGEST CANYON?

Most lists of natural wonders include the Grand Canyon in the United States. It is the world's largest canyon and the most awe-inspiring. The canyon is 277 miles long and almost a mile deep. It was worn down by the Colorado River over the last 6 million years.

ULURU

Uluru in Australia is an "island mountain," an immense rock left over after the erosion of a mountain.

▷ WHAT IS THE GREAT PEBBLE?

"Uluru" is an Australian Aboriginal word meaning "great pebble." Also called Ayers Rock, Uluru is the world's biggest monolith (single rock) and lies in central Australia.

▷ IS THERE A LAKE UNDER ANTARCTICA?

Scientists have found a lake, about the size of Lake Ontario, hidden under Antarctica. It may contain creatures that lived on Earth millions of years ago.

TOP ? QUESTION

WHERE IS THE MATTERHORN?

The Matterhorn is a magnificent mountain on Switzerland's border with Italy. It was created by glaciers wearing away the mountain from opposite sides.

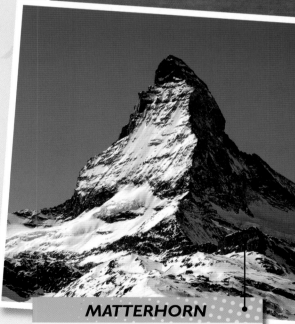

MATTERHORN

The Matterhorn reaches a height of 14,692 feet above sea level.

More natural wonders

Many locations may compete for the fame of being the longest beach or the tallest stalagmite. What we do know for certain is that our natural wonders must be protected for future generations.

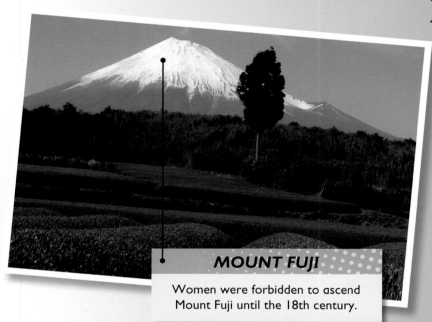

MOUNT FUJI
Women were forbidden to ascend Mount Fuji until the 18th century.

❯ WHERE IS THE WORLD'S TALLEST STALAGMITE?

Many stalagmites claim this honor. The winner may be a 220.5-foot-tall stalagmite in the cave of San Martin Infierno in Cuba.

❯ WHICH IS THE LONGEST BEACH?

At 77 miles long, Cox's Bazar Beach in Bangladesh is the longest sandy sea beach. The beach is used by both fishermen and swimmers.

❯ WHERE ARE THE NEEDLES?

The Needles are a row of chalk stacks, eroded by waves, that lie off the Isle of Wight in southern England.

❯ WHICH JAPANESE WONDER ATTRACTS PILGRIMS?

Mount Fuji in Japan is a beautiful volcanic cone. Many people regard it as a sacred mountain—a dwelling place for the gods—and they make long pilgrimages to the top.

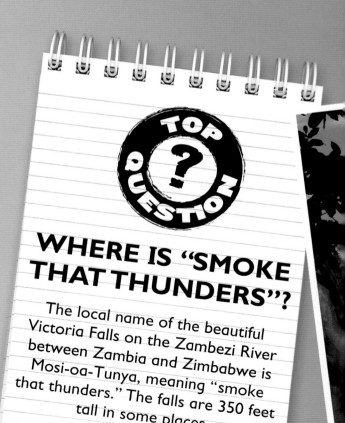

TOP QUESTION ?

WHERE IS "SMOKE THAT THUNDERS"?

The local name of the beautiful Victoria Falls on the Zambezi River between Zambia and Zimbabwe is Mosi-oa-Tunya, meaning "smoke that thunders." The falls are 350 feet tall in some places.

➤ WHAT IS THE GREAT BARRIER REEF?

The Great Barrier Reef is the world's longest group of coral reefs and islands. It lies off the northeast coast of Australia and is about 1,200 miles long.

GREAT BARRIER REEF

The reef is made of billions of tiny organisms, known as coral polyps. It supports a wide variety of wildlife.

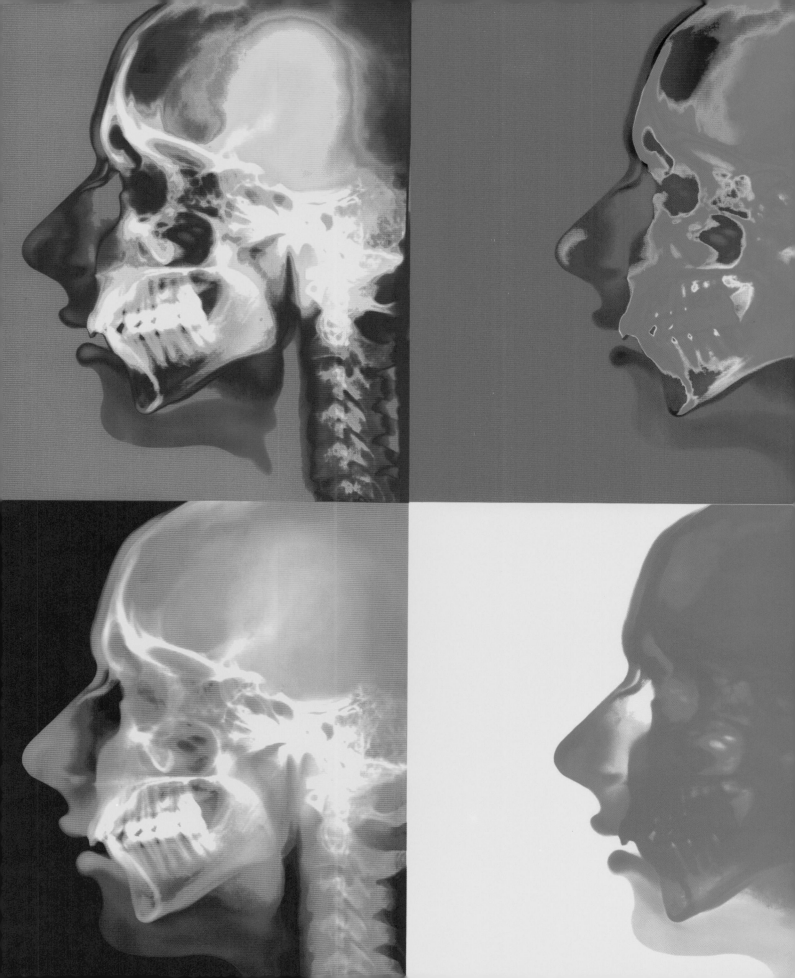

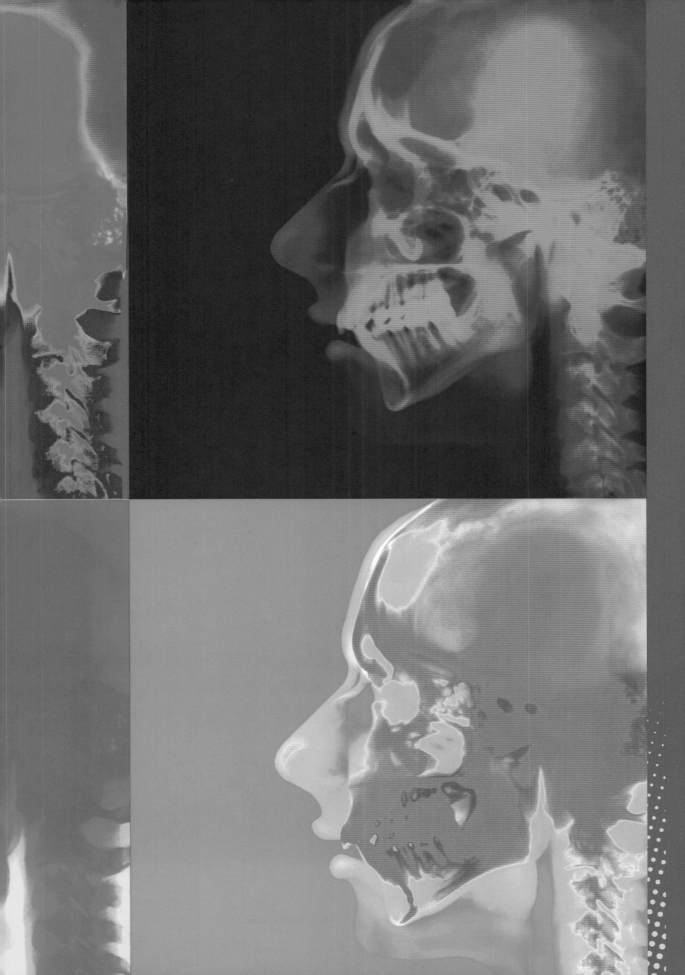

The human body

Skin, hair, and nails >

Skin, hair, and nails are part of the body's defenses. Skin forms a protective barrier. Hair keeps us warm. Nails protect our fingers and toes as well as helping us to grasp objects. Skin, hair, and nails contain keratin, a protein that makes them strong.

> WHAT DOES SKIN DO?

Skin stops the moisture inside the body from drying out and prevents germs from getting in. Tiny particles of melanin help to shield your body from the harmful rays of the Sun. The more melanin you have, the darker your skin and the better protected you are.

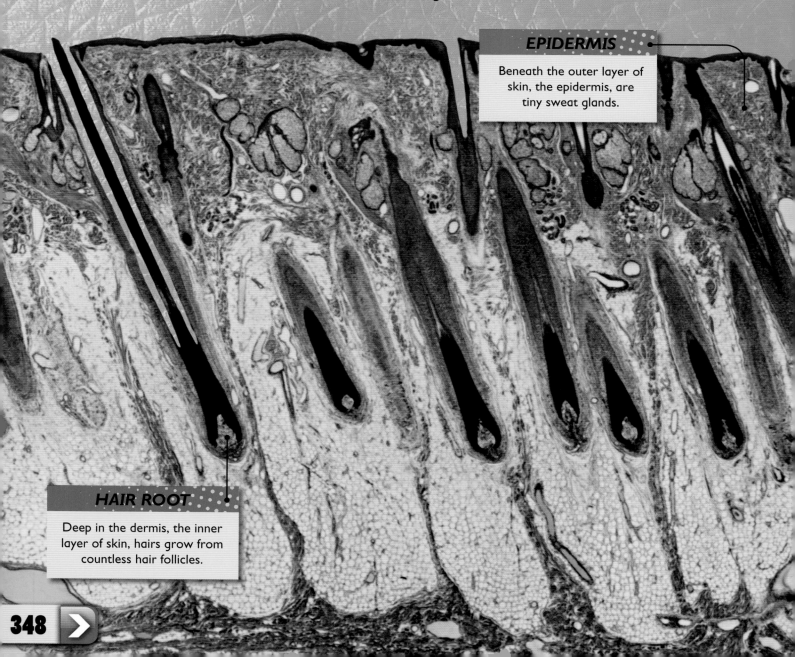

EPIDERMIS

Beneath the outer layer of skin, the epidermis, are tiny sweat glands.

HAIR ROOT

Deep in the dermis, the inner layer of skin, hairs grow from countless hair follicles.

➤ WHY DOES HAIR FALL OUT?

No hair lasts more than about six years. Every day you lose about 60 hairs, but since you have about 100,000 on your scalp, you hardly notice. After a while, new hairs grow from hair follicles.

➤ WHAT GIVES HAIR ITS COLOR?

The color of your hair is determined mainly by the pigment (colored substance) it contains. Hair color depends on melanin, which is a pigment in two forms: one lighter, causing blond or red hair, the other darker, causing brown or black hair.

MAGNIFIED HAIR

The hair shaft is protected by a hard outer layer.

➤ WHY DOES SKIN HAVE PORES?

Skin has tiny holes, called sweat pores, to let out sweat. When you are too hot, glands pump out sweat, or water, which cools you as it evaporates.

➤ HOW FAST DO NAILS GROW?

A fingernail grows about 0.04 inches every 7 days. As new nail forms behind the cuticle, under the skin, it pushes the older nail along.

FINGERPRINT

The uniqueness of fingerprints has led to their being used for identification.

TOP ? QUESTION

ARE FINGERPRINTS UNIQUE?

Yes! A fingerprint is made by thin ridges of skin on the tip of each finger and thumb. The ridges form a pattern of lines, loops, or whorls, and no two people have the same pattern.

The skeleton

Bones provide a strong framework that supports the body and protects the brain, lungs, and other vital organs. You can move and bend different parts of the body because the bones meet at joints.

WHAT IS A JOINT?

Where two bones meet, their ends are shaped to make different kinds of joints. Each kind of joint makes a strong connection and allows a particular kind of movement. For example, the knee is a hinge joint that lets the lower leg move only back and forward. The hip is a ball-and-socket joint that allows you to move your thigh in a circle.

THE SKELETON

All the bones together are called the skeleton. An adult has about 206 bones.

WHY DON'T JOINTS SQUEAK?

Joints are cushioned by soft, squashy cartilage. Many joints also contain synovial fluid, which works like oil to keep them moving smoothly and painlessly.

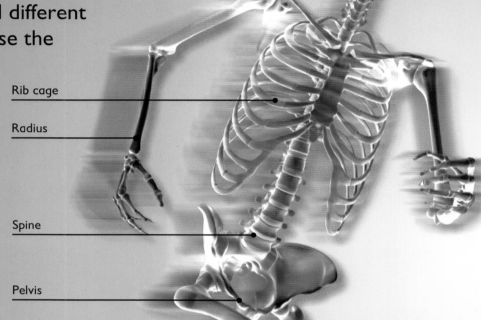

Skull

Rib cage

Radius

Spine

Pelvis

Femur (thigh)

Patella (knee cap)

Fibula

Tibia (shin)

Tarsals (foot bones)

BROKEN BONE

Bones can break because of a fall or accident. A break will mend fully in up to 18 months.

HOW MANY VERTEBRAE ARE THERE IN THE SPINE?

A vertebra is a knobbly bone in your spine. The 33 vertebrae fit together to make a strong pillar, the spine, which carries much of your weight.

➤ WHICH IS THE LONGEST BONE?

The thigh bone, or femur, in the upper part of the leg is the longest bone in the body. It accounts for more than a quarter of an adult's height.

➤ WHAT IS INSIDE A BONE?

Inside the larger bones is a crisscross honeycomb. Blood vessels weave in and out of the bone, keeping the cells alive.

➤ WHAT ARE LIGAMENTS?

They are strong, bendy straps that hold together the bones in a joint. Nearly all the body's joints have several ligaments.

VERTEBRAE X-RAY

The discovery that X-rays could be used to photograph bones was made over 100 years ago.

The skeleton is covered with muscles that move your bones and give your body its shape. Muscles in the legs allow us to run, jump, and kick. Different kinds of muscles make the heart beat and move food through the intestines.

➤ HOW DO MUSCLES WORK?

Muscles work by contracting. Each muscle is connected to at least two bones. When they contract, muscles get shorter and thicker and so they pull the bones together, causing the body to move.

➤ WHICH IS THE BIGGEST MUSCLE?

The biggest muscle is the gluteus maximus in the buttock. You can use it to straighten your leg when you stand up, and it makes a comfortable cushion to sit on.

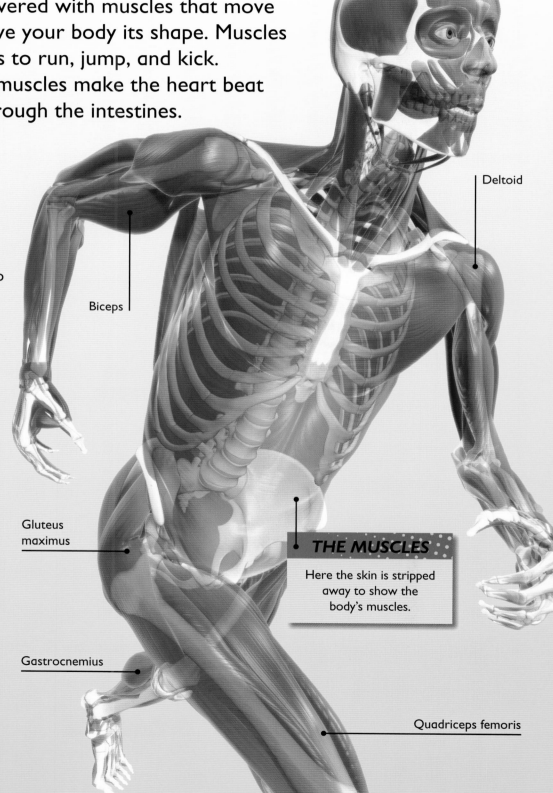

Deltoid

Biceps

Gluteus maximus

Gastrocnemius

THE MUSCLES

Here the skin is stripped away to show the body's muscles.

Quadriceps femoris

WHY DOES EXERCISE MAKE MUSCLES STRONGER?

A muscle is made of bundles of fibers that contract when you use the muscle. The more you use the muscle, the thicker the fibers become. They contract more effectively, which means the muscle is stronger.

➤ WHY DO MUSCLES WORK IN PAIRS?

Because muscles cannot push, they can only pull. For example, to bend your elbow, you tighten the biceps muscle at the front of your upper arm. To straighten the elbow again, you relax the biceps and tighten the triceps muscle at the back of your upper arm.

➤ WHAT IS A TENDON?

A tendon is like a rope that joins a muscle to a bone. If you bend and straighten your fingers, you can feel the tendons in the back of your hand. The body's strongest tendon is the Achilles tendon, which is above your heel.

➤ HOW MANY MUSCLES ARE THERE IN THE BODY?

You have about 650 muscles that work together. Most actions—including walking, swimming, and smiling—involve dozens of muscles.

STRETCHING

Regular stretching of muscles can make them more flexible.

The nervous system >

Nerves carry information and instructions to and from the brain. Sensory nerves bring information from the eyes, ears, and other sense organs to the brain. The motor nerves control the muscles, telling them when to contract.

SPINAL CORD

The spinal cord is the body's largest nerve. It runs through the center of the spine.

> HOW DOES SMELL WORK?

A smell is made by tiny particles in the air. When you breathe in, these particles dissolve in mucus in the nose. Smell receptors in the nose respond to this and send a message to the brain.

NERVOUS SYSTEM

Hundreds of nerves reach out to all parts of the body. They are connected to the brain by the spinal cord.

> WHAT ARE THE BODY'S FIVE MAIN SENSES?

The five main senses are seeing, hearing, smelling, tasting, and touching. Each sense has a special part of the body, called a sense organ, which reacts to a particular kind of stimulus. For example, eyes react to light and ears react to sound.

> HOW DOES TOUCH WORK?

There are many different kinds of sense receptor in the skin, which between them react to touch, heat, cold, and pain. The brain puts together all the different messages to tell you if something is shiny, wet, cold, and many other things.

> CAN BLIND PEOPLE USE TOUCH TO READ?

Yes. Blind people can run their fingertips over Braille (right)—patterns of raised dots that represent different letters.

SIGNALS

The arms of the cell, called dendrites, collect signals from other nerve cells.

➤ HOW DOES A NERVE WORK?

A chain of nerve cells carries a signal to or from the brain. The electrical impulse is received by the nerve endings and sent through the first nerve cell and along its nerve fiber to the nerve endings of the next nerve cell.

➤ HOW FAST DO NERVES ACT?

A nerve signal is a tiny pulse of electricity. It travels at about 3 feet per second in the slowest nerves to more than 300 feet per second in the fastest.

NERVE CELL

A nerve cell sends and receives messages. The center of the cell is the nucleus.

TOUCHING BRAILLE

Braille was developed by Louis Braille, a blind French schoolboy, in 1824.

The brain >

Your brain controls your body, keeping the vital organs working, collecting information from the senses, and sending messages to the muscles. The brain also controls everything you think and feel, as well as storing memories of the past.

CORTEX

This part of the cerebral cortex controls vision and recognition of colors.

> WHAT DOES THE CEREBRAL CORTEX DO?

The cortex is the wrinkly top part of the brain. It controls all the brain activity that you are aware of—seeing, thinking, reading, feeling, and moving. Only humans have such a large and well-developed cerebral cortex. Different parts of the cortex deal with different activities. The left side controls the right side of the body, while the right side of the cortex controls the left side of the body.

CEREBELLUM

The cerebellum coordinates movement and maintains balance.

TOP ? QUESTION

WHAT DOES THE SKULL DO?

The skull is a hard covering of bone that protects the brain like a helmet. All the bones of the skull except the lower jaw are fused together to make them stronger.

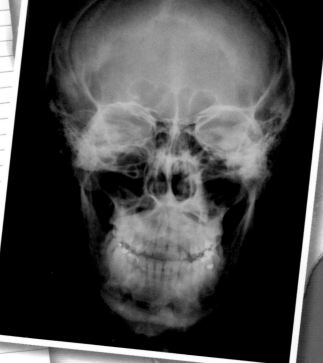

➤ WHY DO YOU REMEMBER SOME THINGS AND FORGET OTHERS?

You usually remember things that are important to you in some way. Some things need to be remembered for only a short while. For instance, you might look up a telephone number, keep it in your head while you dial, and then forget it.

HYPOTHALAMUS

The hypothalamus controls hunger, thirst, and body temperature.

➤ WHY ARE SOME PEOPLE LEFT-HANDED?

Most people are right-handed—the left side of their brain is dominant. In left-handed people, the right side of the brain is dominant. The part of the brain that controls speech is usually on the dominant side.

➤ WHY DO SOME PEOPLE SLEEPWALK?

People may walk in their sleep because they are worried or anxious. If someone is sleepwalking, you should gently take them back to bed.

SLEEPING

The brain blocks most incoming signals while you sleep, unless they are so strong they wake you up.

➤ WHY DO YOU NEED TO SLEEP?

The truth is that scientists don't yet really know! Sleeping performs some mental function still to be identified. A ten-year-old sleeps on average nine or ten hours a night, but sleep time can vary between four and twelve hours.

The eyes >

You see an object when light bounces off it and enters your eyes. The black circle in the middle of the eye is called the pupil. Light passes through the pupil and is focused by the lens on to the retina at the back of the eye. The retina sends signals to the brain.

> HOW DO YOU SEE COLOR?

Different nerve cells in the retina, called cones, react to the colors red, blue, and green. Together they make up all the colors. The cones only work well in bright light, which is why you can't see color when it gets dark.

THE EYE

The eye is protected by the eyelid. The eyelashes prevent dust and dirt from entering.

Eyelashes

Sclera (white of the eye)

Iris

> WHY DO YOU BLINK?

You blink to clean your eyes. Each eye is covered with a thin film of salty fluid, so every time you blink, the eyelid washes the eyeball and wipes away dust and germs. The water drains away through a narrow tube into the nose.

Tear duct

Pupil

WHY DO YOU HAVE TWO EYES?

Two eyes help you to judge how far away something is. Each eye gets a slightly different picture, which the brain combines into a single three-dimensional, or 3D, picture—one that has depth as well as height and breadth.

WHY DOES THE PUPIL CHANGE SIZE?

The pupil becomes smaller in bright light to stop too much light from damaging the retina. In dim light the pupil opens to let in more light. The iris is a circular muscle that controls the size of the pupil.

EYEBALL

Nerves in the retina send signals along the optic nerve to the brain.

TOP QUESTION ?

HOW BIG IS AN EYEBALL?

An adult eyeball is about the size of a golf ball, but most of the eyeball is hidden inside your head.

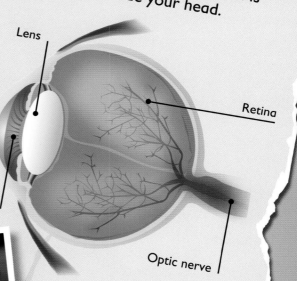

Lens

Retina

Iris

Optic nerve

WHY DO PEOPLE HAVE DIFFERENT COLORED EYES?

The iris is the colored ring around the pupil. The color is made by a substance called melanin. Brown irises have a lot of melanin, while blue irises have little. Very occasionally, someone has irises of different colors (left).

The ears >

Sound reaches your ears as vibrations in the air. The vibrations travel to the eardrum, which makes the bones in the middle ear vibrate, too. These pass the vibrations to the fluid around the cochlea in the inner ear. Nerve endings in the cochlea send signals to the brain.

> HOW DO EARS HELP YOU TO BALANCE?

Three tubes in the inner ear, called the semicircular canals, are filled with fluid. As you move, the fluid inside them moves. Nerves in the lining of the tubes detect changes in the fluid and send signals to the brain.

TOP QUESTION ?

HOW IS SOUND MEASURED?

The loudness of a sound is measured in decibels. The sound of a pin dropping is less than 10 decibels, while a personal stereo makes about 80 decibels. A noise over 120 decibels can damage your hearing.

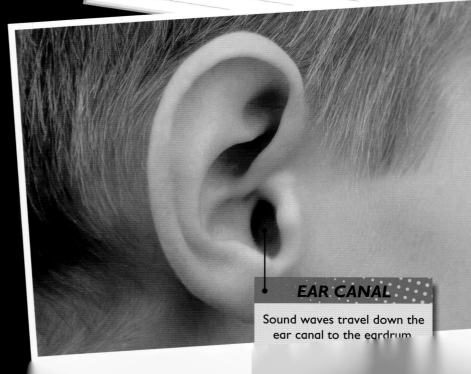

BALANCING
A gymnast balances with the help of semicircular tubes in the inner ear.

EAR CANAL
Sound waves travel down the ear canal to the eardrum

WHY DO YOU GET DIZZY?

If you spin around and around and then stop, the world seems to carry on spinning. This is because the fluid in the semicircular canals is still moving as though you were still spinning.

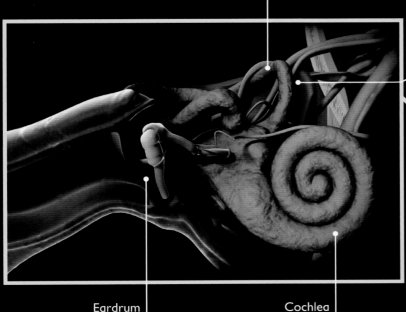

Semicircular canals

Eardrum

Cochlea

INNER EAR

The cochlea is filled with fluid and lined with nerve endings, which take signals to the brain.

OUTER EAR

The outer ear is known as the auricle or pinna.

WHAT IS EARWAX?

This yellow-brown wax is made by glands in the skin lining the ear canal. Wax traps dirt and germs and is slowly pushed out of the ear.

WHY DO YOU HAVE TWO EARS?

Two ears help you to detect which direction sounds are coming from.

WHY DO YOUR EARS POP?

If you are flying in an aircraft and it changes height quickly, you may go a bit deaf, because the air inside and outside the eardrum is at different pressure. Your ears "pop" when the pressure becomes equal again.

The digestive system >

The digestive system breaks down food into simple nutrients that the body can absorb. The process starts when we chew and swallow food, continues in the stomach and intestines, and ends when waste products are expelled from the body as feces.

> WHAT HAPPENS TO THE FOOD WE EAT?

After it is swallowed, food goes down the esophagus into the stomach. Here it is broken down into a soupy liquid, before being squeezed through a coiled tube called the small intestine. The nourishing parts of the food are absorbed into the blood and the rest passes into the large intestine. About 24 hours after swallowing, the waste, called feces, is pushed out of the body.

> HOW DO YOU DETECT TASTE?

As you chew, tiny particles of food dissolve in saliva and trickle down to the taste buds on the tongue. The taste receptors react and send messages about the taste to the brain.

TASTE BUDS

The tongue has about 10,000 microscopic taste buds. Buds on different parts of the tongue react to different tastes.

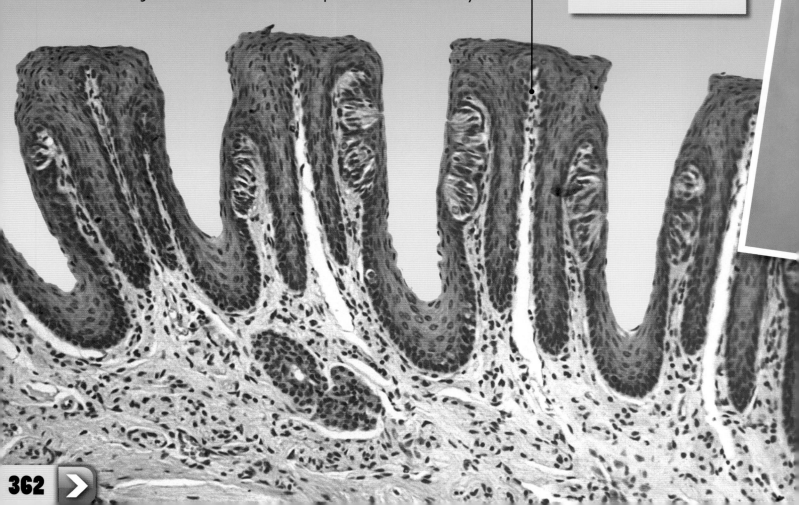

➤ WHY DOES VOMIT TASTE REALLY SOUR?

When you vomit you bring back partly digested food into your mouth. It is sour because it is mixed with acid made by the stomach lining. The acid helps to break food down into smaller pieces.

➤ WHAT IS THE EPIGLOTTIS?

The epiglottis is a kind of trapdoor that closes off your windpipe when you swallow. It stops food going down into the lungs, rather than down the esophagus to the stomach.

CHEWING

When you chew food, it becomes a mushy ball, ready to travel down the esophagus.

HOW LONG ARE THE INTESTINES?

The small intestine is more than three times as long as the whole body! In an adult this is about 20 feet. The large intestine is a further 5 feet, and the whole tube from mouth to anus measures about 20 feet.

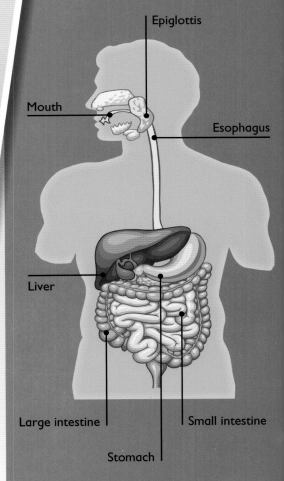

Epiglottis

Mouth

Esophagus

Liver

Large intestine

Small intestine

Stomach

➤ WHY ARE TEETH DIFFERENT SHAPES?

Different teeth do different jobs to help you chew up food. The broad, flat teeth at the front slice through food when you take a bite. They are called incisors. The pointed canine teeth grip and tear chewy food such as meat. The large premolars and molars grind the food between them into small pieces.

The lungs and breathing >

The air contains oxygen, which the body needs to stay alive. When you breathe in, you pull air through the mouth or nose into the windpipe and down to the lungs. Here the oxygen is passed into the blood, then carried to all parts of the body.

> HOW LONG CAN YOU HOLD YOUR BREATH?

You can probably hold your breath for about a minute. The longer you hold your breath, the higher the carbon dioxide level in your blood rises, and the more you feel the need to breathe out.

> WHAT HAPPENS TO AIR IN THE LUNGS?

The air you breathe in travels from the windpipe into tiny tubes, or bronchioles, in the lungs. At the end of each bronchiole are minute balloons called alveoli. As these balloons fill with air, oxygen passes from them into the blood vessels that surround them. The blood then carries the oxygen around the body. At the same time, waste carbon dioxide passes out of the blood and into the lungs. It leaves the body in the air you breathe out.

BREATH CLOUD

The air you breathe out contains water vapor. On a cold day, this condenses into a mist of tiny water droplets.

> WHY DO YOU COUGH?

You cough when mucus, dust, or other particles clog the air passages between your nose and lungs. The sudden blast of air helps to clear the tubes.

❯ HOW DO YOU TALK?

When you breathe out, the air passes over the vocal cords in the voice box, or larynx, in the neck. When the cords vibrate, they make a sound. Changing the shape of your lips and tongue makes different sounds, which can be put together into words.

❯ WHY DOES RUNNING MAKE YOU PANT?

Muscles use up oxygen as they work. When you run, your muscles are working hard and need extra oxygen. Panting makes you breathe in up to 20 times more air, to supply your muscles with the oxygen they need.

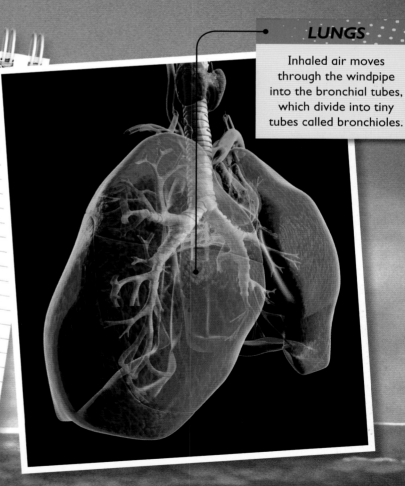

LUNGS

Inhaled air moves through the windpipe into the bronchial tubes, which divide into tiny tubes called bronchioles.

TOP QUESTION ?

WHY DO THE LUNGS HAVE SO MANY ALVEOLI?

In order to provide a huge surface across which oxygen and carbon dioxide can move in and out of the blood. In fact, the lungs have more than 700 million alveoli.

The heart and blood >

The heart's job is to pump blood to the lungs and then all around the body. The right side of the heart takes in blood from the body and pumps it to the lungs. The left side takes blood filled with oxygen from the lungs and pumps it around the body.

> HOW OFTEN DOES THE HEART BEAT?

A child's heart usually beats about 80 times a minute, a bit faster than an adult's (70 times a minute). When you run or do something strenuous, your heart beats faster to send more blood to the muscles.

RED BLOOD CELL

Each tiny drop of blood contains up to 5 million red blood cells. These are the most common type of blood cell.

> WHY IS BLOOD RED?

Blood gets its color from billions of red blood cells. These cells contain a substance called hemoglobin, which takes in oxygen in the lungs. Blood that is rich in oxygen is bright red, and as it is pumped around the body, the oxygen is gradually taken up by the body's cells. By the time the blood returns to the heart, it is a darker, more rusty red.

TOP QUESTION ?

WHAT DO WHITE BLOOD CELLS DO?

They surround and destroy germs and other intruders that get into the blood.

> WHAT IS PLASMA?

Just over half the blood is a yellowish liquid called plasma. It is mainly water with molecules of digested food and essential salts dissolved in it.

> WHAT IS THE HEART MADE OF?

A special kind of muscle, called cardiac (heart) muscle, which never gets tired.

DEFENCE

White blood cells are part of the immune system, protecting us from infection.

Artery

Vein

> WHAT IS A CAPILLARY?

Blood travels around the body through tubes called arteries and veins. These branch off into smaller tubes that reach every cell of the body. Capillaries are the tiniest blood vessels of all. Most capillaries are thinner than a single hair.

CARDIOVASCULAR SYSTEM

Oxygen-rich blood leaves the heart along arteries (red in this diagram) and used blood returns along veins (in blue).

The kidneys and liver >

The kidneys filter the blood to remove wastes and extra water and salts. The liver is a chemical factory that does more than 500 different jobs, including the processing of food and the removal of wastes and poisons from the blood.

> WHAT IS URINE?

Each kidney has about a million tiny filters, which between them clean about a quarter of your blood every minute. The unwanted substances combine with water to make urine, which trickles down to the bladder.

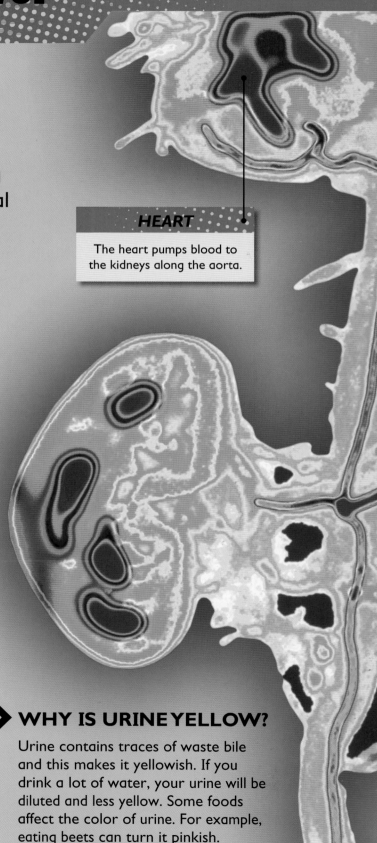

HEART
The heart pumps blood to the kidneys along the aorta.

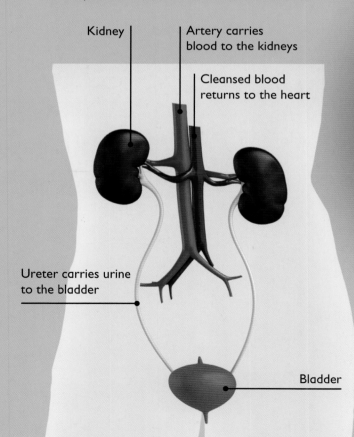

Kidney

Artery carries blood to the kidneys

Cleansed blood returns to the heart

Ureter carries urine to the bladder

Bladder

> WHY IS URINE YELLOW?

Urine contains traces of waste bile and this makes it yellowish. If you drink a lot of water, your urine will be diluted and less yellow. Some foods affect the color of urine. For example, eating beets can turn it pinkish.

➤ WHAT DOES THE LIVER DO?

One of the liver's most important functions is the processing of digested food (see the diagram on p.363). The intestines pass digested food to the liver, where some nutrients may be released into the blood and the rest are stored to be used later. The liver also processes poisons in the blood and changes unwanted proteins into urea. The kidneys then remove poisons and urea from the blood and make them into urine.

➤ WHAT IS BILE?

Bile is a yellow-green liquid made by the liver and stored in the gall bladder. From there it passes into the small intestine, where it helps to break up fatty food.

KIDNEYS

This medical thermographic image shows raised temperatures caused by activity in the body. It reveals the kidneys at work, processing the blood.

➤ WHY DO YOU SWEAT WHEN YOU ARE HOT?

Sweating helps to cool you down. When the body becomes hot, sweat glands pump lots of salty water on to the skin. As the sweat evaporates, it takes extra heat from the body.

SWEATING

When you exercise, the body gets hot, making you sweat. Drinking replaces the lost water.

HOW MUCH DO YOU NEED TO DRINK?

You need to drink about 2–3 pints (5 large glasses) of watery drinks a day. Most water is lost in urine and feces, but sweat and the air you breathe also contain water.

Reproduction ➤

A baby begins when a sperm from a man joins with an egg from a woman. The cells of the fertilized egg embed in the lining of the mother's womb. Slowly the cells multiply into the embryo of a new human being.

➤ WHERE DOES A MAN'S SPERM COME FROM?

Sperm are made in the testicles, two sacs that hang to either side of the penis. After puberty, the testicles make millions of sperm every day. Any sperm that are not ejaculated are absorbed back into the blood.

➤ WHAT IS A FETUS?

A fetus is an unborn baby from eight weeks after conception until birth. In the first seven weeks, it is called an embryo. From about 24 weeks onward, babies may survive in an incubator if they are born early, but most stay in the mother's womb for the full 38 weeks.

PREGNANCY

A baby usually grows in its mother's womb for 38 weeks.

➤ WHERE DOES THE EGG COME FROM?

When a girl is born she already has thousands of eggs stored in her two ovaries. After puberty, one of these eggs is released every month and travels down the Fallopian tube to the womb.

> HOW DOES AN UNBORN BABY FEED?

Most of the cluster of cells that embeds itself in the womb grows into an organ called the placenta. Food and oxygen from the mother's blood pass through the placenta into the blood of the growing baby.

NEWBORN

The average newborn weighs about 7.5 pounds. Most newborns need to sleep a lot.

> WHAT ARE GENES?

Genes are a combination of chemicals contained in each cell. They come from your mother and father and determine all your physical characteristics, including the color of your hair, how tall you will be, and even what diseases you might get later in life.

HOW FAST DOES AN UNBORN BABY GROW?

You grow faster before you are born than at any other time. Three weeks after the egg is fertilized, the embryo is the size of a grain of rice. Five weeks later, almost every part of the baby has formed—the brain, eyes, heart, stomach—yet it is only the size of a thumb. By the time it is born, the baby will probably be about 20 inches long.

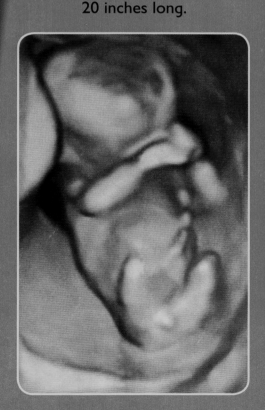

Glossary >

Aboriginal
One of the original inhabitants of Australia. Aboriginals were already there when European settlers arrived.

Aquatic
Something that lives in water.

Artery
Blood vessel that carries blood away from the heart.

Asteroid
A piece of rock in the Solar System, varying in size from a grain of dust to 600 miles across.

Atmosphere
A layer of gas held around a planet by gravity. The Earth's atmosphere is over 500 miles thick.

Atom
Once thought to be the smallest part of a substance. We now know that atoms are made up of smaller parts known as subatomic particles.

Beak
The jaws of a bird, made of bone, which it uses for feeding.

Camouflage
Coloring that allows an animal to blend in with its background.

Carbohydrate
A substance found in foods such as sugars, wheat, and rice. Animals eat carbohydrates to obtain energy.

Cardiovascular system
The network of blood vessels that, along with the heart, carries blood around the body.

Carnivore
An animal that eats other animals.

Cell
The tiny unit from which all bodies are made. The smallest animals have just one cell, and the largest have many millions.

Climate
The pattern of weather in an area. All plants and animals are suited to their native climate.

Colony
A group of animals living together in a shared home.

Conifer
A tree that has needle-shaped leaves.

Continent
One of the Earth's seven large land areas, which are Africa, Antarctica, Asia, Australia, Europe, North America, and South America.

Crustacean
An animal without a backbone that has a body covered by an outer skeleton. Crustaceans include crabs, lobsters, crayfish, shrimp, krill, and barnacles.

Democracy
A system of government in which leaders are chosen by people in elections. A government in which the leader is not elected is called a dictatorship.

Desert
An area of land that receives little rain. As life needs water to survive, fewer plants and animals live in deserts.

Diaphragm
The dome-shaped sheet of muscle that lies beneath the lungs. During breathing, the diaphragm flattens to increase the volume of the lungs and to pull air into them.

Digestion
The process of breaking down food into very small particles in the body. They can then pass into the blood to provide the body with all the substances it needs to stay healthy.

DNA
Short for deoxyribonucleic acid. DNA is arranged in a twin spiral shape, called a double helix, and contains the genetic instructions for every cell.

Echo
The repeated sound heard when a soundwave bounces off a hard surface such as a cliff or tunnel.

Echolocation
A means of finding objects by making high-pitched sounds or clicks and listening to the echo. Bats, whales, and dolphins use echolocation to find food.

Electricity
The movement of tiny particles called electrons through a substance such as metal. This causes an electrical current that can be used as a source of power.

Electron
A subatomic particle. Along with protons and neutrons, electrons make up atoms. Electrons have a negative electrical charge and play a vital role in electricity and magnetism.

Endangered
When a species, or kind, of animal is so few in number that it is in danger of disappearing.

Equator
An imaginary line that runs around the middle of the Earth.

Evaporate
To change from a liquid into a gas, for instance when water turns into steam in a boiling saucepan.

Evolution
The process by which animals and plants adapt and change over many generations. Those that are best suited to their surroundings survive and produce young, while others die out.

Extinction
When a species can no longer survive due to overhunting or when there is a change in its habitat.

Feces
Waste products left over from the digestive system.

Fin
A part of the body of a fish that is used for swimming.

Force
A push or a pull that makes an object speed up or slow down.

Fossil
The remains of an animal or plant that has been preserved in rock or another substance, often for millions of years.

Galaxy
A group of millions of stars held together by gravity.

Gene
The code within a cell that tells it what kind of cell it should become. In this way, our genes decide how our bodies will look.

Germs
Tiny living things, such as bacteria, that cause diseases in animals and plants.

Gland
A cell or organ in the body. A gland makes chemicals that tell other parts of the body what to do.

Grassland
A type of habitat that is dominated by grasses and has very few trees.

Gravity
The force of attraction between any two objects, such as the pull between the Earth and the Moon.

Greenhouse effect
The warming of the Earth, also known as "global warming" due to the presence of the gas carbon dioxide in the air, which stops heat escaping from the atmosphere. Pollution from burning oil and coal is causing an increase in the greenhouse effect.

Habitat
The place where an animal or plant lives.

Herbivore
An animal that eats only plants.

Glossary

Herd
A large group of hoofed mammals that live together.

Hibernation
A sleep that some animals go into to survive the winter. The animal's heart rate slows down.

Ice caps
The layers of ice and snow that cover the North and South Poles.

Incubation
Keeping eggs warm so that they will hatch successfully.

Insect
An animal without a backbone that has three body parts, three pairs of legs, and usually two pairs of wings.

Magma
The molten, or liquid, rock under the surface of the Earth that sometimes rises up through volcanoes.

Mammal
An animal with a backbone that usually has hair on its skin. Female mammals make milk to feed their young.

Microscopic
Too small to be seen with the naked eye.

Middle Ages
A period in history that is often defined as spanning from around AD 500 to 1500.

Migration
A regular journey made by an animal.

Molecule
Tiny particle that makes up a substance. A molecule can be as small as just two atoms held together by a chemical bond.

Moon
A planet's natural satellite.

Muscle
A part of the body that is able to contract (shorten) and relax (lengthen) to produce movement.

Nerve
A bundle of fibers in the body that carries electrical signals to and from the brain.

Neutron
A subatomic particle found in the nucleus of an atom. Neutrons carry no electrical charge.

Nocturnal
When an animal is active at night and rests during the day.

Omnivore
An animal that eats both plants and animals.

Organ
A part of an animal or plant that performs a particular task. The heart, for example, pumps blood around the body.

Photosynthesis
The process plants use to make chemicals using the Sun's energy. This forms the basis for all other life as it is the only way in nature to take energy from the Sun.

Plankton
The tiny plants and animals that are found floating close to the surface of ponds, lakes, and seas.

Polar
Related to the cold areas around the North and South Poles.

Population
The total number of people or animals living in a particular place.

Predator

An animal that hunts and eats other animals.

Prey

An animal that is hunted by another animal for food.

Proton

A subatomic particle found in the nucleus of an atom. Protons carry a positive electrical charge.

Rain forest

Dense forest found in areas with high rainfall around the equator.

Renewable energy

A source of energy, such as wind power, which cannot be used up.

Reptile

An animal with a backbone that has four legs and a body covered by scales. Female reptiles lay leathery eggs.

Satellite

Any object that orbits a planet, held by the planet's gravity.

Scavenger

An animal that eats dead plants or animals.

Sediment

Small pieces of rock or soil that settle at the bottom of rivers and oceans.

Senses

The ways humans and animals are able to experience the world around them. Humans have five senses: sight, hearing, touch, smell, and taste.

Shoal

A group of fish that swim together.

Skeleton

The framework of a body that holds it together. Some skeletons are inside the body, while others are outside.

Solar System

The part of space that includes the Sun, the planets that circle the Sun, and all the moons and asteroids in between.

Streamlined

When something is smooth and tapered and can move through water or air with very little effort.

Temperate

Areas of the world that have a mild climate and four seasons.

Tentacle

A long, feeler-like structure found on certain animals, such as jellyfish.

Tradition

A way of doing things, such as making music, cooking, or a system of government, that is passed down from one generation to another.

Transparent

The word for any matter, such as glass or water, that lets light pass through it.

Tropical

Areas of the world that lie around the middle of the Earth, near the equator, and are hot all year round.

Tusk

An extra-long tooth found on some animals, such as elephants.

Vein

Blood vessel that carries blood back to the heart. The larger veins have valves inside them to stop blood flowing the wrong way.

Venom

A harmful liquid that some animals make to kill prey or to defend themselves.

Vertebrae

The name of the bones that make up the spine, or backbone. They protect the spinal cord.

Vertebrate

Any animal that has a bony skeleton and a backbone. Animals without a backbone are called invertebrate.

Index

cats 198–199
caves 319, 325, 329
caviar 102
cellulose 163
Celsius scale 175
centurion 117
cerebral cortex 356
chameleon 213
cheese 100
cheetah 199
chemical formulae 153
chemical reactions 150, 152–153
Chicago 111
child workers 135
chimpanzees 211
China 62, 80, 90, 93, 99, 106, 124–125, 136, 305
Chinese language 74, 75
chlorophyll 244
chocolate 257
chopsticks 101
Christianity 88, 89, 91, 95
cities 63, 78–79, 123, 338
climate change 289, 331, 336–339
clogs 106
cloth 260, 263
clothes 104–107, 262
clouds 149
coal 167, 309, 339
coasts 328–329, 341
coco de mer 264
coffee 257
cold deserts 271
Cold War 137
color 176, 177, 178, 358
comets 33
communication 76–77
compounds 150–151, 153, 160–163
condensation 148
conduction 175, 184

Confucius 90
coniferous trees 279, 287
constellations 44, 47
continental drift 302–303
continents 65, 302, 319
Cook, Captain James 130
Copernicus, Nicolaus 13
core, Earth's 11, 22
cork 262
corona 19
cotton 262, 263
coughing 364
countries 66–69
courts 72, 73
coyote 197
craters 15
Crick, Francis 160
cricket bats 263
crocodiles 230–231
crops 82–83, 100, 254, 256
Crusades 123
crust, Earth's 11, 22
CT scan 180
Curie, Marie 145
currencies 80
curry 100

D

dams 158, 159, 341
dance 96, 97, 99
day 12
Dead Sea 150, 319
Death Valley 270
decibels 360
deciduous forests 284–287
deltas 327
democracy 70, 71, 73
Denmark 67
dependencies 66, 69

desert 123, 253, 270–75, 334–35, 341
desertification 271, 339
dhows 128
diamonds 310, 311
digestion 258, 362–363
dingo 196
dinosaurs 298, 299, 312–313
dioon plant 266
dissolving 151
Diwali 92
dizziness 361
DNA 160
dogs 196–197
dolphins 222, 223
drama 96, 97, 98
drinks 102, 256, 257, 369
drums 98
duckweed 264
dust storms 334

E

eagles 238, 240, 241
ears 360–361
Earth 10–13, 52, 58, 187, 294–345
earthquakes 304–305
earwax 361
eating 362–363
echo 189
echolocation 189, 223
eclipse 16, 17, 19
ecosystems 268–293
eggs 370
Egypt, Ancient 114–115
Einstein, Albert 170
elections 70, 73
electric eels 227
electricity 156–159, 182–185
electrolysis 153

Index

Index >

Acknowledgments

t = top, b = bottom, l = left, r = right, m = middle

Cover images courtesy of SCIEPRO/Getty Images (dinosaur), Corey Ford/Stocktrek Images/Getty Images (shark), SEBASTIAN KAULITZKI/Getty Images (brain). All other cover images courtesy of iStockphoto and Shutterstock

1 DaddyBit/iStockphoto, 2 Sebastian Duda/iStockphoto, 3 Julien Grondin/iStockphoto, 4–5 Andreas Sandberg/iStockphoto, 6–7 NASA/Jeff Hester and Paul Scowen Arizona State University, 8–9 ESA/NASA/SOHO/JPL, 10 NASA/JPL/Caltech, 11t Eraxion/Dreamstime.com, 11b NASA, 12 ESA/NASA/SOHO, 12–13 Girts Pavlins/Dreamstime.com, 13 Laurent Dambies/Dreamstime.com, 14 NASA, 15l NASA/JPL/USGS, 16l NASA, 16r Liaj/Dreamstime.com, 17 Johnny Lye/Dreamstime.com, 18 NASA, 19l and b Steve Albers/NASA, 19r Hinode JAXA/NASA/PPARC, 20–21 Luke Pederson/Dreamstime.com, 21t Marbo/Dreamstime.com, 21m Hinode JAXA/NASA, 21b NASA/SOHO, 22–23 NASA/JPL, 22 Beriliu/Dreamstime.com, 23 NASA/JPL/Caltech, 24–25t NASA/JPL/USGS, 24–25b NASA/JPL/Arizona State University, 25 and 26 NASA/JPL, 27t NASA/JPL/University of Arizona, 27b NASA/JPL, 28–29 NASA, 29t NASA/JPL, 29b NASA/JPL/University of Colorado, 30 and 31l NASA, 31t NASA/JPL/Caltech, 31r ESO/Getty Images, 32–33 David Gilder/Dreamstime.com, 32 NASA, 33l T. Rector (University of Alaska Anchorage), Z. Levay and L. Frattare (Space Telescope Science Institute) and National Optical Astronomy Observatory/Association of Universities for Research in Astronomy/National Science Foundation, 33r NASA Johnson Space Center, 34–35 NASA/ESA, 36 COBE Project/DMR/NASA, 37l and r NASA/Adolf Schaller for STScI, 38 and 39t NASA/ESA, 39b NASA/JPL/Caltech/SSC, 40–41 Andreus/Dreamstime.com, 41t Fermi National Accelerator Laboratory, 41b United States Federal Government, 42 NASA/Jeff Hester and Paul Scowen Arizona State University, 43t NASA/JPL/Hubble, 43bl NICMOS Group (STScI, ESA)/NICMOS Science Team (University of Arizona)/NASA, 43bm JPL/NASA/NOAO/ESA and The Hubble Heritage Team (STScI/AURA), 43br NASA/C.R. O'Dell and S.K. Wong (Rice University), 44l Serge Brunier/NASA, 44r Thomas Tuchan/iStockphoto, 45 NASA/ESA/Hubble Heritage (STScI/AURA)-ESA/Hubble Collaboration, 46–47 Manfred Konrad/iStockphoto, 46 URA/STScI/NASA/JPL, 47 NASA/ESA/A. Field (STScI), 48 NASA/J.P. Harrington and K. J. Borkowski University of Maryland, 49t NASA/JPL/Caltech, 49b NASA/ESA, 50t NASA, 50b NASA/ESA/AURA/Caltech, 51 Shaun Lowe/iStockphoto, 52t NASA, 52b and 53 NASA/ESA/The Hubble Heritage Team (STScI/AURA), 54–55 HST/NASA/ESA, 55l NASA/JPL/Caltech, 55r Dave Long/iStockphoto, 56t NASA/CXC/SAO, 56b J. Bahcall (IAS, Princeton)/M. Disney (Univ. Wales)/NASA, 57 Manfred Konrad/iStockphoto, 58–59 Endi Dewata/iStockphoto, 59l NASA/JPL, 59r NASA, 60–61 Greg Wood/AFP/Getty Images, 62–63 Joshua Haviv/iStockphoto, 62 Eric Feferberg/AFP/Getty Images, 63 Robert Churchill/iStockphoto, 64l Steffen Foerster/Dreamstime.com, 64r Jerry Cooke/Pix Inc./Time Life Pictures/Getty Images, 65 DNDavis/Dreamstime.com, 66–67 Bruce Hempell/Dreamstime.com, 67 Asdf_1/Dreamstime.com, 68–69 Denis Babenko/Dreamstime.com, 69t Joel Blit/Dreamstime.com, 69b iStockphoto, 70t English School/Bridgeman/Getty Images, 70b Richard Simkin/Bridgeman/Getty Images, 71 Sygma/Corbis, 72 Franck Fife/AFP/Getty Images, 73t Graeme Robertson/Getty Images, 73b Marekuliasz/Dreamstime.com, 74 Stougard/Dreamstime.com, 75t Natalia Bratslavsky/Dreamstime.com, 75b Maria Weidner/iStockphoto, 76t Paul Moore/Dreamstime.com, 76b Brailean/Dreamstime.com, 77 scanrail/iStockphoto, 78 Christopher Howey/Dreamstime.com, 78–79 Elpis Ioannidis/Dreamstime.com, 79 Itinerantlens/Dreamstime.com, 80t Webking/Dreamstime.com, 80b Tiburonstudios/Dreamstime.com, 81 Tall Tree Ltd, 82t Karen Winton/Dreamstime.com, 82b Alena Yakusheva/Dreamstime.com, 83 Chris Harvey/Dreamstime.com, 84 Will Sanders/Getty Images, 84–85 Dreamstime.com, 85 Nivi/Dreamstime.com, 86–87 Eric Meola/The Image Bank/Getty Images, 88–89 Tiero/Dreamstime.com, 89t iStockphoto, 89b Lambert (Bart) Parren/Dreamstime.com, 90–91 Aidar Ayazbayev/iStockphoto, 90 Craig Hanson/Dreamstime.com, 91 Catherine Jones/Dreamstime.com, 92–93 Nikhil Gangavane/Dreamstime.com, 93t Howard Sandler/iStockphoto, 93b Christophe Testi/Dreamstime.com, 94l Shawn O'Banion/iStockphoto, 94r Adriana Barsanti/iStockphoto, 95 Jose Gil/Dreamstime.com, 96 Pavel Aleynikov/Dreamstime.com, 97t Bruno Vincent/Getty Images, 97b Paula Connelly/iStockphoto, 98t Paul Gauguin/The Bridgeman Art Library/Getty Images, 98b Museum of New Mexico, 99 Oliver Strewe/Lonely Planet Images/Getty Images, 100–101 Vojko Kavcic/Dreamstime.com, 101t Edward Shaw/iStockphoto, 101b Monkey Business Images/Dreamstime.com, 102 Ioana Grecu/Dreamstime.com, 103t Daria Khlopkina/Dreamstime.com, 103b Will Hayward/Dreamstime.com, 104–105 Shariff Che' Lah/Dreamstime.com, 104 Alan Tobey/iStockphoto, 105 Eric Ryan/Getty Images, 106t iStockphoto, 106b Terraxplorer/iStockphoto, 107 Pierdelune/Dreamstime.com, 108–109 Andrew Buckin/Dreamstime.com, 109l Pcphotos/Dreamstime.com, 109r Bananaman/Dreamstime.com, 110–111 Daniel Boiteau/Dreamstime.com, 111t iStockphoto, 111b Jakich/Dreamstime.com, 112–113 Robert Everts/Getty Images, 114–115 Alessandro Bolis/Dreamstime.com, 115l Webking/Dreamstime.com, 115r Karen Moller/iStockphoto, 116–117 Jeremy Walker/Getty Images, 116 Moemrik/Dreamstime.com, 117 James Steidl/Dreamstime.com, 118–119 Philippe Bourseiller/Getty Images, 119t Denise Kappa/iStockphoto, 119b European/Getty Images, 120–121 Pavalache Stelian/Dreamstime.com, 121t Robyvannucci/Dreamstime.com, 121b Carolyne Pehora/Dreamstime.com, 122 David Pedre/iStockphoto, 123t Norbert Speicher/iStockphoto, 123b French School/Getty Images, 124–125 Robert Churchill/iStockphoto, 125l David Lentz/iStockphoto, 125r Jason Gulledge/iStockphoto, 126 DaddyBit/iStockphoto, 127t George Gower/Getty Images, 127b Erick Nguyen/Dreamstime.com, 128–129 Mike Carlson/Dreamstime.com, 129t Luciano Mortula/Dreamstime.com, 129b Rb-studio/Dreamstime.com, 130 Mansell/Time & Life Pictures/Getty Images, 131l William Wang/Dreamstime.com, 131r Matthew Scholey/Dreamstime.com, 132 Sundown/Dreamstime.com, 133t Michael Thompson/Dreamstime.com, 133b Coomerguy/Dreamstime.com, 134–135 Time Life Pictures/Mansell/Getty Images, 134 English School/Getty Images, 135 Rod Lawson/Dreamstime.com, 136t Dan Braus Photography/iStockphoto, 136b Popperfoto/Getty Images, 137 NASA, 138–139 SMC Images/Getty Images, 140–141 Fabrizio Zanier/iStockphoto, 141t Dorling Kindersley/Getty Images, 141b Getty Images, 142–143 Tatiana Nikolaevna Kalashnikova/Dreamstime.com, 143b Photowitch/Dreamstime.com, 143b Topical Press Agency/Getty Images, 144–145 Mark Schneider/Getty Images, 145 Ian Wilson/Dreamstime.com, 145 Hulton Archive/Getty Images, 146–147 Panoramic Images/Getty Images, 147l Sergey Rogovets/Dreamstime.com, 147r Johnny Lye/Dreamstime.com, 148 NASA/MSFC, 149l Kelpfish/Dreamstime.com, 149r Mat Monteith/Dreamstime.com, 150–151 Yory Frenklakh/Dreamstime.com, 150 Ivan Mateev/iStockphoto, 151 Vladimir Lukovic/Dreamstime.com, 152 Zoom-zoom/Dreamstime.com, 153l iStockphoto, 154l Rade Lukovic/iStockphoto, 154r Ilya Rabkin/Dreamstime.com, 155t Ken Lucas/Getty Images, 155b Victor Boswell/National Geographic/Getty Images, 156 Andrea Danti/Dreamstime.com, 157t Dobresum/iStockphoto, 157b AFP/Getty Images, 158–159 Andrew Edelstein/iStockphoto, 159t Darren Baker/Dreamstime.com, 159b Trevor Fisher/iStockphoto, 160–161 Sebastian Kaulitzki/Dreamstime.com, 161t Martin McCarthy/iStockphoto, 161b Dan McCoy/Rainbow/Getty Images, 162–163 Lance Michaels/Dreamstime.com, 162 David Hancock/Dreamstime.com, 163 Oliver Sun Kim/iStockphoto, 164–165 cookelma/iStockphoto, 166 NASA, 167t David Coleman/Dreamstime.com, 167b Jeff Hower/iStockphoto, 168–169t Brandon Laufenberg/iStockphoto, 168–169b Rafa Irusta/iStockphoto, 169 Marcin Kempski/Dreamstime.com, 170l Steven Wynn/iStockphoto, 170r Anders Aagesen/iStockphoto, 171t Romilly Lockyer/Getty Images, 171b technotr/iStockphoto, 172 and 173b NASA, 173t Drazen Vukelic/Dreamstime.com, 174t Andrey Pali/Dreamstime.com, 174b Andra Cerar/Dreamstime.com, 174–175 Jinyoung Lee/Dreamstime.com, 175 Chiya Li/Dreamstime.com, 176 Richard Griffin/Dreamstime.com, 176–177 Gary Vestal/Getty Images, 177 Norman Pogson/Dreamstime.com, 178l Paul Phillips/Dreamstime.com, 178r Adam Gryko/Dreamstime.com, 179l Katharina Wittfeld/Dreamstime.com, 179r Lukasz Tymszan/Dreamstime.com, 180 Cammeraydave/Dreamstime.com, 181 Gofer/Dreamstime.com, 182 Feng Yu/Dreamstime.com, 182–183 Martin Eaves/Dreamstime.com, 183 Shannon Neal/Dreamstime.com, 184 Josef Bosak/Dreamstime.com, 185t Francis Black/Dreamstime.com, 185b Krystian Nawrocki/iStockphoto

Acknowledgements >

186 iStockphoto, 187t Irochka/Dreamstime.com, 187b Dreamstime.com, 188 Pixhook/iStockphoto, 189 Javarman/Dreamstime.com, 190–191 Ronald Wittek/Getty Images, 192–193 Ken Cole/Dreamstime.com and John Pitcher/iStockphoto, 192 Sters/Dreamstime.com, 193 Ryszard Laskowski/Dreamstime.com, 194 Anthony Hathaway/Dreamstime.com, 195l Valerie Crafter/iStockphoto, 195r Sandra von Stein/iStockphoto, 196 Kitch Bain/iStockphoto, 197l Karel Broz/Dreamstime.com, 197r Anita Huszti/Dreamstime.com, 198t Yong Chen/Dreamstime.com, 198b Jean-Marc Strydom/Dreamstime.com, 199 Ian Jeffery/iStockphoto, 200–201 Neil Bradfield/iStockphoto, 200 Edward Duckitt/Dreamstime.com, 201 Jayanand Govindaraj/Dreamstime.com, 202 Chris Fourie/Dreamstime.com, 203t Romkaz/Dreamstime.com, 203b Lee Dirden/Dreamstime.com, 204 Yegor Korzh/Dreamstime.com, 205t Nicole Duplaix/National Geographic/Getty Images, 205b Gary Unwin/Dreamstime.com, 206 Martin Harvey/Corbis, 207l Ewan Chesser/Dreamstime.com, 207r Rusty Dodson/Dreamstime.com, 208 Eric Delmar/iStockphoto, 209t Can Balcioglu/Dreamstime, 209b Xavier Marchant/Dreamstime.com, 210 Eric Gevaert/Dreamstime.com, 211l Peter-John Freeman/iStockphoto, 211r George Clerk/iStockphoto, 212t Anna Yu/iStockphoto, 212b Hudakore/Dreamstime.com, 213 Sebastian Duda/iStockphoto, 214 Paul McCormick/Getty Images, 215l Joe McDaniel/iStockphoto, 215r Nico Smit/Dreamstime.com, 216–217 Tim Laman/National Geographic/Getty Images, 218 Tom Dowd/Dreamstime.com, 219t Morten Elm/iStockphoto, 219b John Pitcher/iStockphoto, 220 Jens Kuhfs/Getty Images, 221t Ken Moore/Dreamstime.com, 221b Dale Walsh/iStockphoto, 222 Evgeniya Lazareva/iStockphoto, 222–223 David Schrader/iStockphoto, 223 Paul Nicklen/National Geographic/Getty Images, 224 Romilly Lockyer/Getty Images, 224–225 Jeff Hunter/Getty Images, 225 Casey and Astrid Witte Mahaney/Lonely Planet Images/Getty Images, 226 Carol Buchanan/Dreamstime.com, 227t Jacek Chabraszewski/Dreamstime.com, 227b Sergey Kulikov/iStockphoto, 228 Mark Kostich/iStockphoto, 229t Tommounsey/Dreamstime.com, 229b iStockphoto, 230 Greg Niemi/iStockphoto, 231t Anup Shah/The Image Bank/Getty Images, 231b Mark Higgins/iStockphoto, 232 Kim Bunker/iStockphoto, 233 Jason Edwards/National Geographic/Getty Images, 234–235 Kim Bunker/iStockphoto, 235t Jerome Whittingham/Dreamstime.com, 235b Thomas Bjornstad/Dreamstime.com, 236t Janne Hämäläinen/iStockphoto, 236b Paul Edwards/Dreamstime.com, 237 Roberto A. Sanchez/iStockphoto, 238–239 iStockphoto, 239l Andrew Howe/iStockphoto, 239r Rui Saraiva/Dreamstime.com, 240 J.C. McKendry/iStockphoto, 241l Jeff Foott/Getty Images, 241r Derek Dammann/iStockphoto, 242–243 Adam Jones/Visuals Unlimited/Getty Images, 244 Peter Garbet/iStockphoto, 245t Ppmaker2007/Dreamstime.com, 245b Richard Griffin/Dreamstime.com, 246 Mikeexpert/Dreamstime.com, 247l Janehb/Dreamstime.com, 247r Tommounsey/Dreamstime.com, 248 Liang Ma/Dreamstime.com, 249t Karoline Cullen/Dreamstime.com, 249b Scheiker/Dreamstime.com, 250–251 Gumenuk Vitalij/Dreamstime.com, 251t Brenda A. Smith/Dreamstime.com, 251b Bill Kennedy/Dreamstime.com, 252 Isabel Poulin/Dreamstime.com, 253l Tessa Rath/Dreamstime.com, 253r Colleen Coombe/Dreamstime.com, 254 Larry Ye/Dreamstime.com, 255t Sandra Cunningham/Dreamstime.com, 255b Laura Bulau/Dreamstime.com, 256l Angela Vetu/Dreamstime.com, 256r Oneclearvision/iStockphoto, 257 Rene Hoffmann/Dreamstime.com, 258 Chris Hellier/Corbis, 259t Kai Zhang/Dreamstime.com, 259b Carrie Bottomley/iStockphoto, 260 Peter Elvidge/Dreamstime.com, 261t Feng Hui/Dreamstime.com, 261b Pasticcio/iStockphoto, 262–263 Marek Cech/iStockphoto, 263t Peter Pattavina/iStockphoto, 263b Mark Kolbe/iStockphoto, 264 Maxim Malevich/Dreamstime.com, 265l Ken Cole/Dreamstime.com, 265r Dean Pennala/Dreamstime.com, 266 Vova Pomortzeff/Dreamstime.com, 266–267 Lesya Castillo/Dreamstime.com, 267 Alan T. Duffy 1970/Dreamstime.com, 268–269 J.A. Kraulis/All Canada Photos/Getty Images, 270–271 Henk Van Mierlo/Dreamstime.com, 271t Dmitry Pichugin/Dreamstime.com, 271b iStockphoto, 272–273 Eric Isselée/Dreamstime.com, 273l Pixelite/Dreamstime.com, 273r Jim Parkin/Dreamstime.com, 274t Sburel/Dreamstime.com, 274b Robert F. Sisson/National Geographic/Getty Images, 274–275 Dmitry Pichugin/Dreamstime.com, 276–277 Uwe Halstenbach/iStockphoto, 276 Diane Diederich/iStockphoto, 277 Mark Atkins/Dreamstime.com, 278–279 David Ciemny/iStockphoto, 278 Vincent Vanweddingen/iStockphoto, 279 Eric Boucher/Dreamstime.com, 280 Julia Britvich/Dreamstime.com, 281t Avner Richard/Dreamstime.com, 281b Carmentianya/Dreamstime.com, 282–283 Sergey Anatolievich/Dreamstime.com, 282 Gail Johnson/Dreamstime.com, 283 Lauren Jones/Dreamstime.com, 284–285 Andrei Calangiu/Dreamstime.com, 285t Simone van den Berg/Dreamstime.com, 285b Christophe D./Dreamstime.com, 286t Geopappas/Dreamstime.com, 286b Tom Davison/Dreamstime.com, 287 Bronwyn8/Dreamstime.com, 288 Kenneth McIntosh/iStockphoto, 289t Vinicius Tupinamba/Dreamstime.com, 289b Tradkelly/Dreamstime.com, 290 Joseph C. Justice Jr./iStockphoto, 291l Co Rentmeester/Time & Life Pictures/Getty Images, 291r iStockphoto, 292–293t Kai Zhang/Dreamstime.com, 292–293b Deborah Benbrook/Dreamstime.com, 293 Kwest19/Dreamstime.com, 294–295 Richard Bouhet/AFP/Getty Images, 296 Antonio Petrone/Dreamstime.com, 297 O. Louis Mazzatenta/National Geographic/Getty Images, 298 and 298–299 Bob Aimsworth/Dreamstime.com, 299 Kevin Walsh/Dreamstime.com, 300–301 Paul Prescott/Dreamstime.com, 302–303 Panoramic Images/Getty Images, 303 Randall L. Ricklefs/McDonald Observatory, 304 Archive Holdings Inc./Getty Images, 305t Dario Mitidieri/Reportage/Getty Images, 305b iStockphoto, 306–307 Julien Grondin/iStockphoto, 307l Adeline Yeo Hwee Ching/Dreamstime.com, 307r Snem/Dreamstime.com, 308 Andy Butler/iStockphoto, 309t Scott Rothstein/Dreamstime.com, 309b J. Duggan/Dreamstime.com, 310t Piotr Majka/Dreamstime.com, 310m Fabrizio Argonauta/Dreamstime.com, 310b Evgeny Terentyev/iStockphoto, 311 Pavlos Rekas/Dreamstime.com, 312–313 Tanya Weliky/Dreamstime.com, 313t Bob Aimsworth/Dreamstime.com, 313b Ismael Montero/Dreamstime.com, 314–315 iStockphoto, 315t Mark Kostich/iStockphoto, 315b Popperfoto/Getty Images, 316–317 Kazuyoshi Nomachi/Corbis, 316 and 317 iStockphoto, 318 NASA, 318–319 William Britten/iStockphoto, 319 Alexal/Dreamstime.com, 320–321 Frank Krahmer/Getty Images, 322–323 Chenyhscut/Dreamstime.com, 322 Pancaketom/Dreamstime.com, 323 Joe Gough/iStockphoto, 324–325 Joshua Haviv/Dreamstime.com, 324 Pierdelune/Dreamstime.com, 325l Jack Dykinga/Getty Images, 325r Joshua Lurie-Terrell/iStockphoto, 326–327 Grafissimo/iStockphoto, 326 Petra Klaassen/Dreamstime.com, 327 NASA, 328–329 Peter Clark/Dreamstime.com, 329t Joe Gough/Dreamstime.com, 329b Stuart Elflett/Dreamstime.com, 330–331 Dr Marli Miller/Getty Images, 330 Reinhard Tiburzy/Dreamstime.com, 331 Dmitry Kozlov/Dreamstime.com, 332–333t Joe Cornish/Getty Images, 332–333b Andreas Sandberg/iStockphoto, 333 Alexander Potapov/Dreamstime.com, 334 Vladimir Kondrachov/iStockphoto, 334–335 Howardliuphoto/Dreamstime.com, 335 Hashim Pudiyapura/Dreamstime.com, 336–337 Alexander Hafemann/iStockphoto, 336 Armin Rose/Dreamstime.com, 337 Anthony Hathaway/Dreamstime.com, 338–339 Daniel Stein/iStockphoto, 338 Corbis, 339 Wolfgang Amri/Dreamstime.com, 340 Jonathan White/iStockphoto, 341t Dave Raboin/iStockphoto, 341b Wessel Cirkel/Dreamstime.com, 342–3 Nick Schlax/iStockphoto, 343t Robyn Mackenzie/Dreamstime.com, 343b Spunky1234/Dreamstime.com, 344 Oksana Asai/Dreamstime.com, 345l Francois Etienne Du Plessis/Dreamstime.com, 345r Dirk-Jan Mattaar/Dreamstime.com, 346–347 Peter Dazeley/Getty Images, 348 Dr Don Fawcett/Getty Images, 349t Clouds Hill Imaging Ltd/Corbis, 349b Anette Linnea Rasmussen/Dreamstime.com, 350 3D4Medical.com/Getty Images, 351l Carolina K. Smith M.D./Dreamstime.com, 351r Peterfactors/Dreamstime.com, 352 3D4Medical.com/Getty Images, 353t Bobby Deal/Dreamstime.com, 353b Emir Memedovski/Dreamstime.com, 354 Dannyphoto80/Dreamstime.com, 355l Andres Balcazar/iStockphoto, 355r Sebastian Kaulitzki/Dreamstime.com, 356 Tihis/Dreamstime.com, 356–357 Dan McCoy/Rainbow/Getty Images, 357 Ryszard Bednarek/Dreamstime.com, 358 Kutay Tanir/iStockphoto, 359t Dannyphoto80/Dreamstime.com, 359b Rosemarie Gearhart/iStockphoto, 360l David Davis/Dreamstime.com, 360r Gordana Sermek/Dreamstime.com, 361 3D4Medical.com/Getty Images, 362 Visuals Unlimited/Corbis, 363l Tracy Hebden/iStockphoto, 363r Oguzaral/Dreamstime.com, 364–365 Kennan Harvey/Getty Images, 365t Vlad Turchenko/Dreamstime.com, 365b 3D4Medical.com/Getty Images, 366–367 Sebastian Kaulitzki/Dreamstime.com, 367l Sgame/Dreamstime.com, 367r Dannyphoto80/Dreamstime.com, 368 Sebastian Kaulitzki/Dreamstime.com, 368–369 Pete Saloutos/Corbis, 369 Stephen Coburn/Dreamstime.com, 370–371 Devan Muir/iStockphoto, 371l Jenna Duetsch/iStockphoto, 371r Koi88/Dreamstime.com, 372t NASA Johnson Space Center, 372b Armin Rose/Dreamstime.com, 373 Sebastian Kaulitzki/Dreamstime.com, 374t Geopappas/Dreamstime.com, 374b Joshua Haviv/iStockphoto, 375l Paul Moore/Dreamstime.com, 375r Nico Smit/Dreamstime.com.